THE INVISIBLES

A HISTORY OF THE ROYAL NEWFOUNDLAND COMPANIES

JAMES E. CANDOW

Breakwater Books
P.O. Box 2188, St. John's, NL, Canada, A1C 6E6
www.breakwaterbooks.com

A CIP catalogue record for this book is available from Library and Archives Canada

Copyright © 2019 James E. Candow

ISBN 978-1-55081-795-9

All Rights Reserved. No part of this publication may be reproduced, stored in a retrieval system or transmitted, in any form or by any means, without the prior written consent of the publisher or a licence from The Canadian Copyright Licensing Agency (Access Copyright). For an Access Copyright licence, visit www.accesscopyright.ca or call toll free to 1-800-893-5777.

We acknowledge the support of the Canada Council for the Arts.
We acknowledge the financial support of the Government of Canada and the Government of Newfoundland and Labrador through the Department of Tourism, Culture, Industry and Innovation for our publishing activities.

Printed and bound in Canada.

Breakwater Books is committed to choosing papers and materials for our books that help to protect our environment. To this end, this book is printed on a recycled paper that is certified by the Forest Stewardship Council®.

In memory of Cyril Byrne

CONTENTS

AUTHOR'S NOTE xi

INTRODUCTION xiii

CHAPTER I
THE LABYRINTH 1

    Army Administration 1

    Regional and Local Organization 4

CHAPTER 2
**THE RISE AND FALL OF THE
ROYAL NEWFOUNDLAND COMPANIES** 11

    Origins 11

    Growing Pains 14

    Signal Hill 16

    Garrison Reduction 21

CHAPTER 3
THE SCUM OF THE EARTH 27

    The Rank and File: An Overview 27

    Pay and Living Conditions 29

Diet 40

Garrison Routine and Duties 43

Parades and Reviews 49

Crime and Punishment 50

The Great Gulf 60

CHAPTER 4
BALLROOMS AND BATTLEFIELDS 63

The Officer Corps: An Overview 63

High Society 70

Garrison Theatricals and the Regimental Band 76

The Sporting Life 81

The Ties that Bound 85

CHAPTER 5
THE COMING OF THE FROST 87

The Firetrap 87

Nineteenth-Century Firefighting 89

The Military-Civilian Relationship 91

The Great Fire of June 9, 1846 94

Aftermath of the Great Fire 102

CHAPTER 6
CIVIL COMMOTION 107

Politics and Society 107

The Poisoning 109

The Neaven Funeral Riot 119

Conception Bay 129

The Reckoning 141

Dénouement 166

CHAPTER 7
CONCLUSION 171

Legacy 171

Patrick Myrick's Limp 175

ACKNOWLEDGEMENTS 177

APPENDIX I
**COMPOSITION OF THE
ROYAL NEWFOUNDLAND COMPANIES, 1845** 181

APPENDIX 2
**COMMANDING OFFICERS OF THE
ROYAL NEWFOUNDLAND (VETERAN) COMPANIES** 182

APPENDIX 3
PLANS OF SELECTED MILITARY FACILITIES, 1861 184

     3.1 Fort Townshend 185

     3.2 Fort William 186

     3.3 Garrison Hospital 187

     3.4 Ordnance Yard 188

ENDNOTES 189

BIBLIOGRAPHY 211

INDEX 231

MAPS AND ILLUSTRATIONS

CHAPTER I

Fig. 1   Government House, Commissariat House, and
Residence of the Collector of Customs, 1831 6

Fig. 2   Private of the Royal Newfoundland Companies
in full dress, marching order, 1860 15

CHAPTER 2

Fig. 3   View of St. John's from Long's Hill, 1831 18

Fig. 4   St. John's, 1844 20

Fig. 5   "The Landing and Reception of His Royal
Highness the Prince of Wales at St. John's
Newfoundland on the 24th. July 1860" 23

CHAPTER 3

Fig. 6   Fort William Barracks from
Military Road, 1831 32

Fig. 7   Government House, 1851 46

Fig. 8   "Narrows, or Entrance of the Harbour of
St. John's, Newfoundland." 48

Fig. 9   Robert Law, circa 1871 66

Fig. 10   "Sleighing at St. John's" 72

| Fig. 11 | St. John's Cricket Club, Pleasantville, Quidi Vidi Lake site, n.d. | 82 |

CHAPTER 5

Fig. 12	The Great Fire of June 9, 1846	95
Fig. 13	Customs House and view of Water Street, October 1841	96
Fig. 14	Colonial Building, 1851	103

CHAPTER 6

Fig. 15	Michael Anthony Fleming	110
Fig. 16	Conception Bay and Environs	
Fig. 17	"Water Street, Harbour Grace, N.F."	129
Fig. 18	"New road made after the attack on Winton 1835/Saddle Hill."	132
Fig. 19	"N[orth] View of the Harbour Grace Court House Aug. 1841."	134
Fig. 20	"The Prince of Wales leaving St. John's, Newfoundland for Halifax, Nova Scotia."	145
Fig. 21	May 13, 1861 Riot	158
Fig. 22	Court House and Market, 1851	161

CHAPTER 7

| Fig. 23 | "St. John's Station – looking northeast from housetop, west of Devon Row, before 1900." | 172 |

AUTHOR'S NOTE

By an amendment to the Canadian constitution on December 6, 2001, Newfoundland was officially renamed Newfoundland and Labrador. Because that change has no bearing on the past, I use the old name throughout this book except when referring to the present.

To avoid using the dreaded "sic" in square brackets, I have reproduced all quotations in their original spellings. Except where I thought it necessary, I have not distinguished between an officer's brevet rank and his rank in the army. Usher's *Dictionary of British Military History* defines brevet rank as a "superior nominal rank formerly given to an officer, but without extra pay. Hence a brevet major would have the status of a major but be paid as a captain." Finally, the research for this book was conducted intermittently over the course of four decades. During that time archivists changed many of the titles and accession numbers of the records I used. Although it has been a challenge to keep pace, I have done everything possible to ensure that the archival references in the endnotes and bibliography are current.

INTRODUCTION

In the spring of 1866, residents of The Goulds, Newfoundland, were appalled when the disappearing snow revealed not just the usual farmers' fields, but also a decomposed human body.[1] Somewhat incongruously—because it suggested unfinished business—the deceased's feet were clad in leather boots, one of which bore the stamp "B, 40 R.N.C."This clue, plus the footwear's martial appearance, led coroner Joseph Shea to the nearby St. John's British Army garrison, where records showed that boots bearing this inscription had been issued to a Private John Hanlin, who had been missing since deserting from his regiment, the Royal Newfoundland Companies, on July 15, 1860. Although a coroner's jury was unable to establish a cause of death or to say whether foul play was involved, it concluded that the remains were almost certainly Hanlin's.

Hanlin's corpse, which had gone undetected for nearly six years, is an apt symbol of his regiment, for despite being stationed in Newfoundland from 1824 to 1862, the Royal Newfoundland Companies have been virtually invisible to historians of the British Army. Worse still, the eminent Canadian military historian Desmond Morton was unaware that Newfoundland even had a British Army garrison, let alone knew its regiment's names.[2] That garrison, incidentally, was Britain's first in what is today Canada. Newfoundland and Labrador residents are not much different than the historians. When they remember their military history, they usually focus on a single engagement that their ancestors fought at Beaumont-Hamel, France, on July 1, 1916.[3] (In Newfoundland and Labrador, the Second World War is second not only chronologically, but also in importance.) This book is a study of soldiers who bore the word *Newfoundland* in their regiment's name, but who crossed the Atlantic in the opposite direction in earlier times, albeit on behalf of the self-same British Empire.

Between 1697 and 1870, 30 British regiments served in various Newfoundland communities, but mainly in St. John's and Placentia.[4] (Established in 1713, the Placentia garrison was withdrawn in 1811.) Despite the army's lengthy presence, Newfoundland's security ultimately rested on the Royal Navy, whose ships began accompanying English fishing vessels to and from the island in the 1640s. The relationship between the navy and the migratory fishery was symbiotic: the navy protected the fishery, whose main product—dried, salted cod—was a valuable commodity in Iberian and Mediterranean markets, while the fishery itself had strategic importance as a training ground for men who could be pressed into naval service in wartime.[5] The Newfoundland squadron's senior officer, who held the temporary rank of commodore, was informally regarded as governor while he was on the station—that is, until 1729, when the practice became official.

Because St. John's had an excellent harbour and was roughly in the middle of the English fishing and settlement zone, it became the headquarters of both the squadron and the unique government over which the governor presided, which included a surrogate court system administered by junior naval officers.[6] Although in peacetime the squadron

INTRODUCTION   xv

contained only two or three ships, it expanded in wartime, when some ships overwintered to protect the small but growing resident population (roughly 10,000 people by 1793).[7] The Newfoundland station would not be permanently staffed until the French Revolutionary and Napoleonic Wars (1792-1815), when, however, Halifax eclipsed St. John's as a naval base because of its usefulness against the United States of America in the War of 1812.[8]

The wars accelerated both the demise of the British migratory fishery and the growth of fishing and sealing by Newfoundland residents, whose numbers rose to 40,568 in 1815, with 10,018 of them in St. John's.[9] With these irreversible changes, Newfoundland could no longer be regarded, as it had been for centuries, as "a great English ship moored near the Banks ... for the convenience of the English Fishermen."[10] It was now a settled society that deserved the same constitutional trappings as its British North American neighbours, a process that began in 1824-25 with the abolition of the surrogate court system, the creation of civil courts, and the commencement of rule by a governor and appointed council—in short, colonial status. Ironically, these same developments undermined Newfoundland's strategic value to Britain. Accordingly, in 1824 the Royal Navy announced that the Newfoundland station would be closing and that Newfoundland would henceforth be part of the North America and West Indies station, headquartered in Halifax and Bermuda.[i] Although one or two Halifax-based ships continued to visit Newfoundland's waters each summer until the eve of the First World War, the British Army's St. John's garrison was once again the colony's only year-round imperial force.

The Royal Newfoundland Companies' lifespan coincided with the colony's achievement of representative government

---

[i] Despite the announcement, the St. John's Naval Office remained open until 1826.

(1832) and responsible government (1855), outwardly progressive milestones that belied times that were as turbulent as they were formative. Elections became outlets for inter- and intra-denominational tensions and local and factional rivalries, spawning violence the police could not always control. On such occasions, the magistrates, as agents of the civil power, requested military aid, plunging the Royal Newfoundland Companies into the maelstrom. Like elections, fires also revealed shortcomings in public services. Civilian firefighting was no more sophisticated than policing, and because St. John's experienced many fires, here, too, the regiment stepped into the breach. When it did, it encountered conditions that were as dangerous and controversial as when it aided the civil power.

When not suppressing riots or battling fires, the regiment's men followed a monotonous routine that would have been familiar to British soldiers in other garrisons during the period. Nearly every aspect of army life was shaped by elaborate regulations and a strict, sometimes brutal, disciplinary code. To cope with the tedium and the repression, men used (and abused) alcohol, while the truly desperate, such as the luckless Private Hanlin, deserted. But the Royal Newfoundland Companies' men had another option not widely available to other British soldiers: they married local women, and they did so in far greater numbers than army regulations allowed. This gave a more personal quality to the regiment's community ties and, in the process, helped to make it unique within the British Army. Unlike the rank and file,[ii] the regiment's officers led lives that were characterized by lax discipline and leisurely pursuits. Officers nonetheless left their own marks on the community, especially in sports, arts, and education.

It is difficult to assign a collective identity to a group

[ii] The non-commissioned men of the army (privates, corporals, and sergeants).

whose numbers may have approached 2,000 during their regiment's existence.[iii] But if there were such an identity, novelist Robertson Davies' concept of "fifth business" would be it. According to Davies, "Those roles which, being neither those of Hero nor Heroine, Confidante nor Villain, but which were nonetheless essential to bring about the Recognition or the dénouement, were called the Fifth Business in drama and opera companies according to the old style; the player who acted these parts was often referred to as Fifth Business."[11] The Royal Newfoundland Companies were not major players in the dramas that unfolded in their lifetime, but when they fired into a sea of rioters in downtown St. John's on May 13, 1861, they unwittingly helped forge a political compromise that would shape Newfoundland society long into the twentieth century. Their legacy would have other dimensions, but none were more important than this fifth business.

[iii] For most of its 38 years, the regiment's strength was approximately 300 men. Assuming an annual turnover rate of 15 per cent, some 1,700 men would have served.

CHAPTER I

THE LABYRINTH

Army Administration

The British Army was more than just a fighting machine. It was also a sprawling bureaucracy whose ungainly structure was the product of a lengthy power struggle between Parliament and the Crown.[1] As complicated as that bureaucracy was, some knowledge of it is necessary to understand the environment in which the Royal Newfoundland Companies functioned.

There were effectively two armies in our period: the infantry and the cavalry, who answered to the Horse Guards; and the professional corps—the Royal Artillery[i] and the Royal Engineers—who answered to the Board of Ordnance. Named after the London building containing the guardhouse and barracks of the royal household's cavalry, the Horse Guards included the offices of the Commander-in-Chief and the Secretary at War. The former, who was appointed by the Crown as its representative,[ii] was charged with the recruitment, training, discipline, and efficiency of the infantry and the cavalry; the latter, a Member of Parliament, was that body's watchdog for army finances. (Parliament voted annually to

---

[i] Known formally as the Royal Regiment of Artillery.

[ii] For constitutional purposes, the monarch was and still is the army's commander-in-chief.

establish the army's size and budget.) The War Office, as the secretary's unwieldy fiefdom was known, occupied so many buildings that messengers at one point accounted for a fifth of its workforce.[2] For the professional corps, the Board of Ordnance oversaw pay and discipline, supplied clothing, weapons, and ammunition, and managed all military lands and buildings at home and abroad.

Numerous other officials also had says in army administration. One of the main ones was the Secretary of State for War and the Colonies, or Colonial Secretary for short. Although his primary responsibility was the civil administration of the colonies, in wartime commanding officers abroad reported directly to him, not to the Commander-in-Chief. He also approved senior regimental appointments in the colonies, and in consultation with colonial governors[iii] decided on the army's size and distribution abroad. (A separate official, the Home Secretary, did the same for troops in Britain.) Since it was more convenient for the Colonial Secretary to deal with a single individual on civil and military matters, he tended to appoint ex-army officers as governors.[3]

In 1862 the Colonial Office staff was a mere 48 bureaucrats, whose workplace at 14 Downing Street was so ramshackle that one employee said, "It is to be hoped the building will fall (for fall I believe it will) at night."[4] Perhaps it was just as well that other government officials and branches, including the navy, had roles in colonial affairs, sometimes exerting more power than the Colonial Office itself.[5] The Chancellor of the Exchequer, who headed the Treasury, influenced the army both as the government's chief financial officer and as the minister responsible for the Commissariat Department, a civilian service that at the garrison level administered contracts for the supply of food, light, fuel, forage, cartage, and transportation of men and *matériel*. The Commissariat was

---

[iii] Technically lieutenant governors during our period, but commonly known as governors.

also custodian of the military chest, from which all military personnel, including pensioners and colonial governors, were paid. The Clothing Board ensured that the clothing sent to regiments conformed to army regulations. The Army Medical Department oversaw regimental and staff surgeons and ordered and controlled medical supplies. Medical officers decided if unfit soldiers should be discharged, and submitted their findings to the Board of Commissioners of the Royal Hospital for Soldiers, which was located in Chelsea and thus commonly known as Chelsea Hospital. Comprised of military men and politicians, the Chelsea commissioners managed the hospital's veterans' home, and also set pension rates.

Baffling though the system was, Parliament's efforts to reform it in the relatively peaceful years after Waterloo were stymied by public apathy, limited finances, and resistance from the arch-conservative Duke of Wellington[iv] and his disciples. But after the Iron Duke's death the spectre of war with Russia alarmed the public and, for a few years at least, gave reformers the upper hand.[6] Administrative changes were already underway in 1854 when British troops joined the Crimean War (1853-56). The military and civil responsibilities of the Secretary of State for War and the Colonies were divided between, respectively, a Secretary of State for War and a Secretary of State for the Colonies. The following year the Secretary at War's position was subsumed in that of the Secretary of State for War, who also took on the Commissariat and Medical departments. As well, the Board of Ordnance was dismantled, with the Royal Artillery and the Royal Engineers now coming under the Commander-in-Chief. There would be no further reforms on a comparable scale until 1868-72, but for now the result was an improved administration that gave Parliament the advantage in its age-old struggle with the Crown.

[iv] Prime Minister 1828-30, Commander-in-Chief 1827-28, 1842-52.

Regional and Local Organization

The St. John's garrison—and, while it lasted, the Harbour Grace detachment—belonged to the Nova Scotia command, whose headquarters were in Halifax. With a strength of nearly 1,400 men in 1835, the Halifax garrison dwarfed the eight others in the region, of which St. John's (276 men) and Fredericton (275 men) were the next largest.[7] The command was usually headed by the Lieutenant General or Major General Commanding in Halifax,[v] who himself answered to the Commander of the Forces, British North America, based in Québec until 1836 and Montreal thereafter.[8] Although the Halifax garrison's standing orders[vi] were supposed to apply to St. John's "as far as they can be rendered applicable to the circumstances of the place," the St. John's garrison also had its own standing orders.[9]

The command structure underwent several changes in our period, often because of the outsized egos of the men involved. After the death of Lieutenant General Sir Benjamin D'Urban at Montreal on May 25, 1849, Nova Scotia Governor Sir John Harvey, a lieutenant general in the army, temporarily assumed the position of Commander of the Forces, British North America.[10] A month later Nova Scotia became a separate command, making Harvey the equal of Lieutenant General Sir William Rowan, newly appointed to the Canada command.[11] Not to be outdone, in January 1852, Newfoundland Governor Sir John Gaspard Le Marchant assumed exclusive command of his colony's troops.[12] Newfoundland's days as a separate command were fleeting, because when Le Marchant replaced Harvey as Governor of Nova Scotia that June, Newfoundland reverted

---

[v] In 1840, during the last few months of Sir John Harvey's tenure as Governor of New Brunswick, command headquarters were in Fredericton.

[vi] As the name suggests, standing orders could be valid for months or years.

THE LABYRINTH 5

to its former status within the Nova Scotia command. The last realignment occurred in 1856, when all British troops in North America were constituted as a separate army division under Lieutenant General Sir William Eyre in Montreal.[13] The division consisted of two brigades, with Colonel Charles Trollope commanding the Canada brigade and now Major General Sir John Gaspard Le Marchant the Nova Scotia brigade, which, as before, included Newfoundland.

Despite the end of naval government in 1824, Newfoundland's governors continued to be drawn from naval ranks until Harvey's appointment in 1841. Harvey had an army background, as did his next three successors, but in 1857 the mould was broken by Sir Alexander Bannerman, a civilian whose appointment came after the Colonial Office had been stripped of its military responsibilities. In theory, a governor's peacetime military role was limited to advising the Colonial Secretary on larger issues such as troop deployment; in practice, governors did not hesitate to poke their noses into garrison affairs. Admittedly, this was a grey area. As the Crown's representative, a governor was titular commander-in-chief of his colony's armed forces, including militias and volunteer companies where these existed.[14] Also, since governors' instructions were often vague and filled with obsolete clauses, and because news travelled slowly before cables circled the globe, office-holders enjoyed considerable leeway.[15]

Around St. John's there were ample signs of the governor's martial side. His private secretary was invariably an army officer, and from about 1780 until 1831 his residence, known as Government House, was inside Fort Townshend. The military orientation of the new Government House and its vast grounds (more than eight hectares) was pronounced.[16] To the south they faced the aptly-named Military Road, built in the 1770s to link Forts William and Townshend; to the northwest they were bordered by the Garrison Hospital;[vii] and to

---

vii That is, until 1852, when a new Garrison Hospital opened on Forest Road.

Source: City of St. John's Archives Photo No. 12-01-003

Figure I: (Left to right) Government House, Commissariat House, and Residence of the Collector of Customs, 1831. By Lieutenant Colonel John Oldfield.

the east they abutted the Royal Engineer and Commissariat establishments, and St. Thomas's Anglican Church.

The governor was not the only official with civil and military responsibilities. Under representative government, the garrison commandant[viii] was a member of the governor's Council,[ix] and he would have been under civil government as

---

[viii] The most senior of the commanding officers of infantry, artillery, or engineers.

[ix] There is disagreement among historians as to whether this was an Executive or Legislative Council. This is not surprising, given that it had advisory (executive) and law-making (legislative) functions. I side with Patrick O'Flaherty, who maintained that under representative government (1832-42, 1848-55) the correct usage is simply "Council." During the short-lived Amalgamated Legislature experiment (1843-48) the Assembly consisted of 15 elected members and ten appointed legislative councillors, although there does not appear to have been a Legislative Council per se. A handful of the legislative councillors were also part of a smaller, appointed Executive Council. After the attainment of responsible government in 1855, there were separate Executive and Legislative Councils. See Patrick O'Flaherty, *Old Newfoundland: A History to 1843* (St. John's: Long Beach Press, 1999), 148, and, by the same author, *Lost Country: The Rise and Fall of Newfoundland, 1843-1933* (St. John's: Long Beach Press, 2005), 3, 25, and 426, n. 69.

well had not the commanding officer at the time, Irish native Lieutenant Colonel Thomas Kirwan Burke, been excluded because he was a Catholic.[17] Lieutenant Colonel Robert Law, on the other hand, was president of the Council from 1848 to 1850, and again from 1853 to 1854. Between 1846 and 1854, Law was also administrator of the colony during the intervals—routinely of several months' duration—between an outgoing governor's departure and his replacement's arrival. (A native of Leixlip, Ireland, and a decorated Battle of Waterloo veteran, Law commanded the Royal Newfoundland Companies from 1841 to 1859, longer than any other person. He will figure prominently in our story.) Under responsible government there was no military representative on either the Executive or the Legislative Council, but the commandant could still become lieutenant governor during the governor's absence, as Law did during the three months between Charles Darling's departure and Sir Alexander Bannerman's arrival.[18]

Although the Royal Newfoundland Companies formed

the bulk of the garrison, the professional corps and the Army Medical Department were also represented. Under the Ordnance umbrella, the Commanding Royal Engineer (CRE) oversaw the design, construction, and maintenance of fortifications and military buildings. His staff comprised a clerk, office keeper, subaltern officer, clerk of the works, foreman of carpenters, and civilian labourers who were hired as needed.[19] Other Ordnance officials included the Deputy Storekeeper, established clerk, assistant clerk, storehouse man, office keeper, gatekeeper, and boat and wharf keeper. Except between June 1852 and January 1862, when the Royal Newfoundland Companies performed the roles, a Royal Artillery company under a captain's command operated the port signalling service and minded the guns that defended the harbour and its entrance channel, The Narrows. The CRE, Deputy Storekeeper, and Commanding Officer of Royal Artillery constituted a board of Respective Officers of the Ordnance, who shared major decisions affecting Ordnance land, buildings, and equipment.[20] Until 1855 the Army Medical Department assigned a surgeon and an assistant surgeon to the Royal Newfoundland Companies; thereafter the medical charge fell to a lone assistant surgeon.[21] The surgeons were recognized as members of the regiment's officer corps and answered to its commanding officer.

The Commissariat Department's chief official in St. John's held the rank of Assistant Commissary General (ACG), reflecting the garrison's intermediate status in the Nova Scotia command. (Halifax boasted a Deputy Commissary General.) The ACG's staff usually comprised one or two deputy assistant commissaries general, clerks, store issuers, warehouse men, and a messenger.[22] Although the Commissariat was a civilian service, its members wore uniforms and held corresponding army ranks (captain, for the ACG). Among the St. John's business community, however, the ACG was known as "the accountant." All monies voted by Parliament for the Royal

Newfoundland Companies found their way to the ACG via the regiment's London-based agent, which for most of its existence was Sir John Kirkland of 80 Pall Mall, London.[23] The agent also functioned as a banker for the regiment's officers and attended to sundry other needs, including supplying the men's uniforms, which throughout the regiment's existence were red with blue facings.[24]

CHAPTER 2

THE RISE AND FALL OF THE ROYAL NEWFOUNDLAND COMPANIES

Origins

It was all the fault of French and American fishermen. Suspended during the French Revolutionary and Napoleonic Wars, France's ancient fisheries on the Grand Banks and along Newfoundland's west and northeast coasts (the "French Shore") resumed with a vengeance after 1815, as did French settlement in St. Pierre and Miquelon. The presence of French fishermen had long plagued relations between Britain and France, but with Napoleon having recently been defeated, Britain was now more concerned with the United States, which it had fought to an embarrassing draw in the War of 1812. Several important issues arising from that conflict were not resolved until the signing of the Convention of 1818. Among other things, that agreement recognized American fishermen's liberty to catch and dry fish along the coasts of Labrador and western and southwestern Newfoundland. The resulting potential for conflict in the fisheries made Newfoundland a factor in Anglo-French and Anglo-American relations for the rest of the century and beyond.[1] In the shorter run, it ensured the survival of the St. John's garrison, which, not coincidentally, had its last hurrah during the American Civil War (1861-65).

The Royal Veteran Companies[i]—as the Royal Newfoundland Companies were originally known—were formed on July 25, 1824, from Chelsea Hospital out-pensioners[ii] and volunteers from regiments recently returned from India.[2] Veterans' regiments had been around since the late seventeenth century, when they were collectively known as the Independent Companies of Invalids.[3] Consisting of men who despite their disabilities were still capable of garrison duty, they were valued because they freed up regular troops for active service abroad. Before long, however, the distinction between invalids and regulars began to blur. In 1715 the invalids' pay became the same as that of regulars, and in the 1720s they began to be posted overseas.[4]

In an effort to remove the stigma associated with "Invalids," in 1802 they were renamed the Royal Garrison Battalions, only to be rebranded two years later as the Royal Veteran Battalions.[iii] These changes also acknowledged that the battalions were attracting relatively young men who had been discharged after the short-lived Peace of Amiens (1802) and who wished to resume their army service. In 1806 the 10th Royal Veteran Battalion was assigned to forts along the border between British North America and the United States, the assumption being that men who had already proven their loyalty would be less likely than regulars to desert, a chronic problem at the border posts.[5] This reasoning, however, would

---

[i] Although the regiment was renamed the Royal Newfoundland Veteran Companies in 1827, many army officials continued to use the original name until 1842, when the regiment was redesignated as the Royal Newfoundland Companies. I employ this last name throughout for generic purposes, and use "the Veterans" when discussing the period before 1842.

[ii] Out-pensioners were men who had been released from the hospital on the assumption that their disabilities were manageable; in-pensioners were so severely disabled that they remained in the hospital, surrendering their pensions for the privilege.

[iii] Then as now, the Crown awarded the "Royal" title to recognize long and distinguished service or exceptional bravery.

not have applied to Newfoundland, since it was geographically remote from the United States and was an island to boot.

While the stationing of the Veterans in St. John's reflected the garrison's intermediate status, there was another context. After 1815 a war-weary British government embraced retrenchment, and the army became a favourite target, as armies usually do after prolonged conflicts. Although the number of soldiers of all ranks declined from 233,952 in 1815 to 102,539 in 1828, the wars had generated unprecedented numbers of pensioners—85,756 in 1825—and they too came under scrutiny.[6] In 1829, with an eye to reducing costs, Secretary at War Sir Henry Hardinge made length of service and good behaviour, not disability, the chief determinants of pensions and pension amounts.[7] From now on a man would receive a basic pension of a shilling a day after 21 years' service and an extra halfpenny for each additional year thereafter, the latter in hopes he would delay taking his pension.[iv] Pensions would be denied to men of "bad" character no matter how long they might serve, and any veteran who agreed to emigrate to Australia or British North America could commute his pension for a lump sum payment.

The "commuted pensioners" scheme found only some 4,000 takers, barely offsetting newcomers to the pension list. There were still 84,534 pensioners in 1831, and in 1833 Secretary at War Sir John Hobhouse became downright draconian, halving the basic pension amount to sixpence per day[v] and requiring an additional six years' service to qualify for a shilling a day.[8] The creation of veterans' regiments for Newfoundland in 1824 and Australia (New South Wales and Tasmania) in 1826 may have been bureaucratic sleight of hand—after all, it merely transferred men from the pension list to the payroll

---

[iv] One shilling equalled 12 pence (or pennies).

[v] In 1847 the army restored the basic pension of a shilling a day for men with 21 years' service.

14　THE INVISIBLES

—but it must be seen in the context of postwar efforts to manage the pension problem.

Growing Pains

The first Veterans' detachment reached St. John's on November 19, 1824, and the second on December 8. When the last stragglers of the 81st Regiment[vi] departed on December 19, the 331 men and officers of the Veterans, together with 58 men of the Royal Artillery, constituted the garrison's armed forces.[9] The regiment soon drew the wrath of Governor Sir Thomas Cochrane, who complained that its men were "totally unfit to perform the duties necessarily imposed on them."[10] Although medical officers had cleared them before they left England, they were beset with health issues after arriving in Newfoundland. Between 1825 and 1836, 132 of them died, for an average annual ratio of 41 deaths per thousand of strength, numbers more commonly seen among troops in disease-ridden tropical garrisons.[11] St. John's ought to have been more in line with the Nova Scotia and Canada commands, where the ratios were, respectively, 15 and 19 per thousand.

Noting that mortality among Newfoundland's civilian population was "on a lower scale than in any portion of the American continent," medical staff dismissed climate as a factor in the Veterans' unusual mortality rates. Instead, they pointed to the men's "advanced age"—nearly half were between 33 and 40 years old, and the rest were over 40—and to "the immediate effects of intemperance," which they blamed for over half the deaths. Although the War Office considered withdrawing the Veterans as early as 1827, it was more concerned with the situation in New South Wales and Tasmania, where the men's quality was even worse, and the experiment an

---

[vi] A caretaker regiment that had been sent from Halifax to mind the shop until the Veterans arrived. From 1818 to 1823, the 74th Regiment had formed the backbone of the St. John's garrison.

Source: Artistic recreation by Carl McIntyre, with research assistance by Wayne Moug and James E. Candow.

Figure 2: Private of the Royal Newfoundland Companies in full dress, marching order, 1860. At an average height of 174 cm. (5 ft. 7 in.), the regiment's men were small by today's standards.

unmitigated disaster.[12] Lost in a haze of bureaucratic neglect, by 1832 the regiment had dwindled to 150 men.[13]

The deployment of the Veterans to Newfoundland and Australia went so badly that the War Office did not create another veterans' unit —the Royal Canadian Rifle Regiment—until 1840. But unlike Australia, where the Veterans were disbanded in 1833, things began to turn around in Newfoundland that very same year, when Horse Guards allowed the regiment to recruit from men returning to England from abroad "or other Corps as may be found fit for Garrison duty."[14] The regiment's commanding officer, Dublin native Lieutenant Colonel William Sall, took this as permission to seek volunteers from the Nova Scotia command. This became the preferred recruitment method, and as it did, the regiment's quality improved. Although Horse Guards apparently had not foreseen that its words would be interpreted this way, the regiment stopped being a burden, and in 1840 the then Commander-in-Chief, the Duke of Wellington, belatedly sanctioned the practice.[15]

Recruits from the Nova Scotia command were encouraged to volunteer by a bounty of 30 shillings—equivalent to a month's salary—and applicants had to be men of "general good character" who had volunteered for permanent service in British North America.[vii] By these means the regiment became so indistinguishable from others in the Nova Scotia command that, in 1842, Horse Guards removed the word *Veteran* from its name.[16] While this did not alter the fact that it was still a veterans' regiment, in 1842 the CRE in St. John's, Lieutenant Colonel Sir Richard Henry Bonnycastle, described the Royal Newfoundland Companies as "a fine healthy looking regiment of comparatively young men … which regiment might take its place in line with some of the best troops of Britain."[17]

Signal Hill

Bonnycastle spoke too soon, as 1842 was a high-water mark for both the regiment and the St. John's garrison. To understand why, we must go back to 1823, when President James Monroe declared that the United States would no longer tolerate efforts by European powers to colonize the western hemisphere or to extend monarchy to it. Although the Monroe Doctrine, as it later became known, was inspired by French and Spanish designs on South America, as well as Russian ones on the Pacific Northwest, its aggressive tone led London to appoint a commission to review British North America's defences.[18] In 1825 the Carmichael Smyth Commission—after its president, Major General Sir James Carmichael Smyth—recommended construction of new defences for Halifax, roads in New Brunswick to facilitate troop movements

---

[vii] In 1860 the bounty was reduced to one guinea, or 21 shillings; the character requirement proved to be too stringent, and in 1845 was relaxed to "fair and general good character."

THE RISE AND FALL OF THE ROYAL NEWFOUNDLAND COMPANIES   17

to the Canadas[viii] during winter, canals on strategic water-ways, and new fortifications for Montreal, Kingston, and the Niagara Peninsula. In the event of war, Halifax and Bermuda were to reprise their roles from the War of 1812 as bases for operations against the eastern seaboard of the United States; along the border between the United States and mainland British North America, operations were to be strictly defensive.

Because time constraints prevented the commissioners from visiting Newfoundland, in 1827 the then Master-General of the Board of Ordnance, the Duke of Wellington, addressed the oversight by ordering Lieutenant General Gustavus Nicolls, CRE at Halifax, to proceed to St. John's, assess the situation, and recommend a new defence system. In his report, Nicolls identified Signal Hill as the key to defending the town.[19] The concept was not entirely new, for the hill had been developed during the French Revolutionary and Napoleonic Wars as a potential citadel for the garrison. Nicolls, however, had something even more elaborate in mind: he wanted extensive new facilities on the summit and an imposing line of Martello towers farther down the hill. When finished, these works would render Forts William and Townshend and several Narrows batteries redundant, enabling the entire garrison to be concentrated on Signal Hill.

The Board of Ordnance was slow to endorse the concentration scheme, mainly because the Royal Engineer establishment was preoccupied with building the new Government House, a structure that historian D.W. Prowse would unfairly dismiss as "a huge pile of unredeemed ugliness."[20] In December 1831, with Government House finally done to Cochrane's satisfaction, the Board informed the respective officers that it had approved a gradual implementation of Nicolls's plan, so that as existing buildings in the town forts became unserviceable, their replacements would be built on Signal Hill.[21]

[viii] Upper and Lower Canada, or present-day Ontario and Quebec.

Source: City of St. John's Archives, Photo No. 12-01-007.
Figure 3: View of St. John's from Long's Hill, 1831. By Lieutenant Colonel John Oldfield. This fine view of the town and harbour was sketched at a time of general prosperity and expansion. The graveyard on the left was the Catholic burial ground from 1813 to 1849.

A decade of construction ensued on the hill, but the work was hampered by the Treasury's refusal to grant all of the requested funds, and by a shortage of skilled labour. None of the Martello towers was ever built, and although barracks and other buildings were eventually completed on the summit, living conditions in this exposed area were so bad that, in January 1842, Governor Harvey reluctantly ordered most of the troops back to the town forts, effectively killing the concentration scheme.[22]

Much scrambling followed. Having formally surrendered Fort William to the colony as a home for the legislature, the Board of Ordnance now had to sheepishly take it back.[23] On the assumption that the fort's days were numbered, the Board had not only allowed it to deteriorate, but had sanctioned extensive civilian encroachments.[24] The latter reflected the fact that St. John's was growing rapidly, its population of 14,946 in 1836 representing a 49 per cent increase over 1815.

The area between Military Road and the harbour was filling in, and the pressure to push north beyond the forts and Government House was increasing. By 1835, houses had been erected so close to Fort William that, according to Lieutenant Colonel John Oldfield, CRE, "The Guns mounted on

Source: London News, May II, 1844, 300/Author's collection.

Figure 4: St. John's, 1844. This view shows Fort Townshend (upper left) prior to construction of the Roman Catholic Cathedral of St. John the Baptist.

the works cannot be fired for alarm or on any other occasion without breaking the windows and otherwise damaging the Houses."[25]

Humans were not the only problem. Chickens now scratched and strutted on the fort's slumping parapet, and the glacis had been conquered by herds of grazing sheep. Since military personnel also cultivated vegetable gardens along the entire length of the fort's north and east sides, its appearance had become a strange hybrid of the martial and the agricultural. Fort Townshend was better off, partly because it was newer, and partly because a small detachment had been retained there "to assist the civil power in preserving the tranquility of the Town" after the bulk of the garrison had decamped to Signal Hill.[26] Nonetheless, the Board's decision to grant adjacent land to the colony for a new gaol and to Roman Catholic Bishop Michael Anthony Fleming for a new church eroded Fort Townshend's agricultural fringe and spoke to its declining military prospects.

Garrison Reduction

As one phase was drawing to a close, another that would sound the garrison's death knell was opening. Britain's embrace of free trade in the 1840s placed its colonies on roughly the same commercial footing as countries outside the empire. This made it easier for Britain to accept colonial demands for responsible government, a process that played out in North America between 1848 and 1855, with Newfoundland bringing up the rear. Although responsible government gave the colonies greater say in their internal affairs, it should not be confused with genuine independence. Governors still exercised considerable power and relinquished it only gradually; Britain reserved the right to disallow colonial legislation and to negotiate treaties, including trade agreements, on the colonies' behalf; and the colonies were expected to fall into line if Britain went to war.[27]

With the colonies having achieved responsible government and commercial independence, it followed—again, from the British perspective—that they must share some of the burdens the Mother Country had formerly borne on their account. The heaviest of these was defence, long the single largest colonial expenditure.[28] Further complicating matters, in 1846-47 resurgent French military power caused invasion fears in Britain, drawing attention to the army's global dispersal—more than two-thirds of the infantry were stationed overseas—and sparking demands to bring the troops home.[29] Although in 1846 the Colonial Secretary, Lord Grey, decided to do just that, the process was delayed in British North America owing to the expansionist tendencies of the United States.[30] These were all too clearly displayed during the Mexican-American War (1846-48) and the Oregon boundary dispute.

The first wave of garrison reduction struck Newfoundland in June 1852 when the lone company of 81 Royal Artillerymen departed, and the second in March 1855 when the Royal Newfoundland Companies were reduced from three companies to two. To cushion the blow, in May 1855 the Harbour Grace detachment was shuttered and its men brought back to the capital. Even though entire garrisons disappeared elsewhere in the Nova Scotia command,[ix] Newfoundland politicians were indignant. In 1856 the Legislative Council not only asked Colonial Secretary Henry Labouchere to increase the garrison, but also to revive the naval station, improbabilities that it sought to justify by noting that France had recently erected batteries at the entrance to St. Pierre harbour.[31] The council's timing could not have been worse, for Britain and France were on rare good terms after just having fought as allies against Russia in the Crimean War; the St. Pierre batteries, in fact, had been built because of fears that a Russian cruiser might escape into the Atlantic Ocean and threaten French colonial possessions.[32] The request for an increased garrison fell on deaf ears, as did the appeal to reinstate the naval station, for as Labouchere reminded the councillors, "As there is already a Naval Establishment at Halifax, it is unnecessary under present circumstances, to incur the expense of forming another so near to that station."[33]

Initially the British failed to get Newfoundland to share the defence burden. In 1846 Governor Harvey's efforts to create a militia upset the colony's fishermen, who objected with good reason that the seasonal nature of their calling was incompatible with militia service.[34] Without the support of the colony's largest occupational group, Harvey's initiative was doomed, and legislation to give effect to it went nowhere. Nothing more was heard on the subject until 1859 when the then

---

[ix] Garrisons were withdrawn from Charlottetown, Prince Edward Island and from Windsor, Sydney, and Annapolis Royal, Nova Scotia.

Source: Library and Archives Canada/Peter Winkworth Collection of Canadiana at the National Archives of Canada/e0III72054.

Figure 5: "The Landing and Reception of His Royal Highness the Prince of Wales at St. John's Newfoundland on the 24th. July 1860." Men of the St. John's volunteer companies can be seen clustered in the middle foreground. True to form, the Royal Newfoundland Companies, drawn up at dockside and thus first to greet the prince, are almost invisible.

Commander-in-Chief, the Duke of Cambridge, threatened to remove some of the existing armament from St. John's unless a militia were formed.[35] Nonplussed, in 1860 a joint committee of the House of Assembly and the Legislative Council rejected the idea on the same basis as in 1846.

Despite the militia impasse, a solution emerged when Newfoundland got swept up in the volunteer fervour that arose in Britain after Napoleon III's military successes against Austria in 1859 stirred fresh invasion fears.[36] In Newfoundland as in Britain, the volunteer movement was largely an urban, middle-class phenomenon: the four companies that were formed in St. John's in 1860 included accountants, office clerks, blacksmiths, printers, tailors, watchmakers, and cabinetmakers, with nary a fisherman to be seen.[37]

The commanding officer of the Royal Newfoundland Companies administered the oath of allegiance to the volunteers, and the regiment's non-commissioned officers helped

24   THE INVISIBLES

to train them. There was some irony here, given that the volunteers' creation coincided with the regiment's last days. It was bad enough that the reductions in the Nova Scotia command had shrunk the pool from which the Royal Newfoundland Companies could recruit, but by now the Royal Canadian Rifle Regiment was also recruiting from the Nova Scotia command, siphoning off men who might otherwise have gone to St. John's. Accordingly, the regiment was in a grim struggle just to maintain an effective strength.

The British government temporarily shelved garrison reduction during the American Civil War, which revived fears about British North America's security. Most of the 11,175 British troops who were despatched to North America ended up in the Canadas, although Newfoundland was allotted 120 Royal Artillerymen who arrived in St. John's on January 21, 1862. This did not alter the fate of the Royal Newfoundland Companies, who by then numbered barely 150 men. The War Office had grown tired of the effort to bring the regiment up to strength, a challenge now worsened by the avalanche of older soldiers retiring to collect their pensions.[38] The only sensible course was to merge the Royal Newfoundland Companies and the Royal Canadian Rifle Regiment, and since the latter boasted 14 companies to the Royal Newfoundland Companies' two, there was no question as to which unit would have to go.

On November 12, 1862, 104 men and officers of the Royal Canadian Rifle Regiment arrived in St. John's from Quebec; four days later, most of the Royal Newfoundland Companies' personnel were officially transferred to their new regiment.[39] A few diehards refused to play along for fear it might jeopardize their pensions, but a general order one week later proclaimed that all remaining personnel were to be "attached" to the Royal Canadian Rifles on November 30 for purposes of discipline and drill.[40] A detachment order of January 29, 1863, made it official, declaring that the Royal Newfoundland Companies had "become extinct by the transfer of the Officers and men to the Royal Canadian Rifle Regiment."[41] The latter would continue to serve in St. John's until the garrison's withdrawal in 1870.

CHAPTER 3

THE SCUM OF THE EARTH

The Rank and File: An Overview

Until the mid-nineteenth century, most of the British Army's rank and file were former agricultural labourers from England, Ireland, and Scotland. The subsequent shift to the urban working class was a function of both the ongoing depopulation of rural Ireland and the growth of cities and towns that accompanied industrialization.[1] Army leaders nonetheless preferred rural recruits, believing them to be fitter and healthier than city dwellers, which, on the whole, they were: by the mid-nineteenth century, average life expectancy at birth for those born in rural areas was 44 years, versus 35 years for those born in cities and towns.[2] The brass also believed that urban recruits were more insubordinate because of their exposure to trade unionism. Regardless of where the men were from, they tended to be uneducated and unskilled, hence the Duke of Wellington's oft-quoted barb that they were "the scum of the earth." That judgment, however, was overly harsh, for whenever these same men fought an enemy, they not only showed great courage, but more often than not emerged victorious.[3]

Since army life exposed men to low pay, stern discipline, service abroad, and risk to life and limb in combat, the question arises: why would anyone would want to enlist in the first place? Whatever the drawbacks—and they were well known at the time—army service ensured a regular income as well as food, shelter, clothing, and, if all went well, a pension at the end of the day. For someone trapped in poverty, these were powerful inducements. The army also appealed to debtors and men trying to escape domestic responsibilities, since upon enlistment they could not be removed from the army for debts under £30, or for leaving their wives and children as parish wards. Men frequently enlisted on impulse, lubricated by alcohol compliments of wily recruiting sergeants; others were tempted by bounty money that was immediately clawed back to pay for their first kit. Although a handful were motivated by patriotism, most enlisted "more out of a sense of hopelessness about finding anything better than from a positive desire to serve queen and country."[4]

Because they were a veterans' regiment, the Royal Newfoundland Companies differed from regiments of the line, who sought raw recruits throughout the United Kingdom. For most of their existence the Royal Newfoundland Companies drew directly from regiments of the line stationed elsewhere in the Nova Scotia command. From this, one might reasonably expect the regiment to have reflected army norms, but the evidence, while fragmentary, suggests otherwise. In 1830 Englishmen accounted for 43.7 per cent of the army as a whole, and in 1840, 46.5 per cent.[5] A survey of 95 randomly-selected men discharged from the Royal Newfoundland Companies between 1826 and 1857 reveals English origins for 37.9 per cent.[6] Scots, who made up 13.6 per cent of the army in 1830 and 13.7 per cent in 1840, were also under-represented in the survey group at 4.2 per cent. At 55.8 per cent of the survey group, the Irish were the only traditional source to be over-represented in the regiment: army averages for Irishmen in 1830 and 1840 were, respectively, 42.2 per cent and 37.2 per cent. Even though figures for the survey group cover 31 years and thus conceal annual or decadal variations, the evidence suggests that, where national origins were concerned, the regiment was an anomaly that tilted toward Ireland.

The predominance of Irishmen in the regiment (or at least in the survey group) probably explains why Roman Catholics were over-represented in the regiment compared to the army as a whole. In 1862, 60 per cent of the army's men were Anglicans, followed by Catholics at 28.2 per cent and Presbyterians at 10.5 per cent. Comparable figures for the Royal Newfoundland Companies in 1861 show that 47 per cent of the non-commissioned officers and men were Catholics, 32 per cent Anglicans, and 21 per cent Presbyterians.[7] This, incidentally, was a marked change from 1851, when the regiment was 41 per cent Anglican, 39 per cent Catholic, 12 per cent Wesleyan, and 6 per cent Presbyterian.[8]

The regiment also appears to have differed from the army as a whole in its occupational origins. Army statistics for 1861 give the following service-wide profile: labourers – 48.4 per cent; mechanics – 24.3 per cent; artisans – 15.1 per cent; shopmen/clerks – 9.6 per cent; boys – 2 per cent; professions – 0.6 per cent. In the Royal Newfoundland Companies' survey group, labourers (including two servants and one sailor) constituted 67 per cent, followed by artisans (including weavers, tailors, and shoemakers) at 25 per cent, and mechanics (coopers, carpenters, plasterers, and bricklayers) at 6 per cent. Slight though the evidence is, it suggests that labourers and artisans were over-represented in the regiment.

Pay and Living Conditions

Only the lowliest unskilled British worker earned less than a soldier, whose basic pay of a shilling a day was set in 1797 and did not budge until 1891.[9] A shilling a day translated to

£18 a year, less than the estimated annual income (£25) of a Newfoundland fisherman in the mid-1830s.[10] Although the soldier's pay was augmented (from 1800) by a daily allowance of one pence for beer, this was more than offset by stoppages (deductions) for things such as haircuts, hospitalization, laundry service, barrack damages, and food that was not part of the daily ration. In 1856 a Royal Newfoundland Companies' private could expect to clear only three and a half pence sterling a day after stoppages.[11] It may be a stretch to say, as a leading authority has, that "[t]o all intents and purposes the soldier received no pay but was paid in kind," but she was not far off the mark.[12]

Fortunately, there were ways to make extra money. Beginning in 1836 a man with an unblemished record could earn good conduct pay of one pence a day after his first five years of service, and an extra pence after each subsequent five-year interval up to and including his 25th year.[i] Each officer was also allowed to have a servant, and men lucky enough to be chosen for these positions received an allowance of one shilling sixpence a week.[13] Servants still had to attend reviews, inspections, and parades, but were exempted from fatigues and guard duty. A servant attending a sick officer was excused from all duties during his master's illness, and if the illness were serious enough he could even accompany his master back home. There was, accordingly, much competition among the men for servants' positions. There were eight servants and one batman[ii] in the regiment in 1832, eleven in 1833, and nine in 1855.[14]

Regimental tailors and shoemakers also received additional pay, although the amounts are unknown. In 1855 the Royal Newfoundland Companies carried three tailors and four shoe-

---

[i] After a regulation change in 1860, good conduct pay was awarded after the first three years of service and every five years thereafter up to and including the 38th year.

[ii] A batman was someone who looked after an officer's horse. That officer was undoubtedly the commanding officer, Lieutenant-Colonel William Sall.

makers, all of them privates.[15] In addition, selected wives of married men could earn up to five shillings a week for doing the regiment's laundry, a welcome addition to a family's income. The regiment's standing orders specified that this work was to be "divided among the well-conducted women, married with the Commanding Officer's consent."[16] Wives of sergeants, tailors, shoemakers, and men employed as servants were ineligible for laundry pay because their husbands already earned more than regulars.

Meagre pay was compounded by crowded and unsanitary living conditions. Until 1845 the army had no regulations for space allocation in barracks, and crowding was universal. Matters were further complicated in St. John's by the unusually high numbers of women and children in barracks, a situation that was especially acute in the regiment's early years. Army norms stipulating that wives could live in barracks and draw rations at a ratio of six per 100 rank and file were initially waived for the Veterans, partly because the regiment was not meant for active service, and partly because so many of the men were older and already married.[17] In June 1832 the regimental barracks in St. John's were home to 337 men, 91 women, and 220 children. This, said Lieutenant Colonel John Oldfield, CRE, was "<u>101</u> persons more than the Barracks are under any circumstances calculated to contain."[18] Sometime before the end of the decade the regiment adopted a new ratio of 20 wives for every 100 men, and although this was still high, it was no longer open-ended.[19] When the regiment's constitution was altered in 1842, it adopted a ratio of 12 per 100, the same as for the Royal Canadian Rifle Regiment.[20]

Initially the veterans were quartered in wooden barracks at Forts William and Townshend. In 1827, 48 men lived in the relatively new (1814) north barracks at Fort William, and an unknown number in the eighteenth-century south barracks (capacity 136), which they shared with some civilian artificers.[21] At Fort Townshend the Royal Artillery had already

Source: City of St. John's Archives, Photo No. 12-01-005.

Figure 6: Fort William Barracks from Military Road, 1831. By Lieutenant Colonel John Oldfield. The barracks are to the left of centre.

laid claim to the best barracks, and although the only other one (capacity 196) was rat-infested, it was here that the rest of the regiment lived with another group of civilian artificers. Although there were two turn-of-the-century barracks atop Signal Hill, these had been appropriated as hospitals for convalescing veterans.

The barracks picture began to change after the Board of Ordnance sanctioned the Signal Hill concentration scheme.

In December 1831 the Board approved the evacuation of the now thoroughly dilapidated south barracks at Fort William, with a view to moving its occupants to Signal Hill. The hospitals there were to revert to their original role as barracks, one for officers and one for soldiers.[22] The buildings on the hill were cleaned and whitewashed in the summer of 1832, and the move began that October, if not sooner.[23] In the spring of 1833 the Veterans and artillerymen who comprised the garrison were distributed as follows: Signal Hill - 9 officers and 228 rank and file; Fort William - 3 officers and 22 rank and file; Fort Townshend - 12 officers and 180 rank and file.[24]

The use of the wooden barracks on the hill was meant to be temporary, pending construction nearby of an imposing masonry barracks with separate ranges for officers and men. That building was completed in 1840 and ended up housing men from both the regiment and the Royal Artillery. Each of the 16 rooms in the soldiers' range was 6.4 metres long, 5.5 metres wide, and 3 metres high, with a door at one end, a fireplace at the other, and two windows along the outside wall.[25] Given its capacity of 197 men, there would have been 12 men per room, or 8.9 cubic metres[iii] per man. This was less than the army standard, adopted in 1845, of 450 cubic feet (12.7 cubic metres) per man, and even that was less than the space allotted to convicts in Victorian gaols.[26] Moreover, since women and children were present in most if not all of the rooms in the masonry barracks, the crowding would have been even worse than the figures suggest.

Married couples occupied the corners of the rooms and were separated from the men by suspended sheets or anything else that could serve for privacy.[27] Since each family was entitled to only two single beds, children often slept on the floor, although it was common for young boys to slip into beds vacated by men on guard duty.[28] For adolescent girls the lack of privacy meant that they had to contend with prying eyes and probably sexual advances. Even though the army frowned on marriages generally, it was amenable to those between men and the widows of fellow soldiers, and likewise their daughters, some of whom became child brides.[29]

Until the army began to adopt single iron bedsteads in the late 1820s, men slept in twos, threes, and sometimes fours in wooden double berths, several of which were still being used in St. John's as late as 1835.[30] The iron bedstead was welcomed for privacy reasons and because it could be folded against the wall during the day to create extra space. The other standard

---

iii 315 cubic feet

THE SCUM OF THE EARTH   35

furnishings were communal wooden benches and tables at which everyone ate, and a wooden tub that, until 1840, doubled as a wash basin by day and a urinal by night. The rooms in St. John's were heated by Cape Breton coal, rationed in such miserly amounts that it occasionally had to be supplemented by wood that the men procured themselves.[31] Because most trees near St. John's had long since been felled for firewood, men had to trek deep into the country if they wanted their own wood. Candles were the only light source besides glowing coal, and during winter each man received an extra blanket or rug to help ward off the cold in the rooms.[32]

On Signal Hill the communal well, washhouse (for laundry), ash pit (for garbage), and men's and women's privies were situated in a walled yard adjacent to the south end of the soldiers' range. Anyone wishing to use these facilities was obliged to go outside the barracks, since there was no access from inside. The women's privy (for four) and the men's (for seven) flanked the ash pit, which was emptied, not always thoroughly or on time, by a civilian contractor. (Archaeologists are forever grateful that contractors did such poor jobs.) The privies and ash pit were barely six metres from the cookhouse and a well that provided both washing and drinking water. At Fort William and Fort Townshend like facilities were located behind the barracks but farther back than on the hill.[33]

Perched on the eastern edge of the summit some 150 metres above sea level, the masonry barracks occupied what was arguably the most exposed location in all of St. John's—and that took some doing. The barracks bore the full fury of Signal Hill's remorseless winds. Not only were these often gale force, but they circulated in such a way that they tended to force smoke from the fireplaces back down the chimneys and out into the rooms. Nothing that the Royal Engineers tried brought any lasting improvement, and things came to a head in January 1842 when 15 men were hospitalized because of extreme cold in their rooms, and the baby of Royal Artillery gunner Robert Sears suffocated from smoke inhalation.[34] After inspecting the barracks, coroner Aaron Hogsett expressed dismay at "the dampness and smallness of the apartments ... which he thought were far from being healthy and fit for the troops."[35] These events were the last straw for Governor Sir John Harvey, who ordered the removal of the men and their families from the barracks, and their dispersal between the old wooden barracks on the hill and the Royal Artillery barracks at Fort William.

The next attempt to improve accommodations occurred in the mid-1850s when the Board of Ordnance decided to convert to barrack purposes a hospital that had been built in George's Valley, Signal Hill, in 1843. At 42.7 metres long, 12.2 metres wide, and two storeys high, the hospital was, in the words of the CRE, Sir Richard Henry Bonnycastle, "the best stone building in the Colony."[36] Although it was in a relatively sheltered location, it experienced the same problem with smoky chimneys as the abandoned masonry barracks on the summit. In 1845 Bonnycastle's successor, Major Alexander Watt Robe, concluded that while the hospital was no longer fit to receive patients, there was no reason why it could not serve as a barracks.[37] This seems baffling at first glance, but Robe must have felt that the shortage of good barracks was a more pressing concern than the need for a new garrison hospital. The hospital was duly converted back to a barracks, and by 1851 housed 106 men of all ranks belonging to the Royal Newfoundland Companies and the Royal Artillery.[38] That same year there were 250 men of all ranks at Fort Townshend and 126 at Fort William. In 1855, after the Royal Artillery had been withdrawn and the Royal Newfoundland Companies reduced, George's Barracks, as it was known, became home to 28 married men, non-commissioned officers, and their families.[39] This coincided with the report of a Committee on Barrack Accommodation for the Army that recommended separate quarters for married families. It was a dark day for

THE SCUM OF THE EARTH   37

army traditionalists, who had opposed dedicated married quarters because they might have "the deleterious effect of making marriage more appealing to soldiers."[40]

After 1855 the majority of the regiment's men continued to be housed in the town forts, where conditions remained challenging despite the reduced numbers living there. In 1856 Lieutenant Colonel Law advised Governor Darling that the Fort William barracks was "in a most decayed state," and in 1858 he reported that smoky chimneys had made some rooms at Fort Townshend "almost uninhabitable."[41] While George's Barracks was newer and roomier, the frequent issuing of general orders prohibiting the families who lived there from burning "bogwood" suggests that the fuel ration was inadequate and that the rooms, even if they were no longer smoky, were still cold.[42]

The army hierarchy opposed marriage in the ranks because of the additional cost and because the presence of wives and children supposedly undermined discipline.[43] Against this, critics replied that the wives did useful work, inhibited desertion, and elevated the tone of barracks life. Married men of the Royal Newfoundland Companies fell into three categories: (1) married with the commanding officer's leave (permission), entitling their wives and children up to age 14 to be "borne on the strength," that is, to live in barracks, to draw rations, and perhaps to have access to limited medical attention; (2) married with leave but with their families off the strength; and (3) married without leave and with their families off the strength. In 1852 the Royal Newfoundland Companies had 308 non-commissioned officers and men, of whom 36 were in the first category, 19 in the second, and a staggering 62 in the third.[44] This meant not only that 38 per cent of the men were married, but that 20 per cent were married without leave. Since the best estimate for the army as a whole in this period is that only 7 per cent of men were married without leave, it is clear that the Royal Newfoundland Companies were outliers.[45]

38   THE INVISIBLES

While soldiers in the second and third categories almost always lived in barracks and their families in town, those in the second could at least look forward to their loved ones being taken on strength when vacancies arose in the first category. But men married without leave were destined to spend their service years apart from their families except when off duty or given night passes.[46] In 1850 several wives—and doubtless children—of men married without leave were living in the Kings Road and Tarahan's Town[iv] neighbourhoods, near Forts William and Townshend respectively, and infamous for their extreme poverty.[47] These women's marginal status was underscored in 1854 when the police force attempted to make a cash donation to the regiment "for the relief of the poor of the corps."[48] In rejecting their offer, Lieutenant Colonel Law maintained that "there are no cases of distress in barracks," and advised that "the mens wives who are married without leave ... are not recognized or entitled to any indulgence from the service — I beg therefore you will apply the money in question to the relief of the distressed as you may deem fit."[49]

When barracks became too crowded even by the army's lax standards, commanding officers were allowed to shift properly married couples and their families into civilian accommodations. Beginning in 1849 the army gave such families a lodging allowance of one pence per day, and although this was increased to four pence by 1862, it was still insufficient. A few married men of the Veterans lived outside of barracks in 1832, but there is no evidence of the practice after that date.[50] Johanna Smith, wife of a soldier in the regiment, died in a private home at River Head in January 1847.[51] That home, however, is unlikely to have been hers, for even properly married women were removed from barracks if about to give birth or if suffering from infectious diseases.

[iv] Named after the landlord and publican Thomas Tarahan, Tarahan's Town was a neighbourhood roughly bound by Queens Road and Prescott, Gower, and Cathedral streets.

A soldier's wife who gave birth outside barracks could at least look forward to returning after the delivery. The same could not be said of another group of women who do not appear in army statistics and whose circumstances were especially bleak: those who bore illegitimate children fathered by soldiers. In Newfoundland it was customary (from 1834) for such soldiers to pay something toward their children's maintenance. But as the case of Virtue Pippy of Mosquito (now Bristol's Hope), Conception Bay, makes clear, the initiative lay with the mother and the system was stacked against her.[52] In February 1842, Pippy gave birth to a female child fathered by Private James Reynolds of the Royal Newfoundland Companies' Harbour Grace detachment.[53] On March 2, she walked the five kilometres to Harbour Grace and begged magistrates Thomas Danson and James Power to make Reynolds pay child support. The magistrates spoke with Reynolds and concluded somewhat cryptically that "his circumstances ... prevented our compelling him to provide a sufficient maintenance for the said child." That did not sit well with Virtue's father, Joseph Pippy, who on hearing it beat her and forced her to take the baby to Harbour Grace, where, on May 9, she laid it in front of the barracks and crept away.

Virtue Pippy was apprehended, gaoled, and reunited with her child while the magistrates awaited instructions from St. John's. There her case was taken up by Colonial Secretary James Crowdy, who learned from Lieutenant Colonel Law that Reynolds cleared five and a half pence a day after stoppages, "from which it is obvious," Law said, "that he can afford but very little, if any thing, towards the support of the child in question."[54] Crowdy nonetheless felt that Reynolds must do something, and Law finally convinced the soldier to pay five shillings (Newfoundland currency)[v] a month for as long

---

[v] Newfoundland currency was approximately four-fifths the value of sterling. See A.B. McCullough, *Money and Exchange in Canada to 1900* (Toronto: Dundurn Press, 1984), 291-92.

40   THE INVISIBLES

as he remained in the colony.[55] Given that the money was issued not to Pippy but to her father, it is questionable how much if any she received, or for how long.

Diet

In 1813 the army established a daily ration of three-quarters of a pound (0.3 kg) of meat per man and one pound (0.5 kg) of bread, amounts that did not fundamentally change during our period.[56] The salted beef and pork consumed in St. John's was imported from England until the early 1850s, when some bright light in the Treasury decided that domestic meat might be cheaper.[57] Despite subsequent tender calls for fresh local beef, potential contractors were free to substitute "Beef slaughtered at Halifax, Nova Scotia … as though the Cattle had been slaughtered by himself."[58] Accordingly, fresh meat remained a rarity. If a man wanted luxuries such as tea, coffee, sugar, and other vegetables, stoppages were applied to his pay. The daily ration had limited nutritional value, and the meat, which included fat, bone, and gristle, was usually tasteless because it was boiled in copper pots, ovens for roasting and baking food being unknown in the St. John's barracks until 1861.[59] But at least it was dependable. Problems tended to arise, however, when men whose families lived outside barracks shared their rations with them, since this adversely affected the men's health and their ability to perform their duties.[60]

Royal Newfoundland Companies' soldiers were fortunate in being able to supplement their diet with tastier and more nutritious fare. Owing to the difficulty of getting fresh vegetables, the Board of Ordnance allowed men (and officers) to grow vegetables on military property, a tradition that had a long history in St. John's.[61] In 1766 the Board appropriated 50 acres (20 hectares) of land around Fort William for gardens, and in 1775 it acquired an additional 150 acres (61 hectares)

THE SCUM OF THE EARTH   41

around Fort Townshend for the same purpose. The official designation of the Signal Hill Peninsula as military property in 1807 led to more such land being set aside in Ross's and George's valleys.[62]

Despite the expansion of commercial agriculture around St. John's in the early nineteenth century, in 1851 an anonymous member of the Royal Engineer establishment could still speak of "the extreme difficulty of procuring vegetables at this Station."[63] Besides, the men were not interested in paying for something that they could grow for themselves, and understandably clung to their privileges. The only vegetables mentioned in the records are potatoes, but it would be surprising if the men did not cultivate a few carrots, turnips, and cabbages for variety and because they were suited both to the short growing season and to winter storage. Men stationed on Signal Hill stored vegetables in cellars underneath the barracks, and there must have been similar facilities in the town forts.[64]

Well-behaved men of the Royal Newfoundland Companies qualified for passes entitling them to be absent from barracks from 4:00 p.m. to 9:00 p.m. to go fishing.[65] Archaeological evidence from Signal Hill confirms that the men who were posted there took full advantage.[66] At the site of the old wooden soldiers' barracks on the summit, fish bones accounted for 21 per cent of all skeletal remains, with cod by far the dominant species. (Mammal species accounted for two-thirds of the remains.) Since archaeologists uncovered no trout bones and only one salmon bone, "fishing" by soldiers meant fishing for cod; based on the abundance of skull and vertebral elements, it was probably brought back head on and gutted. Because other regiments had used the barracks since its construction around 1800, it is impossible to say what proportion of the bones the Royal Newfoundland Companies contributed. As the fish passes suggest, however, it may have been substantial.

Tender calls for supplying food to the St. John's garrison describe a much broader range of food than the regulation issue of bread and meat.[67] The winning contractor was also required to provide rice, peas, flour, salt, tea, coffee, pepper, barley, onions, turnips, potatoes, and brown sugar. Soldiers wanting to consume such things would have been hit with stoppages that few if any could have afforded. These foods, therefore, were likely to be eaten only if a man was hospitalized, when he also had access to milk, oatmeal, fresh meat, and ale, porter, and brandy.[68] There was, however, a catch, because stoppages for men in hospital were as high as nine pence per day.[69] Although this was intended to prevent "malingering," it effectively denied pay to men who were legitimately sick or injured.

As challenging as life in the St. John's garrison was, the soldiers and their families were healthier than most of their brethren in other garrisons, the regiment's formative years excepted. The high mortality rates of those years were an anomaly that had more to do with the quality of the men who had been sent out than with living conditions in St. John's, and the change in the recruitment method in 1833 paid immediate and lasting dividends. There were only 18 deaths between 1832 and 1834 (versus 46 in the preceding three years), and the mortality ratio of 11.5 per thousand between 1837 and 1846 was in line with North American norms.[70] In 1856 Lieutenant Colonel Robert Law was not exaggerating when he declared that "From an experience of 21 years here I must say that the general health of the Troops has been excellent," and that "there is no more healthy Station in Her Majesty's Dominions than Newfoundland."[71] That judgment echoed the findings of army statistician Lieutenant Colonel Alexander Tulloch, who only two years earlier had described Newfoundland as "one of the healthiest and quietest of any in H[er] M[ajesty's] dominions."[72]

Garrison Routine and Duties

As with virtually all aspects of army life, the soldier's daily routine and ordinary duties were strictly regulated. In 1850 the Royal Newfoundland Companies' summer routine consisted of breakfast at 8:00 a.m., morning parade 10:00 a.m., dinner 1:00 p.m., evening parade 4:00 p.m., and evening tea[vi] 5:20 p.m.[73] Shorter daylight hours made for a compressed schedule during winter, which lasted from December to May in the Nova Scotia command. Breakfast was at 8:30 a.m., morning parade 10:00 a.m., dinner 1:00 p.m., and evening tea 4:00 p.m. Tattoo was indicated by the firing of a gun at 9:00 p.m. in summer and 8:00 p.m. in winter, at the sound of which all men were expected to be back in barracks for roll call.[74] A morning gun (reveille) fired at daybreak had originated in 1813, and a noon gun was added in 1842.[75] In the aggregate, the morning, noon, and evening firings constituted the "daily gun."

Regardless of the season, men were supposed to use the time between meals and parades to clean their arms and accoutrements, tidy their barrack rooms, receive instruction, and perform sundry minor duties. Free time was supposedly limited to the hours between evening tea and tattoo, but resourceful soldiers found ways around the rules. In Halifax, for example, men were known to hit the grog shops as early as 11:00 a.m. to get in some fun between morning parade and dinner.[76] It would be surprising if St. John's were different.

Of the men's numerous duties, guard (or sentry) duty was both the most common and the most tedious. Sentries had to ensure that no men left the grounds before morning parade unless on duty or bearing passes; to stop all but officers or civilians on business from entering barracks after tattoo roll call; to prevent men from leaving during snowstorms; and

---

[vi] The army had officially adopted evening tea in the 1840s, and although a few regiments offered it before then, we do not know if the Royal Newfoundland Companies were among them.

44 THE INVISIBLES

to supervise prisoners in the guardroom cell.[77] Guards were maintained on a 24-hour basis, with each private rotating two hours as a sentry followed by four hours of rest or sleep in the guardroom, for a daily total of eight hours on and 16 off. Men mounted guard in full dress, which they also had to wear while resting or sleeping in case of alarm or surprise inspection by an officer. The sergeant or corporal in charge remained in the guardhouse most of the time, emerging occasionally to inspect the sentries; he also escorted them back to barracks when their tour was over.

Because the guard's day was so long, the army tried to ensure that each man had several consecutive nights in bed before his tour. In larger garrisons such as Halifax this could be as many as nine nights, but as St. John's was a small garrison it was sometimes a struggle to achieve even three.[78] This was especially so in the regiment's early years, when so many men were on the sick list, and again after 1855 as the effects of garrison reduction were felt. Also, during snowstorms and cold weather it was impossible to adhere to the standard rotation of two hours on and four hours off. In January 1827, for example, the sentries were relieved every 15 minutes.[79] Given that there were cases of men freezing to death at their posts, such measures were essential.[80]

The guard scheme in 1832 was as follows:

> Main guard (Fort Townshend): No. 1 at front gate and guardhouse; No. 2 at rear gate and magazine. Two sentries (one sergeant, one corporal, six privates).

> Governor's guard: Nos. 1 and 2 at Government House; No. 3 at guardhouse; No. 4 at "Chest" (Commissariat House). Four sentries (one sergeant, two corporals, one gunner [Royal Artillery], 12 privates).

> Fort William guard: No. 1 at entrance and com-

mandant's quarters; No. 2 at saluting battery and stores. Two sentries (one corporal, one gunner, six privates).

Signal Hill guard: No. 1 at guardhouse and garrison cells; No. 2 at magazine. Two sentries (one sergeant, one corporal, one gunner, six privates).

Hospital guard: Entrance gate. One sentry (one corporal, three privates).[81]

Twenty-nine years later the only notable changes were that the hospital guard had been dropped and a new guard had been added at the colonial penitentiary, which had opened in 1859 and was notoriously insecure in its early years.[82]

Other standard duties included piquets, fatigues, and work parties. Mounted daily, piquets were small groups of men who were part military police and part emergency force. In 1850 the regimental piquet consisted of one sergeant, one corporal, and 12 privates.[83] From this group, three sentries commanded by a provost sergeant supervised regimental convicts sentenced to hard labour, while two sentries watched military property within and adjacent to the forts, including fences and gardens. A company piquet of one non-commissioned officer and two privates was available at night to go looking for men absent without leave after tattoo roll call. The regiment also maintained fire piquets at Signal Hill and Forts William and Townshend, groups of men who remained in barracks and were on call in case of fire.[84] If a fire was large enough, however, all available men were expected to fight it. Fatigue parties were struck as required to perform miscellaneous tasks under the command of a non-commissioned officer. These included washing the guardrooms and the guardroom furniture; removing snow from military property and keeping both Military Road and Signal Hill Road clear in winter; transporting coal from the Commissariat fuel yard to the barracks; and picking

Source: Provincial Resource Library, Newfoundland and Labrador Collection, C68/PAI88.

Figure 7: Government House, 1851. Guards are barely visible at either end of the building.

up groceries from shopkeepers and bringing them back to the barracks.[85] Work parties were struck to provide labourers for the Royal Engineers, and varied in size according to the demands of the times. They would have been at their peak during the 1830s construction boom on Signal Hill, although unfortunately their size at that time is unknown. They would, however, have been considerably larger than in 1858, when the regimental work party was a paltry single non-commissioned officer and four privates, numbers that reflected both the regiment's reduced state and the lack of construction activity at the time.[86] To put things in perspective, in the first decade of the nineteenth century, when the garrison was larger and construction activity frenetic, the work party sometimes contained as many as 90 men.[87]

Peace establishment or not, this was still the army, and

THE SCUM OF THE EARTH   47

knowledge of firearms was paramount. On July 19, 1856, the men had their first practice with the 1853 pattern Enfield rifle, prior to which they had used smoothbore percussion cap muskets.[88] As no one was qualified to give instruction in the new weapon's use, Lieutenant Arthur Saunders Quill was appointed acting instructor. Quill, who at the time was also the regiment's adjutant, must have been the commanding officer's favourite. He had only joined the regiment in 1851, and since he had had no prior army service, he probably knew no more about the rifle than the men he was supposed to be training.[89] This could not continue, and in 1858 Lieutenant Edward Daly underwent formal training at the School of Musketry in Hythe, from which he returned on November 24 to assume the instructor's position.[90] On June 29, 1858, the Newfoundland government granted Lieutenant Colonel Robert Law some 38 acres (15.4 hectares) of land known as Camp Nagle's Hill for a rifle range.[91] Thereafter the men's annual training was conducted at the camp between March and September.[92] Despite all this, there was some question about regimental marksmanship, because on September 26, 1862, the regiment lost a shooting match to the volunteer rifle companies by a single shot.[93] This led to much gloating by the volunteers, with the regiment struggling to save face by alleging that some volunteers had used illegal rifles.[94]

In a departure from army norms, the men also performed artillery duties while the Royal Artillery was absent from St. John's between June 3, 1852, and January 21, 1862. At the time of the artillery's withdrawal, the regiment was fortunate in that one of its own, Lieutenant John Gillespie, had previously served in the artillery.[95] Gillespie was duly appointed instructor for a "gun party" and held the position until March 1856, when he yielded to Sergeant Alexander Stewart of the Royal Artillery, who was sent from Halifax on special duty.[96] Training took place once a week between May 1 and October 31. Service in the gun party was undoubtedly a welcome change from the men's normal routine, and its appeal would have been further enhanced after 1856 when the party's members received pay raises equivalent to their corresponding ranks in the Royal Artillery. In 1859 the gun party consisted of five non-commissioned officers and 40 privates, who were posted at Queen's Battery, Signal Hill and at Fort Amherst, overlooking the southern entrance to The Narrows.[97]

Like the Royal Artillery before its withdrawal, the gun party provided artillery salutes on special occasions, operated the port signalling service from atop Signal Hill, and fired the fog gun (from Fort Amherst) and the daily and fire alarm guns (from Queen's Battery).[98] Military responsibility for the signalling service was a legacy of its late seventeenth-century origins, when it served entirely military functions.[99] Despite the transition to signalling for commercial purposes—a *fait accompli* by 1819—the military continued to provide labour

Source: Frontispiece to Volume I of Richard Henry Bonnycastle, *Newfoundland in 1842: A Sequel to 'The Canadas in 1841'* (London: Henry Colburn, 1842).

Figure 8: "Narrows, or Entrance of the Harbour of St. John's, Newfoundland." Left to Right: Signal Hill, The Narrows, and Fort Amherst.

and expertise while the colony and the mercantile firms did what they could to defray expenses. As firefighting and aid to the civil power would show, signalling would not be the only case of military duties overlapping the civil realm.

Parades and Reviews

It would be a mistake to assume that all was drudgery, for the army thrived on pomp and ceremony. The most common manifestation of this occurred on Sunday mornings when the men made their way to and from their church of choice in divine service parade. Although the army recognized only Anglicanism and Presbyterianism before 1836, soldiers had been attending the Roman Catholic Chapel in St. John's since at least 1800.[100] The chapel was replaced by the Cathedral of St. John the Baptist in 1855. As there was neither a kirk nor a Presbyterian minister until 1843, until then Presbyterian soldiers would initially have gone to the tiny Anglican Church of St. John the Baptist, and from September 21, 1836, to St. Thomas's Anglican Church, newly erected to serve both the Anglican community and the garrison, and known until 1870 as the Garrison Church.[101]

In addition to morning and evening parades, which were held inside the forts, the regiment conducted field exercise parades twice a week during summer, weather permitting.[102] These are likely to have taken place on the spacious parade ground immediately west of Fort Townshend. In winter, field exercise parade gave way to twice-weekly route marches— marching out of the forts and then back along a prescribed route—weather again permitting. On the ceremonial front, the regiment greeted distinguished visitors at the waterfront and provided an honour guard at opening and closing sessions of the legislature. For sheer spectacle, however, nothing could touch the garrison reviews, in which the entire regiment performed marches and field evolutions before large crowds on both the Fort Townshend parade ground and the Government House lawn. The first of these appears to have taken place on August 3, 1836, at the Fort Townshend site, so impressing Governor Henry Prescott that he issued a quart of rum to every non-commissioned officer and man in the regiment.[103] After 1856 the garrison review coincided with the annual visit of the Brigadier General from Halifax.

Crime and Punishment

The army's peacetime justice system derived from the Mutiny Act, renewed annually by Parliament (until 1879) to define the rights and punishments of officers and ordinary soldiers.[104] For most of our period, punishments were meted out summarily by commanding officers, or more formally by (in ascending order of importance) detachment, regimental, district or garrison, and general courts martial.[vii] For minor offences such as occasional drunkenness or missing church, a commanding officer could impose fines and order extra drill or confinement to barracks for up to two months. St. John's was the site of both garrison and general courts martial. The former required the participation of a minimum of seven commissioned officers and could only hear cases punishable by imprisonment or flogging. Crimes in this category included theft, malingering, self-harm, injuring a fellow soldier, and conduct "of a cruel, indecent, or unnatural kind," a euphemism for sexual offences, which at the time included homosexuality.[105] Because the army tried to strike a balance between suitable punishment and regimental efficiency, prison terms for these crimes rarely exceeded six months.[106]

The general court martial required a minimum of 13 commissioned officers and heard cases punishable by execution

---

[vii] The district or garrison court martial was created in 1829 to replace the general regimental court martial. For simplicity's sake, and also because it was the accepted usage in St. John's, I will refer to it as the garrison court martial.

(by hanging or firing squad), transportation (for seven or 14 years, or for life), or imprisonment at hard labour. Crimes of this nature included mutiny, murder, striking or disobeying an officer, desertion, being drunk or asleep while on duty, and habitual drunkenness (four convictions for drunkenness in one year). Deserters were also likely to be branded, or, more accurately, tattooed with the letter "D" (for "Deserter") or "BC" (for "Bad Character"), the tattoo being applied on the arm, hand, or torso.[107] The general court martial was also the only court that could try an officer. After the reductions to the St. John's garrison between 1852 and 1855, it became a challenge to hold general and sometimes even garrison courts martial, and trials that once would have been held in St. John's were moved to Halifax, with prisoners and witnesses conveyed to and from there at public expense.[108]

The Royal Newfoundland Companies never mutinied, nor did any British regiment stationed in the colony until 1800, when United Irish sympathizers in the Royal Artillery and the Royal Newfoundland Regiment of Fencible Infantry rose unsuccessfully against their officers.[109] (There had also been a quasi-mutiny at the Placentia garrison in 1714.)[110] Between 1826 and 1835 only 76 death sentences were awarded in the entire British Army, and 35 of those were commuted to transportation.[111] The last soldiers of the St. John's garrison to be executed were eight of the aforementioned mutineers from 1800. Army convicts were transported either to Australian penal colonies or to Bermuda, where they served their time aboard decommissioned warships known as hulks.[112] Although the evidence is scarce, in the 1830s men of the St. John's garrison sentenced to transportation seem to have been Bermuda-bound; thereafter, however, they were sent to England, almost certainly as an interim destination en route to Australia.[113] (English felons awaiting transportation were held in a government-run collection depot until ships were ready to take them away.)[114] In 1853 the army abandoned transportation for sentences of less than 14 years, and although it officially ended the practice in 1857 in favour of imprisonment with hard labour, soldiers continued to be transported until 1868.[115] Private Robert McCourt of the Royal Newfoundland Companies, who in 1852 was sentenced to transportation for seven years, appears to have been the last of his regiment to be so punished.[116] The records, unfortunately, do not specify his crime.

Cooperation between military and civil authorities over imprisonment was common throughout the empire during our period, St. John's included. Initially, men of the Veterans who received prison sentences were confined to a military ward in the St. John's gaol, located in the same building as the courthouse.[117] Until 1836, when High Sheriff Benjamin Garrett ended the practice, soldiers sentenced to hard labour were put to work building and maintaining roads in and around St. John's.[118] Thereafter they were employed at menial tasks on Signal Hill and Fort Townshend under military supervision, presumably in shackles as before.[119] Each post also had its own guardroom cells where men were confined to await trial or to serve brief summary sentences. The two cells at Fort Townshend were medieval-type "black holes" under the guardroom floor, whose quality can be gleaned from the example of Private James Kirkpatrick of the Veterans, who perished in one of them while awaiting trial for drunkenness in January 1836.[120]

In the 1830s, army leaders began to have misgivings about shared correctional facilities, believing that contact between soldiers and hardened criminals was unlikely to foster reform; the civil authorities, meanwhile, griped that military prisoners caused overcrowding.[121] Cost concerns delayed the shift to dedicated military prisons, which started in England in 1846 and slowly spread to the colonies. For a fleeting moment it appeared as though St. John's would be in the vanguard of colonial garrisons with their own prisons.

THE SCUM OF THE EARTH   53

In the spring of 1846, the Board of Ordnance approved a request from Major Alexander Robe to convert a portion of the former masonry barracks on Signal Hill into a prison for solitary confinement cases. The conversion had already begun when, on June 9, the courthouse/gaol was lost to a fire that destroyed much of St. John's. At the colonial government's request, the military authorities consented to the use of the Signal Hill facility as a temporary civilian gaol. That supposedly temporary role lasted until 1859, when the colony opened a new penitentiary on Forest Road.

In the fire's aftermath, some military prisoners were confined in new provost cells at Signal Hill and Fort William, while others were shipped to English prisons, both civil and military.[122] Since army regulations adopted in 1844 limited the use of garrison provost cells to sentences of 28 days or less, there must have been many sentences in that range.[123] The district military prisons (as they were known) were for men with sentences from 43 days to six months; men with longer sentences—and thus guilty of more serious crimes—continued to be placed in civilian facilities.[124] Because there was no district military prison in the Nova Scotia command until one opened on Halifax's Melville Island in 1856, long-sentence convicts of the Royal Newfoundland Companies continued to be sent to England. This pattern was so ingrained that the opening of the Melville Island prison seems to have had little or no effect on it.[125]

Few punishments were more controversial than flogging, which was permitted for a broad range of crimes. As the army slowly bent to public pressure, the maximum number of lashes that a regimental court martial could award fell from 300 to 200 in 1832, 100 in 1836, and 50 in 1847.[viii] As resort to flogging declined, there was an increase in the number of men sentenced to imprisonment and, until it peaked in 1845,

---

viii   There was a further reduction to 25 in 1879, and the practice was abolished in 1881.

transportation.[126] Floggings were administered in front of the entire regiment in the mistaken belief that witnessing the spectacle would deter others from bad behaviour. While onlookers routinely fainted, repeated viewings had the unintended effect of fueling resentment among the men toward their officers.[127] And no wonder: the cat-o'-nine-tails was a pernicious device that did so much damage a surgeon had to attend all floggings.

Use of "the cat" was discretionary and thus dependent on the character of individual commanding officers, some of whom refused to use it.[128] Records of regimental courts martial are notoriously scarce throughout the army, and there is only one known case of flogging among the Veterans: on May 19, 1841, Private Edward Edwards received 150 lashes at Fort Townshend for striking a non-commissioned officer.[129] Despite the paucity of evidence, the requirement in the regimental standing orders that a medical officer had to attend parades for corporal punishments suggests that Private Edwards was not an isolated case.[130] Certainly, there was no lack of crime.

As elsewhere in the British Army, alcohol was the single largest threat to regimental discipline. The army, like the Royal Navy, recognized alcohol's role in maintaining morale, hence the beer allowance and, until 1831 in the Nova Scotia command, the daily rum ration, after which rum was issued only as a reward for special achievements.[131] With practices such as these the army trod a fine line—one that its men routinely crossed. In St. John's the preferred beverage was locally distilled rum, available in 1856 for one and a half to two pence (Newfoundland currency) per glass, or six to eight pence for half a pint.[132] Given that men cleared about three and a half pence (sterling) a day, there was a limit to how much they could spare for drink. This, however, deterred no one, not in the regiment's formative years, and not in its closing ones either, because between January 1, 1855, and April 29, 1856, 36 men were tried for habitual drunkenness.[133]

The temptation to drink was especially strong for the men at Forts William and Townshend, both but a stone's throw from downtown. In the early stages of the concentration scheme, Lieutenant Colonel Oldfield dismissed concerns over the quality of the barracks on Signal Hill because "the removal of men, nearly a mile from a large town full of low public houses must tend to health and discipline."[134] In 1831 the former Government House at Fort Townshend was converted into a canteen (that is, a military pub) to encourage men to avoid downtown, and an old building on Signal Hill was appropriated for the same purpose when the barracks there were reoccupied in 1832, only to be replaced by a new facility in 1835.[135] The canteens fell short of expectations because they could never fulfill the pub's traditional role as the "institutional hub of working-class recreation," nor could they provide what civilian establishments offered in spades; namely, female company.[136]

Hard on the heels of the canteen initiative, the army attempted to steer men into more constructive pursuits. A Horse Guards general order of February 5, 1840, called for the establishment of libraries and reading rooms "at each of the principal Barracks throughout the United Kingdom and the Colonies ... to encourage the Soldiery to employ their leisure hours in a manner that shall combine amusement with the attainment of useful knowledge, and teach them the value of sober, regular, and moral habits."[137] There had been a garrison library in St. John's since 1832, but it was privately funded by officers of the Veterans, Royal Artillery, and Royal Engineers, and was for their use only.[138] The new libraries and reading rooms, however, were intended for the non-commissioned officers and men and were supported by army funds and a monthly subscription of one pence per user. In 1855 a visitor to St. John's described the regimental library at Fort Townshend as "a neat little apartment, containing 1,650 well-selected volumes, and a number of newspapers and periodicals."[139]

56   THE INVISIBLES

Given that 20.5 per cent of the army's rank and file in 1857 were illiterate, the number of users was undoubtedly modest.[140] Nor was the reading material much to get excited about: no subversive books were allowed, and initially all titles had to be approved by both the Commander-in-Chief and the Secretary at War. Presumably because these senior officials had more important things to do, they soon delegated this responsibility to the Major Generals Commanding.[141]

In a closely related development, the army also tried to encourage men to attend regimental schools. These were as old as the army itself, but their existence was haphazard and dependent upon the initiative of individual commanding officers and upon other officers' willingness to pay for them.[142] Beginning in 1812, the War Office provided funding for the maintenance of schoolrooms in regimental barracks for soldiers' children, although not for the men themselves. Until the formation of the Corps of Army Schoolmasters in 1846, religious instruction was the main priority, and in St. John's as elsewhere the garrison chaplain—who received a tidy annual stipend of £13—routinely examined the children.[143] Until 1859 the chaplains were always Anglicans. The first Roman Catholic chaplain[ix] to the Royal Newfoundland Companies, Father Jeremiah O'Donnell, assumed his duties in January 1861.[144]

Although the schools were meant for children only, individual soldiers began to attend them, and in 1849 the Duke of Wellington attempted to make their attendance compulsory.[145] This triggered a lawsuit in which the courts ruled that compulsory attendance was incompatible with the Mutiny Act. Afterward, attendance by soldiers varied from regiment to regiment according to the inclinations of the men and their commanding officers. On January 1, 1854, the student body

---

[ix] Technically he was co-chaplain, as there continued to be an Anglican chaplain, who at the time was the Reverend Thomas M. Wood.

of the Royal Newfoundland Companies' regimental school on Signal Hill consisted of 30 male children and 32 female children, but no adults.[146] (Two adults had, however, quit in December 1853.) Four years later the picture was much the same: 38 male children, 28 female children, and, once again, no adults.[147] Where the men of the Royal Newfoundland Companies were concerned, sober habits were apparently a low priority.

Alas for Robert Law, his men had more ways to slake their thirst than by frequenting pubs and grog shops. In 1852 the 81 soldiers whose wives lived outside barracks would have had access to cheap or perhaps even free drink via their in-laws, and even some of the 36 men whose wives resided in barracks probably had local ties.[148] Believing that unsanctioned marriages were the weak link in regimental discipline, Law tried to clamp down on them by recognizing men married without leave as though they were still single, and by restricting their night passes to no later than 11:00 p.m. Subsequent developments suggest that he overreacted. In April 1856, a year after the regiment had been reduced to two companies, it consisted of 219 non-commissioned officers and men, of whom 63 were married without leave.[149] As this was almost the exact number (62) married without leave in 1852, it looks very much as though most, if not all, of those married without leave in 1852 had survived the reduction and stayed in St. John's to be near their wives. Moreover, in 1859 the Army Medical Department drew a correlation between "the high proportion of married men" in the Royal Newfoundland Companies and the "very low" number of admissions—33 per thousand—for venereal disease, a remarkable figure given that the rate for the army as a whole was 422 per thousand.[150] Law's men very well may have been drunkards, but they were honourable ones.

In February 1850, Law prematurely announced that desertion was "a crime happily now of rare occurrence in this

Garrison."[151] Granted, it was not the problem it was in the Canadas, which shared a long, difficult to police, and thus porous border with the United States. Between 1824 and 1862 the annual desertion rate in Newfoundland exceeded Canada's only seven times, with the peak occurring in 1858, when 21 men (out of 211) of the Royal Newfoundland Companies deserted.[152] Although a few daredevils managed to escape to the United States aboard American vessels visiting St. John's harbour, the vast majority fled to the outports (fishing communities beyond St. John's), where the relative and often complete absence of law enforcement was, superficially at least, an enormous advantage. Most such desertions occurred in spring or early summer, when outport fishermen came to St. John's to get supplies for the upcoming fishing season. Undeterred by the stiff fines that the Mutiny Act prescribed for abetting deserters, some wily fishermen hired soldiers to join their crews, then refused to pay them when the fishing season ended in the fall. Deserters caught in that snare had little choice but to return to St. John's "in the most abject state of misery" to face the music.[153]

Despite Law's objections to unsanctioned marriages, the greatest threat to regimental discipline lay in the recruitment system, or, more accurately, in the abuse of it by commanding officers elsewhere in the Nova Scotia command, who increasingly exploited it to get rid of their worst-behaved men. In August 1845, Law complained to Governor Harvey about some recent volunteers from the 74th Regiment, "who after having been repeatedly tried for gross misconduct have almost all deserted."[154] Harvey weakly reminded Major General Sir Jeremiah Dickson that volunteers for the Royal Newfoundland Companies must be of "fair" character—the actual requirement was "fair and general good character"—and the abuses continued. In July 1850, Law informed Lieutenant Colonel John Bazalgette in Halifax that "there are at this moment in the R[oyal] N[ewfoundland] Comp[anie]s no less than 20 men who have forfeited their service by reason of Desertion & with 7 exceptions before they volunteered to this Corps."[155] These men, he added, "are invariably dissatisfied and restless, & even after having been recommended for and obtained restoration of their services, turn out badly."

One of those bad apples is likely to have been Private Joseph Prime, who joined the regiment in 1848 and was still with it in February 1857. By the latter date he had faced six garrison courts martial and nine regimental ones, and was, in Law's opinion, "unquestionably the most worthless soldier I have ever met with."[156] Law would, however, soon meet worse, because the quality of the volunteers continued to decline. Consider, for example, Private Francis Foster, who came over in October 1857 from the 62nd Regiment, having been duly cleared by that regiment's senior medical officer, as indeed all recruits had to be. Foster was unable to shave himself, could only be entrusted with simple tasks such as emptying the barrack urine tubs, and, as Law subsequently discovered, "had never been regarded in any other light than that of an absolute idiot" while with the 62nd.[157]

At Law's request, Foster was brought back to Halifax and released from the army. It was a small victory, but the larger problem remained, thus Private James Creamer, whose former regiment does not appear in the records, and who with Joseph Prime will be remembered as one of the sorriest men in the regiment's history. Creamer's date with destiny began on the evening of November 22, 1858, when he missed roll call at Fort Townshend, only to appear at the gate at midnight deranged and naked, in which condition he had made his way through the town's streets.[158] He refused orders to dress himself, and when he appeared before his commanding officer the following morning he allegedly said: "What has become of your fucking family? She is a whore on the Continent." For missing roll call, for "disgraceful conduct of an indecent kind," and for "insubordinate and improper language" toward his commanding officer, Creamer was sentenced by general court martial to eight years imprisonment in England.

In 1858, with Halifax and London still deaf to Law's complaints, desertion reached epidemic proportions. That May, Law reported that nine of the ten deserters still at large had only recently arrived as volunteers from the 36th Regiment.[159] In September a thoroughly exasperated Law repeated a request he had first made to command headquarters in 1856, namely, that the system of recruiting from within the Nova Scotia command should be discontinued and that the regiment should instead be allowed to recruit "in the Mother Country in the usual manner."[160] But to this he now added the further suggestion that only married men should be allowed to volunteer, as this would, he believed, "entirely obviate Desertion." Here was belated acknowledgment that the recruitment system was largely to blame for the regiment's disciplinary woes, and that married men, far from being the cause, were part of the solution.

The Great Gulf

Law may have had his epiphany, but that did not alter the fact that marriages between soldiers and local women created a gulf across which military discipline could not reach. The extent of that gulf was revealed by an outbreak of violence between townsmen and soldiers of the Royal Newfoundland Companies in 1849. The first sign of trouble occurred on the night of November 19 when some townies rained stones on two privates as they made their way up Garrison Hill toward Fort Townshend, injuring one so badly that he had to be hospitalized for over a month.[161] There were isolated attacks during the next few weeks, including another stoning on Garrison Hill. Then it intensified. In the early evening of December 9, Private Owen Mullen left Fort William and started walking toward Fort Townshend via Military Road.

As he passed Rawlins's public house, Mullen noticed that five or six townies had begun to follow him. They subsequently overtook him and proceeded to shove him down Garrison Hill, where he was struck with a stone or a stick before he escaped by slipping into Buckley's public house.[x]

The following night, there were five separate attacks on men of both the Royal Newfoundland Companies and the Royal Artillery, the worst one involving Private Michael McMahon of the Companies. While walking alone on Military Road, McMahon observed a group of townies, some of them toting sticks, coming toward him across a field. He tore off down Kings Road, only to meet another group armed with sticks and a shovel. Not long after veering west toward Fort Townshend, he felt something sharp—probably the shovel—rip through his thigh. He began to bleed heavily but by now was close enough to the fort that he was able to reach the gate, and after gaining entry was taken to hospital.

The violence peaked on Tuesday, December 11, starting with a couple of isolated incidents along the established lines, and culminating in an outright brawl. By this date Law had created special patrols to comb the streets and prevent "quarrels" between soldiers and locals.[162] Sometime between 7:00 p.m. and 8:00 p.m. on the 11th, one such patrol encountered a large group of soldiers and townies on Kings Road doing pitched battle with shovels, stones, and fists. The patrolmen, who were carrying rifles, managed to stop the donnybrook and the mob reluctantly dispersed. Now on heightened alert, the patrols spent the remainder of the evening rounding up soldiers and escorting them back to barracks for their protection.

The magistrates who investigated the violence took numerous depositions, but to a man none of the combatants would say why they had been fighting.[163] This did not stop

---

[x] If it seems like there were a lot of public houses at the time, it is because there were: 104 to be precise.

the magistrates from offering their own explanations. In part they attributed the trouble to the recent closure of the Fort Townshend canteen, which had led greater numbers of soldiers to drink in the public houses, where the explosive combination of alcohol and gambling was prone to cause acts of revenge for losses or slights, real and imagined. But the magistrates also remarked that the civilians they interviewed were "confined for the most part to Tarrahan's Town and the Kings road in which localities, several Soldiers wives, who are not permitted to live in Barracks reside." So there it was: the magistrates were suggesting that military-civilian marriages were the root of the problem. Alcohol and gambling may have been the ostensible cause, but there could just as well have been other factors such as jealousy, feuds, and gang wars rooted in intra- and inter-family dynamics. The motives must ultimately remain obscure, but the inability of military and civil officials to be certain about them speaks to the limits of their authority.

CHAPTER 4

BALLROOMS
AND BATTLEFIELDS

The Officer Corps: An Overview

Despite a longstanding belief that officers in the first half of the nineteenth century were predominantly members of the aristocracy and landed gentry,[i] revisionist scholarship has shown the growing participation of middle-class professionals, who by the 1850s formed the majority of all officers.[1] It is nonetheless difficult to avoid the conclusion that too much has been made of this discovery, since most members of the middle class, army officers included, admired the upper classes and aped their gentlemanly ways.[2] It had also long been thought that most officers achieved their rank not by seniority or merit, but by purchase—that is, they outright bought their commissions, enabling them to join the army without prior military experience. Once again, modern research maintains that promotion from the ranks, usually with purchase but sometimes without, was "more important than suspected."[3] This tepid qualification does not mean much, because pur-

---

[i] Aristocrats were nobles who invariably owned land; the gentry were landowners but not nobles.

chase still accounted for some three-quarters of all officers' commissions during the period.[4] Also, most commissions acquired without purchase occurred during wartime, when the pressure to quickly replace casualties took precedence over the career aspirations of the well-to-do back home.[5] This is borne out by the career of Robert Law, who joined the army as a private in 1808 and attained the ranks of ensign (1809), adjutant (1810), and lieutenant (1811), all without purchase during wartime, before purchasing his commissions as captain (1821), major (1834), and lieutenant colonel (1844); the ranks of major general and lieutenant general, which he attained in 1859 and 1868 respectively, were awarded on the basis of seniority.[6]

Given the state of officers' pay, which was unchanged from 1806 to 1914 and was seen as little more than an honorarium, it is just as well that most had access to outside money. One source from the 1830s estimated that an annual private income of between £200 and £300 was required.[7] In England a first-class clerk earned more than twice as much as a lieutenant colonel.[8] The discrepancies were not so great in Newfoundland, but even so, the salary of chief magistrate Peter Carter (£350 in 1844) was greater than that of every officer except Law (£365), and a Customs Department clerk (£180) made more than an ensign (£95) or a lieutenant (£118), and almost as much as a captain (£211).[9] Nor could an officer look forward with certainty to a pension, since pensions were awarded only to the wounded or the highly decorated. Successive governments took the view that the proceeds from the sale of an officer's commission were a de facto pension, and while those proceeds could be significant, they were no substitute for a regular amount that could carry a man with dignity to the end of his days.

Before 1830 any officer could, regardless of how long he had served, opt to transfer to the half-pay list, where, as the name suggests, he could earn half his pay while sitting at home. After 1830 an officer needed three years' service to transfer to the half-pay list; after 1840, 18 years; and after 1852, 21 years. The ostensible purpose of the list was to create a reserve that the nation could draw upon in wartime; in reality, it proved to be "more a means to retirement."[10] Unless they were independently wealthy, men who remained on the list—and most did—found it insufficient, and to avoid difficulties had either to re-enter the workforce or emigrate to a country where the cost of living was cheaper.

The army in this period was mainly an imperial force, and this was reflected both in the national origins of the officers and in their itinerant careers. For example, of the Royal Newfoundland Companies' 16 officers in 1852, six had been born in England, five in Ireland, two in Scotland, and one each in Ceylon (today's Sri Lanka), Gibraltar, and the Cape of Good Hope (now part of South Africa).[11] Robert Law's example is again instructive. Before coming to Newfoundland in 1834, he had served in Spain, France, The Netherlands, Portugal, and Ceylon. When he left in 1859 he was 72 years old, but he nonetheless remained in the army and commanded the 2nd West India Regiment and the 71st Regiment of Foot before passing away in Dublin in 1874.

Law and his fellow officers lived lives that could not have been more different than those of the men they commanded. At the core of those lives was the concept of the gentleman, which for the British was virtually "a second religion."[12] In 1851 the respected military authority J.H. Stocqueler advised that an officer who focused solely on military affairs would be taking "a very narrow and imperfect view of his position," given that his moral authority over his men depended on modelling himself after "the British gentleman."[13] The officer, Stocqueler continued, should be "urbane in manners and courteous to all; he must be just and honourable in his most trifling dealings, his word must never be doubted." Furthermore, when mixing with civilian society, he "should be

Source: *The Royal Highland Fusiliers Museum, Glasgow.*

Figure 9: Robert Law, circa 1871. Law was commanding officer of the Royal Newfoundland Companes from 1841 to 1859. When this photo was taken, he was a lieutenant general and colonel of the 71st (Highland) Regiment of Foot (Light Infantry).

BALLROOMS AND BATTLEFIELDS   67

remarked for unobtrusive courtesy and easy elegance of manners; he should be distinguished in ballrooms as well as in battle-fields, and be as familiar with polite accomplishments as with professional attainments."

Like most officers, Robert Law needed no encouragement to follow Stocqueler's guidelines, for the habits they described came naturally. The Law surname is of Scottish origin and is a derivative of Lauriston,[ii] famous as the birthplace of economist John Law.[14] Robert was a descendant of the Reverend Robert Law (1638-1678), who studied at Dublin's Trinity College and afterward became Church of Ireland rector of Annahilt, County Down. Reverend Law's son John (1660-1716), who was rector of Tyholland, County Monaghan, changed the spelling of the family's surname to Lawe. His son Robert Lawe (1710-1786) bucked the call of the church and became Inspector of Barracks, a thoroughly corrupt position that made its holders rich via the misuse of public funds.[15] He used his wealth to buy property, including land at a place he insipidly called Robertsville, near Leixlip, County Kildare, where he also established a calico factory.[16] His marriage to Martha Wrightson produced 12 children, among them another Robert (1747-1826), who styled himself "Esquire," denoting gentlemanly status. He and his wife Elizabeth (surname unknown) in turn had six children, including yet another Robert—our Robert, finally—who was baptized in St. Mary's Anglican Church, Leixlip, on February 4, 1787, and who, by the time he joined the army in 1808, had adopted the earlier spelling of the family name.[iii]

It is significant that Robert Law enlisted as a private instead of purchasing a commission, because this suggests that

---

[ii] Now part of Edinburgh.

[iii] Army records showing Law's birthdate as January 29, 1789, appear to have the wrong year. I would suggest, however, that the month and day are correct because they correspond with his baptism date. I thank Helen Ryan, parish administrator of St. Mary's Anglican Church, Leixlip, for supplying Law's baptism date.

68 THE INVISIBLES

his family's money only went so far. There can, however, be no doubting his Protestant ascendancy credentials, or his gentrified ways. His marriage to Ann Hewitt in Dodford, Northamptonshire, on October 26, 1819, was performed by a Church of England minister, and when his daughter Elizabeth Lucy married Lieutenant Edmund Heathcote of HMS *Eurydice* in St. John's on July 12, 1844, the service was conducted by the Anglican Bishop of Newfoundland, Edward Feild.[17] (Feild, incidentally, had only just arrived in St. John's on July 4, and if this was not the first marriage he performed as bishop, it was one of them.) An account of *some* of Law's personal property in 1838 gives insight into his lifestyle.[18] It included an ebony inlaid chess and backgammon table with turned ivory pieces; a pair of mahogany card tables; a concert piano; hall lamp and clock; silver-plated candlesticks and coasters; a set of extendable mahogany dining tables for 16; drawing- and dining-room chairs; ivory-hafted forks and knives; cut-glass decanters; a floral blue set of dinner glassware; a fine china tea and dessert set; dozens of bottles of port, madeira, and other wines; a sedan chair; and a covered sleigh. If this collection did not say "gentleman," nothing ever did.

With the bulk of regimental duties being handled by a phalanx of non-commissioned sergeants and corporals, commissioned officers had ample time to practise the leisurely arts.[19] Except for the regimental ensign,[iv] even junior officers had little to do other than attend muster parades and carry out perfunctory duties such as inspecting the men's meat rations. Their lot became only slightly more onerous after January 1, 1857, when they were forced to take weekly exams on army rules and procedures; until then, they treated most forms of study as a joke.[20] Nor were they likely to be constrained by family obligations. Commanding officers frowned on marriages

---

[iv] The ensign kept the regiment's records and was the link between the commanding officer and the non-commissioned officers entrusted with carrying out orders.

by colleagues below the rank of major, since, among other things, these tended to complicate life in the mess.[21] When commanding officers relented, they ensured that prospective wives had appropriate social pedigrees.

Desperate to retain a working complement of officers during the Royal Newfoundland Companies' difficult last years, Law approved several marriages, including one by a junior officer. On October 2, 1857, Assistant Surgeon William Mackenzie Skues married Margaret, youngest daughter of merchant Christopher Ayre, in St. Thomas's Garrison Church.[22] Chief magistrate Peter Carter's daughters were also acceptable, and no wonder, for the Carters were local royalty. (Peter's son, lawyer Frederic Carter, would become premier in 1865.) On February 4, 1858, Carter escorted Fanny Maria down the aisle of St. Thomas's in order that she might marry Ensign Arthur Bambrick Mitchell; four years later, in the far grander setting of the Anglican Cathedral of St. John the Baptist, he gave Elizabeth Jane away to be the bride of the regiment's own Lieutenant William Gilmore.[23] Law may have been desperate, but his officers were not going to marry just anybody.

As demonstrated by Ensign Arthur Bambrick Mitchell's irregular behaviour, officers enjoyed a blatant double standard in disciplinary matters. Between July 1856 and April 1857 Mitchell, who, significantly, lived outside barracks, was reprimanded three times, including once for performing his duties while dressed in civilian clothes.[24] He escaped punishment after penning a letter of apology to Law, but a year later was back before him again, this time for failing to appear for duty because he was at a tea party. Law, whose patience was wearing thin, let Mitchell go with a warning that the *next* time he would be forced to reside in barracks "where, being on the spot, your duties can be more readily discharged."[25] With that the disorderly ensign seems to have learned his lesson, and in December 1859 he was rewarded with a promotion

70   THE INVISIBLES

to lieutenant in the Royal Canadian Rifle Regiment.[26] Such were the gentleman's perquisites.

High Society

In the relative absence of meaningful responsibilities, officers spent most of their time socializing, sometimes for hedonistic ends, but also for altruistic ones; if the two could be made to coincide—and they could—then so much the better. As was the case throughout the army, the social life of the Royal Newfoundland Companies' officers revolved around the mess, a private club that was based, when it operated,[v] in Fort Townshend.[27] Alcohol flowed freely there, and officers, unlike the men they commanded, could get blind drunk without fear of getting flogged.[28] Private though it was, the mess could also be thrown open to civilian invitees from the town's middle and upper classes, and when it was, the entertainment could be quite lavish. On February 16, 1830, for example, 120 people attended a ball at the Fort Townshend mess. Dancing commenced shortly after 8:00 p.m. and continued into the early morning hours, and throughout the night "choicest wines, viands, and refreshments of various kinds were provided in the greatest profusion."[29] One of the grandest mess entertainments was a dinner on August 16, 1845, in honour of Willem Frederik Hendrik, Prince of the Netherlands, whose appearance in St. John's was allegedly the first royal visit to the city,[vi] and which, like all subsequent ones, provoked an emotional response bordering on hysteria.[30] In addition to the prince, dinner guests included Governor Sir John Harvey,

---

[v]   The mess suspended operations from time to time for different reasons, and was also briefly located on Signal Hill.

[vi]   Technically, the first royal visitor was Prince William Henry (the future King William IV), who as a youthful Royal Navy lieutenant spent a few debauched months on the Newfoundland station in 1786-87. His stay bore no resemblance to the formal visit of Prince Hendrik, which was the prototype for all that followed.

High Sheriff B.G. Garrett, executive councillor and merchant William Thomas, and the Reverend Charles Blackman, garrison chaplain and rector of St. Thomas's. The fort was illuminated and extensively decorated, the troops performed a *feu de joie*,[vii] there was a fireworks display, and the food was "sumptuous and stylish in the extreme, comprising all the luxuries and delicacies of the season."[31]

All this leisure came at a cost, for officers had to subscribe to a mess fund to pay for the institution's upkeep. In the 1850s "dining" members contributed the equivalent of a day's pay every two months, for an annual subscription of six days' pay, while non-dining members gave the equivalent of a day's pay every three months, for an annual subscription of four days' pay.[32] Dining members also had to pay a daily fee of one shilling three pence each, which, incidentally, was more than a private earned in a day. The subscription and daily fee were just the tip of the iceberg. Officers had countless other financial commitments, such as purchasing mess furnishings and dinnerware, and contributing to charities, the regimental band fund, and special events. Membership, however, had its privileges. Officers received a daily allowance to cover the cost of forage for their horses, and in Newfoundland the legislature remitted the duties on wines consumed in the mess. These amounted to £50 sterling in 1851, no doubt making for happy times when it was shared among the members.[33] Moreover, the mess subscription rate was low compared to other British regiments—eight days' pay per year was the norm—and the cost of living in St. John's was said to be 60 per cent cheaper than in England.[34]

Upper- and middle-class civilians were only too happy to repay the military's hospitality. The heaviest socializing occurred in winter, when, according to an employee of a mercantile firm, "we have nothing to do but to think of passing

---

[vii] A lengthy salute achieved by firing rifles one at a time in rapid succession.

the time in the best and merriest way we can until the middle of April, at which period the spring goods arrive from England."[35] The author of those words, John A Pearson, claimed that sleighing was "the favourite amusement of the country. You may go for miles and miles over the fields of frozen snow, across the ponds and rivers ... without the least fear of danger." That judgment was not shared by Lieutenant Colonel Sir Richard Henry Bonnycastle, who had been spoiled by winter conditions in Kingston, Upper Canada, where, he said, "the snow is more constantly on the ground."[36] While conceding that sleighing on Quidi Vidi Lake and Twenty Mile Pond (now Windsor Lake) "is sometimes very good," Bonnycastle complained that even at those locations "no ice amusements ... can long be practised, as a snowstorm or a sudden thaw spoils the ice." Bonnycastle's carping aside, we know that officers went sleighing, because —as with Robert Law—sleighs and harnesses were almost always part of

Source: Library and Archives Canada/Peter Winkworth Collection of Canadiana at the National Archives of Canada/e000996320.

Figure 10: "Sleighing at St. John's." Sleighing was the favourite winter pastime of army officers and members of the middle and upper classes. Believed to have been painted around 1848, this watercolour plainly shows that the poor used dogs instead of horses, and for work rather than recreation.

their personal belongings, as, on occasion, were buffalo skins.[37] Sleighs, of course, were useless without horses to pull them, and as only the well-to-do could afford horses, sleighing reinforced ties between officers and the local middle and upper classes, while emphasizing the social distance between them and everyone else.

We have an excellent idea of what a private dinner party was like in St. John's, thanks to an account of one by Lieutenant Colonel Robert Barlow McCrea, commanding officer of the Royal Artillery between 1862 and 1864.[38] McCrea belonged to a whist club that met every Monday during winter, with hosting duties rotating among the 16 members, whom he described as "sober and substantial, good fellows every one of them." Club meetings, which were little more than excuses for orgies of eating and drinking, began with the members' arrival at 7:00 p.m., when they were greeted with tea, coffee, and sweets. Card playing ensued shortly thereafter, and during the games the members honed their concentration with generous quantities of port. The governor at the time, Sir Alexander Bannerman, donated a dozen bottles for the season's first meeting. We can assume that the air was blue with smoke, because St. John's was awash in Cuban cigars smuggled in by Spanish ships.[39] Served late in the evening, the main meal consisted of a minimum of four dishes accompanied by "two pyramids of mashed potatoes browned to perfection." The favourite dishes were turkey ("never under sixteen pounds"), baked ham, roast duck, chicken pie, stewed oysters, and wild goose with lemon sauce. A course of Stilton cheese and celery followed, and the meal concluded with tea and lemons "if procurable." Before venturing out into the cold winter night, members fortified themselves one last time with whiskey toddies.

Other social engagements were more public. During the 1840s, Government House was the site of weekly dinners in winter, and balls were held there whenever a dignitary of sufficient status was in town.[40] Army regulations required officers attending such functions to appear in full dress, swords included; mercifully, the swords could be removed for dancing.[41] Summertime visits by French and British naval vessels just in from the French Shore always begat a ball or a dinner or both, and one could be forgiven for thinking that the crews of those vessels came to St. John's—which was, after all, a long way from the French Shore—for no other reason *than* to socialize. (Elizabeth Lucy Law was hardly the only woman from St. John's high society to marry a Royal Navy officer.)[42] Sometimes the patrol vessels themselves were given over to dining and dancing, as on October 24, 1828, when nearly a hundred of the "rank and fashion" of the garrison and the town converged on HMS *Tyne*.[43] Dancing commenced at 2:00 p.m. on the gun deck, suitably decorated for the purpose, and continued until 3:30 p.m., when the starboard side was opened to reveal "a magnificent banquet hall" offering fruit, meat, and wine. After eating, the guests returned to the gun deck for more dancing, followed by tea and coffee in the late afternoon. When the festivities drew to a close at 6:00 p.m., many of the energetic guests left not for home but for an evening at the theatre.

Fraternal societies vied to attract officers to their balls, parades, and banquets. At the 1855 St. Patrick's Day celebration of the Benevolent Irish Society, Major Edward D'Alton —at the time, the acting commanding officer—and Ensign Arthur Saunders Quill of the Royal Newfoundland Companies shared head-table honours with society president, merchant, banker, and legislative councillor, the Honourable Laurence O'Brien; the Roman Catholic Bishop, John Thomas Mullock; merchant and president of the St. George's Society, Robert Prowse; and numerous other luminaries.[44] Many such functions were held to raise money for charity, and the officers' willingness to contribute was of a piece with the garrison's long-standing support for the poor.[45]

BALLROOMS AND BATTLEFIELDS   75

Officers were also partial to societies that promoted individual and societal improvement, notably the Agricultural Society and the Mechanics' Institute. Founded in 1842, the Agricultural Society encouraged commercial farming as a way to broaden Newfoundland's economic base, a noble ambition but with limited prospects. It was nonetheless a logical cause for the officers, who always had the largest gardens on Ordnance land. When the Agricultural Society's first meeting convened on January 13, 1843, the press reported that it was attended by "the Judges, many of the Military, the Merchants, and a large assemblage of the citizens of all classes."[46] In June of that same year, when some 4,000 people descended on Green Field Farm for the society's inaugural exhibition, the military was represented by the Royal Newfoundland Companies' band—compliments of the officers' mess—and the Royal Artillery, who supplied the tents containing the exhibits.[47] For good measure, the officers of the patrol vessel HMS *Electra* were present to lend moral support and, as always, to seek courting opportunities.

The officers' support for the Agricultural Society was equalled if not exceeded by that for the Mechanics' Institute. Originating in Britain in the 1820s and eventually spreading to the colonies—the one in St. John's was formed in 1849— the Mechanics' Institute sought to educate members of the middle and (especially) working classes via public lectures and the establishment of libraries.[48] The movement itself was part of a trend toward rational recreation, i.e., the use of so-called respectable forms of recreation to create positive social change.[49] The executive of the Newfoundland institute declared their intention to disseminate "useful knowledge among all classes in this community," not only via lectures and a library, but also by the "formation of a Museum, especially illustrative of the natural history of Newfoundland."[50]

The institute became the darling of military officers, including those of the Royal Newfoundland Companies. On

March 21, 1851, Assistant Surgeon Gilbert William Spence gave a public talk on astronomy, and in 1852 he topped that with an entire lecture series on chemistry, said to be "the first systematic course delivered before the Institute."[51] His fellow officer, Lieutenant Martin Petrie, was Curator of Apparatus in 1853; when Petrie ascended to the vice-presidency the following year, Spence took his old position. In 1861 the Mechanics' Institute merged with the St. John's Library Society and the Young Men's Literary and Scientific Institute to form the St. John's Athenaeum, to which it donated its collection of over 700 items, among them a Beothuk skull and a stuffed giraffe.[52] Ten years later the Athenaeum sold its collection to the Newfoundland government, and in this manner it later became part of the original Newfoundland Museum's holdings.

Garrison Theatricals and the Regimental Band

From about the mid-eighteenth century, theatrical activity was a familiar accompaniment to the British military presence in North America.[53] Its earliest manifestations in what is now Canada were in Halifax (1773) and Montreal (1774).[54] Its appearance usually coincided with a level of social, economic, and demographic development that would not be found in St. John's until the transitional years of the early nineteenth century.[55] Although a professional acting troupe[viii] led by Scottish natives James and Mary Ormsby performed in St. John's in 1806, the first documented local amateur production took place on March 18, 1817, when the "young Gentlemen of the Navy and the Town" staged Nicholas Rowe's *The Fair Penitent* in a converted storehouse before a "crowded and

---

[viii] My concern here is full-length plays normally staged in purpose-built facilities. In Newfoundland there was also a folk tradition of Christmas mummering that embodied theatrical aspects. The earliest mention of Newfoundland mummering is from 1812, or around the same time that its formal counterpart emerged. See G.M. Story, W.J. Kirwin, and J.D.A. Widdowson, eds., *Dictionary of Newfoundland English* (Toronto: University of Toronto Press, 1982), s.v. "mummer."

respectable" audience.[56] The show's profits were given to the Society for Improving the Conditions of the Poor, an action that, deliberately or not, helped to disarm self-righteous types who viewed the stage as the devil's playground, and who, judging from some of the hostile reactions to the staging of *The Fair Penitent*, were alive and well in St. John's.[57]

With the closure of the Royal Navy's Newfoundland station in the mid-1820s, it fell solely to the "gentlemen" of the army and the town to maintain the dramatic arts, which they were able to do in the new (since 1823) Amateur Theatre. The garrison of course included people other than army officers. One such was Deputy Assistant Commissary General William Stevens, who in November 1833 was fêted for "his exertions on the boards of the Amateur Theatre for a series of 17 years," wording that suggests he may have acted in *The Fair Penitent* in 1817.[58] A delegation representing "The Shareholders and Amateurs" of the theatre, among them Lieutenant Stephen Rice of the Veterans, presented Stevens with an address on behalf of "80 of the most respectable Civil and Military Inhabitants of the Town."[59]

By the late 1830s the amateurs, likely with help from the garrison, were staging plays every two weeks in winter.[60] Curiously, by this time fewer "respectable" people were attending the shows, a phenomenon that Sir Richard Henry Bonnycastle blamed on "the acerbity with which religious and political differences have been maintained of late years."[61] Members of the working class nonetheless continued to throng the pit, and a rapt audience they were, since, according to Bonnycastle, "not a word nor an indication of row or noise occurs" during performances. Their good behaviour may have been a legacy of the local practice, adopted in 1824, of ending shows in mid-performance if audiences became unruly.[62] Rich and poor alike took a forced break from all amusements after the Great Fire of June 9, 1846, destroyed the Amateur Theatre. There does not appear to have been any amateur thespian activity

78   THE INVISIBLES

for several years afterward, although professional troupes from British North America and the United States occasionally made the rounds.

Things began to change in April 1853, if not before, when the garrison theatricals of the Royal Newfoundland Companies were held in the recently constructed British Hall.[63] Given the time of the year, this may have been a one-off, but the theatricals resumed in earnest in 1854, again in the British Hall, and with profits dutifully reserved for "the relief of the poor."[64] The season commenced as usual in the dead of winter (January 30) with a production of *Don César de Bazan*, by the French playrights Dumanoir and d'Ennery,[ix] featuring Major Edward D'Alton in the title role. Edward Shea of the *Newfoundlander* gushed that the performance "attracted a fashionable and very crowded house," signalling that wealthy patrons must have returned to the fold. Shea's additional observation that "The Corps has evidently incurred very heavy expense in new and beautiful dresses" is a reminder that men usually played the female roles in garrison theatricals.[65] The doors generally opened at 7:00 p.m. and the curtain rose 30 minutes later; admission was two shillings for reserved seats, one shilling three pence for box seats, and nine pence for access to the pit.

The 1854 season ran until the end of May and was nothing if not ambitious, *Don César de Bazan* being but one of 11 productions. Among the others were *The Brigand*, by J.R. Planché; *Grimshaw, Bagshaw, and Bradshaw*, by Thomas Morton; *Used Up; or, L'Homme Blasé*, by Dion Boucicault; *Bombastes Furioso: A Burlesque Tragic Opera*, by William Barnes Rhodes; and *King O'Neil; or, The Irish Brigade*, by Catherine Gore. The repertoire, then, was long on farce, melodrama, and comic opera, frothy stuff to be sure, but no different from what was popular elsewhere in British North America in the period.[66]

---

ix Presumably this production was one of three English versions of the play.

There were usually two plays every evening—a mainpiece and an afterpiece—sprinkled with ancillary entertainments such as the song and dance antics of the Ethiopian Serenaders, which borrowed from the American minstrel troupe of the same name, and was almost certainly performed in blackface. The favourite by far, however, was D'Alton's *Don César de Bazan*, which was staged again on April 24 "By Particular Request" and supposedly "For the last time."[67] But demand was so great that a third performance was added on May 22, with the public being admonished beforehand that it was "Positively for the last time."[68] And so, finally, it was.

The next season went off in much the same vein, but after that the garrison theatricals entered a fallow period. In 1855 at least four officers transferred to regiments of the line in order to join the Crimean War, and this, together with the reduction of the regiment in March left only a skeleton group of six officers to face the New Year. Similar pressures forced the closure of the officers' mess between spring 1855 and spring 1857.[69] One of those officers was Edward D'Alton, who appears to have been the driving force behind the theatricals. Alas, D'Alton retired from the army in 1856, and when he sailed for home *Don César* went with him.[70] There were no further garrison theatricals in St. John's until 1864, when officers of the Royal Canadian Rifle Regiment revived the tradition.[71]

The garrison theatricals may have taken a hiatus, but the regimental band lived on. Music's role in the British Army dated to the functional use of fifes, drums, and bugles in the sixteenth century; by the eighteenth century regimental non-combatant bands were Britain's "single largest employer of musicians by a substantial margin."[72] Founded in 1833, the Royal Newfoundland Companies band succeeded Sir Thomas Cochrane's "governor's band."[73] Financed by the officers' mess fund and committed first and foremost to the mess, the band graced civilian functions subject to the commanding officer's permission. An order placed with an English supplier in 1856 specified that the band's sheet music was to be arranged for eight performers playing trumpet, trombone, cornet, saxophone, ophicleide, and baritone saxophone or tuba.[74] The failure to mention drums does not mean that the band did not employ drummers, because in all likelihood it did.[75]

The band practised three days a week under a professional bandmaster, receiving instruction in waltzes, polkas, quadrilles, and quick steps in addition to military marches, airs, and songs, of which "Rule, Britannia" and the national anthem were the gold standards.[76] Typically for regimental bands, its membership included teenaged male apprentices who were the sons of soldiers in the regiment.[77] For these soldiers, securing such placements for their sons assured them of military careers and set them on an educational and cultural path that otherwise might never have been possible. Soldiers who were bandsmen—and they were all from the rank and file—not only escaped much of the tedium of garrison routine, but also could earn additional income depending on the officers' generosity.[78]

The band was a fixture at fraternal societies' parades, dinners, and dances, and from 1841 to 1847 gave bi-weekly summertime concerts on the Government House mall.[79] It regularly graced the city's pre-eminent sporting event, the St. John's Regatta, performed at the garrison theatricals, and supplied backing for touring outfits such as the Krollman Singers and Mr. Bunting's Wax Figures. Like the garrison reviews, the band's performances were not entirely benign, because intentionally or not, they reinforced loyalty to church and state, and were important elements of what William Tecumseh Sherman called the "passive" threat of military force.[80]

The public loved the band regardless, as proven by events in the summer of 1860, when the recently appointed commanding officer of the Royal Newfoundland Companies, Major John James Grant, cancelled the band's appearance at that year's regatta. After lamenting that the band's absence was "a matter of very general regret and disappointment," the *Newfoundland Express* attempted to educate Grant on its significance, allowing as he "may not be aware of the wants of this community in that respect.[81] In many large cities," it continued, "there are professional bands, whose earnings in a great measure depend upon receipts from public entertainments, Regattas, &c. Here the want of any such band has hitherto been met by the Military Band." In fairness to Grant, he was not totally insensitive. Only a few months earlier he had been a head table guest at the annual St. Patrick's Day dinner of the Benevolent Irish Society, where the band performed "and contributed much to the hilarity of the Evening."[82]

The Sporting Life

English historians have identified sport as another of those "cultural pastimes for which the prosperous gentry and the new leisured middle class hungered."[83] Like theatre and music, sporting activities were an important part of the lives of army officers in British North America, Newfoundland included.[84] Although army and navy officers from Halifax and even England hunted and fished in western Newfoundland, officers of the Royal Newfoundland Companies did not have to go that far, since there was game and fish aplenty in the town's vicinity.[85] The inclusion of double-barrelled shotguns and fishing gear among our officers' personal belongings shows that they seized the opportunities.[86] Our concern here, however, is not so much with hunting and angling as it is with the organized sports of cricket and horse racing, where, as with theatre (and music), army garrisons exerted considerable influence.

Cricket was "the most popular summer sport of the pre-1867 era" in British North America, Newfoundland included.[87] Officers are almost certain to have been among the founders of the St. John's Cricket Club, whose existence was first noted in 1824, and whose earliest matches were held on the Fort Townshend parade ground.[88] Visits by naval patrol vessels occasioned matches between town clubs and combined teams of army and navy officers, along with inter-service matches. On September 14, 1843, for instance, the officers of HMS *Electra* played the garrison officers on the Government House lawn before an audience that included Governor and Lady Harvey "and nearly all the higher classes of the community, together with an immense crowd of all shades and standing."[89] By 1854 there was an official Garrison Cricket Club, which remained active in the 1860s when there were at least three other clubs besides the Garrison and St. John's clubs.[90] The St. John's cricketers who competed in Halifax in 1871—and who may have been Newfoundland's first "national" sports team—owed their existence to military and naval influence.[91]

From the upper-class perspective, one of cricket's advantages was that it attracted working-class spectators, thereby helping to reinforce the social order.[92] This was also true of

Source: Rooms Provincial Archives I.12.001.

Figure II. Caption: St. John's Cricket Club, Pleasantville, Quidi Vidi Lake site, n.d. Cricket's popularity in nineteenth-century Newfoundland owed much to the influence of army and navy officers.

horse racing, which, despite its reputation as the sport of kings, was popular with all classes and "reminded the community who was at its head."[93] As with other aspects of popular culture, organized horse racing appeared in St. John's when the requisite social, economic, and demographic conditions prevailed. The so-called "St. John's Races" were first noted in 1818, with army officers serving as race stewards.[94] These early races were ad hoc affairs with no fixed name, course, or schedule, and took place in late summer or fall after an organizing committee had been struck, chosen a track—usually at some farm on the town's outskirts—and raised prize money. That they were community events was evidenced by the 1827 races at Casey's Farm, with one newspaper noting that as race time approached "the different roads leading to the farm were thronged by the young and the old."[95] The course itself "presented an animated and gay scene, lined as it was, on both sides, with tents, and decked with flags innumerable." Nor were people in a hurry to leave, for when the races concluded they were followed by wrestling matches and running and leaping contests that provided "considerable amusement."

Military involvement in the sport was a constant. On September 16, 1828, when the "Amateurs of the Turf" gathered in the Commercial Room to organize that fall's race, the garrison was represented by the commanding officer of the Veterans, Lieutenant Colonel Thomas Burke; the regimental assistant surgeon, Dr. Henry Mackesey; Lieutenant Stephen Rice of the Veterans; and the CRE, Lieutenant Colonel Henry Vigoureux.[96] Robert Law followed in Burke's footsteps, as, probably, had William Sall. In 1845, when the races were held in Mount Pearl, Law was vice-president and steward of the St. John's Turf Club, whose executive was a who's who of the town's mercantile elite, among them future premier Charles Fox Bennett.[97]

Although it may have been uncommon, there is evidence that officers participated in the races themselves. In 1828, when the competition was called both the "Avalon Races" and the "St. John's Races," Henry Vigoureux owned one of the mounts in the pony race, and in the match race, Stephen Rice rode a horse owned by his father-in-law, Dr. William Carson;[x] his rival jockey was Lieutenant John Collington of the Royal Artillery.[98] That year's event, incidentally, took place on October 15 at "the new Avalon course" at the Grove, a farm on the north side of Quidi Vidi Lake.

The races were not only popular for breaking the routine of everyday life, but also because they created opportunities for gambling. A sport unto itself, gambling was the underbelly of the gentleman's world, contradicting everything it stood for and possessing the ability to destroy a family's wealth and social status.[99] That army officers were prone to its attractions was borne out on March 30, 1826, when Captain Mark Rudkin and Ensign John Philpott of the Veterans fought a duel atop Robinson's Hill[xi] to settle a dispute over how the pot was to be divided in a card game.[100] (The game was lanscolet, or lammy for short.) After Philpott was killed in the exchange, Rudkin was charged with murder, and both men's seconds were charged with being accessories. Their trial, the first to be heard by the recently reorganized Supreme Court, was the talk of the town, and when they were released after being found not guilty, they received a rapturous welcome from a throng of supporters outside the courthouse. For years afterward people gave a wide berth at night to Robinson's Hill because it was said to be haunted by Philpott's ghost.[101] Legend also had it that Rudkin, in an act of gentlemanly contrition, returned to England, retired from the army, tracked down Philpott's mother, and gave her an allowance for the rest of her life. That she actually resided in Corsica was beside the point.[102]

---

[x] Rice had married Frances (Fanny) Coulston Carson on July 18, 1825.

[xi] The crest of Robinson's Hill is today circled by Roche Street. I am grateful to Bob Cuff for identifying its location.

The Ties that Bound

Officers, no less than the rank and file, were a vital part of the community. Even if they moved in different circles, some of their activities and causes benefited all classes; witness their charitable giving, participation in the Agricultural Society and Mechanics Institute, the regimental band, garrison theatricals, cricket, and horse-racing. St. John's may have been located on the continent's periphery, but its residents were familiar with the news of the world and, as Robert Barlow McCrea's dinner party shows, they were not unsophisticated. Small wonder, then, that when officers left Newfoundland for good—as almost all did—they received gifts and testimonials that invariably praised their contributions to charity and entertainments. The outpouring of good will when Robert Law was about to leave in May 1859 after 25 years in the colony was especially poignant.[103] In general, the disdain with which the army was regarded in nineteenth-century England seems to have been absent in Newfoundland, perhaps because officers' contributions had a bigger impact in the smaller setting. Their presence was also a visible reminder of the British connection that was an essential element of Newfoundland's emerging colonial nationalism. Theirs were the ties that bound.

CHAPTER 5

THE COMING OF THE FROST

The Firetrap

By 1815 St. John's was Newfoundland's largest town, and over the ensuing decades it would slowly but surely come to dominate the island's two major industries—cod fishing and sealing—and the domestic and international commerce that revolved around them. Be that as it may, until 1888 St. John's had no municipal government, and the services that were normally associated with it were instead the colony's responsibility. It did not always give them the attention they deserved, and sometimes it simply left them to the voluntary sector. This was true of firefighting, in which the shortcomings of the volunteer firefighting companies caused military firefighters to bear a disproportionate share of the load. The town's vulnerability to fire ensured that the load would be heavy.

The best early nineteenth-century description of St. John's and its combustible potential can be found in an 1809 inspection report by Jenkin Jones of the London-based Phoenix Assurance Company:

The body of the Town is comprized in the Lower Street [i.e., Water Street], which is from one extreme of the Harbour to the other, not much less than One Mile and three quarters long — This Street ... is formed on one side, by the Stores and Buildings on the Wharfs, on the other by Rows of Buildings used for Retail Shops. Altho' called a Street, it is in fact only a crooked and narrow Alley, in some places, contracted to 6 feet wide, in others, expanding to as much as 12 or 18 feet. This Street runs nearly in the direction of the prevailing winds, and is a funnel thro' which they blow occasionally with great violence. —

The Buildings are uniformly, throughout the Town of Wood, and have the Roofs covered in with Shingles, — there is not a private Building of a different description in the whole place. —

St. John's has of late years rapidly encreased in population, and the properties on the Water side have become of great value. — In proportion with these causes, the Buildings upon them have become more numerous, and indeed a more crowded range of Wharfage and Stores, I have yet seen in no place.[1]

When another Phoenix Assurance Company inspector, J.J. Broomfield, visited in 1845, he was no more impressed than Jones, declaring St. John's "the worst built town I have seen since I left England."[2] Broomfield must have been unaware that the British North American seaports of Saint John and Québec had equally dangerous concentrations of wooden buildings, not to mention timber, shingles, and other forest products piled sky-high on their waterfronts awaiting shipment to market.[3] For the nineteenth century as a whole, Québec led all British North American towns with 13 conflagrations, followed by Saint John (seven), Montreal (five), and St. John's (three). Fires, however, came in all sizes, and it was said of St. John's that "an annual fire was as regularly looked for as the coming of the frost."[4]

Nineteenth-Century Firefighting

Seemingly minor fires often became major ones owing to the primitive state of firefighting technology and social cleavages in the community. The early fire engine was a wooden reservoir on wheels that firefighters towed to the scene; the use of horses as draught-power came later in the century with the adoption of steam engines.[5] Five men could haul an engine when conditions were perfect, but in winter, when streets were barely passable, it could take up to 30.[6] The main water sources in St. John's were wells and small streams that coursed down the hillside toward the harbour. If a source was nearby, water could be pumped directly from it into the reservoir, but as often as not it became necessary to establish a bucket brigade of "water men" in order to fill it. These were formed into two lines, with full buckets passing up one line and empty ones going down the other to be replenished and recirculated. Depending on a fire's scale, bucket brigades could range from tens to hundreds of water men, most of whom were recruited on the spot from among onlookers.

A manual pump was employed to force the water out of the engine's reservoir, through a leather hose, and onto the fire. Working the pump was so demanding that 40 men were assigned to each engine in St. John's, the same as in Saint John and Toronto.[7] Up to 12 men at a time worked the "brakes," as the pump handles were known, and when they grew exhausted another team would take their place, and so on until the fire was extinguished or the building lost. The water pressure achieved by this method was so weak that the engine had to be placed as close as possible to the fire, increasing the danger to the men. Still, a pump could project water 46 metres into the air, high enough to reach the roofs or windows of most buildings of the period, albeit without much force by the time it got there.[8]

Other techniques were used to keep fires from spreading and to safeguard property. One of the most common was to drape wet blankets or carpets over the roofs and sides of adjacent buildings to keep them from igniting. To this end, the Royal Newfoundland Companies reserved all unserviceable blankets so they could be used in firefighting.[9] More dramatically, "saw and hatchet" men created firebreaks by tearing down buildings in the fire's path. To accomplish this act of creative destruction, the men would saw through a building's interior support beams, attach hooks to it, and pull it down with hawsers. If the building refused to fall, some qualified military firefighter, usually an artilleryman or engineer, would set a gunpowder charge and blow it up.[10] Civilian and military firefighters brought canvas bags to fire scenes, filling them with valuables saved from the flames and removing them for safekeeping until the fire was over. This was necessary because some urban residents viewed fires as opportunities for plunder, much as baymen viewed shipwrecks as licence to take surviving valuables. After witnessing a fire in St. John's in 1839, the British geologist J.B. Jukes reported that:

> The behaviour of the military and the fire companies was good, and to their exertions and those of the more respectable inhabitants was owing the preservation of the town. I was, however, much struck with the stupid indifference of a large part of the lower class of the population.... No inducement or excitement beyond that of present pay and reward seemed to rouse one of the hundreds of great idle fellows that stood around to stir hand or foot for the preservation of the houses and property about. I was afterwards told, indeed, that by far too many of the population looked upon a fire as a godsend, more especially if it reached or

threatened a merchant's store, when a regular system of plundering was carried out unblushingly, and, as it were, by prescriptive right.[11]

Since it was common for booty to be carried off to nearby outports after and sometimes during fires, the Royal Newfoundland Companies delegated men to guard property on the spot, to police roads and bridges leading from town, and occasionally even to watch the harbour entrance.[12]

The Military-Civilian Relationship

In part because of their greater numbers, discipline, and experience, military firefighters led firefighting efforts in St. John's. Once a month during parade, the commanding officer read aloud the garrison orders for procedures to be followed in case of fire.[13] The military was responsible for the related roles of fire detection and sounding the fire alarm. The alarm—two guns "fired quick"—was sounded from Fort William or Queen's Battery.[14] During the Royal Artillery's ten-year absence from St. John's (1852-62), the Royal Newfoundland Companies exercised sole responsibility for these functions. At the sound of the alarm, the fire piquets proceeded with their engines to the scene, and once there were bound "to protect such property as may be committed to their charge, and their Fire Engines to co-operate with those of the City."[15] As well, all off-duty men were to report to the scene and place themselves at the disposal of the fire wardens "or other competent civil authorities." With the exception of these off-duty soldiers, military firefighters took priority over civilian ones. After a fire in 1855, the press reported that "the Phoenix company took the commonly-viewed honourable position of supplying the Military Engine with water."[16] This contrasted with the pecking order in Halifax, where the military took directions from the Chairman of the Board of Fireworks.[17]

The higher status of military firefighters in St. John's reflected the feeble state of the civilian fire companies. The earliest mention of these comes from Jenkin Jones's 1809 report, where he noted that there were three fire engines "with Fire Companies attached," plus an unspecified number of engines belonging to the military.[18] The timing is significant here, for the furious economic expansion of the war years gave rise to a spate of safety-related developments, including an improved pilotage service and the colony's first lighthouse (at Fort Amherst).[19] The Society of Merchants established a fire company in 1811—often wrongly called Newfoundland's first—and the business community was also behind additional companies that were formed in the 1820s, all voluntary and financed by public subscription.[20] The subscribers, however, were mainly those very same businessmen, and, conveniently enough, the fire companies were only obliged to protect subscribers' property.

In 1833 the House of Assembly attempted to broaden coverage by passing legislation creating four fire companies (one for each ward) in which membership was compulsory for all householders.[21] The new companies were supposed to be financed by a property assessment, but because so many property owners reneged on their payments, the equipment of the newly-formed companies continued to be second-rate. Despite membership being compulsory, it lagged because there were no penalties for refusing to participate. The military did what it could to help the fire companies by donating used fire engines to them and setting examples of organization and discipline.[22] Their shortcomings nonetheless persisted.

Military attendance at fires was invariably followed by public expressions of gratitude by individuals whose property had been saved, and on occasion by financial remuneration. After Private Thomas Brennan of the Veterans was accidentally killed while fighting a fire on September 18, 1839, the Chamber of Commerce (successor to the Society of Merch-

THE COMING OF THE FROST   93

ants) gave his widow the then princely sum of £30.[23] After that same fire, the chamber also donated £100 to the Veterans and the Royal Artillery to compensate them for damage to their clothing. Over time, contributions from the chamber, private citizens, and insurance companies accumulated in a fund from which the commanding officer of the Royal Newfoundland Companies met his men's demands for routine fire-related compensation.[24]

Given the importance of the military's firefighting role, community leaders were understandably mortified when news of the Signal Hill concentration scheme leaked out in the mid-1830s. Editor Henry Winton of the *Public Ledger* protested that

> the measure proposed is the most injudicious that can possibly be adopted, inasmuch if carried into effect it will deprive us of that invaluable assistance which we have so frequently derived from the exertions of the troops in cases of fire which in a wooden town such as this must ever be attended with very serious results.[25]

Winton stepped up his opposition to the concentration scheme after a fire on September 20, 1835, during which a Private O'Regan of the Veterans was killed while attempting to rescue a child from a burning house. Winton thanked the regiment, "who, it will be remembered are upon all similar calamities, our main stay and support," and noted that during the fire the Royal Artillery

> were also present and lent their aid for the common good; but they had to run from Signal Hill, a distance of nearly two miles—(*whither it has been very sagaciously proposed to remove all the garrison!*) before they reached the scene of conflagration, and after all, the service which they really performed was vastly

more than could have been expected of them, after such exertion.[26]

The Chamber of Commerce joined the cause at its September 30 meeting, passing a resolution acknowledging that military firefighters constituted "an organized body, perfectly under command and separated from those local interests and feelings which naturally tend to affright and cause confusion among the inhabitants of the town."[27] The chamber was concerned that removing the garrison to Signal Hill would deprive the town of timely assistance during fires "and in the Winter most probably of their aid altogether, as the roads are at that season often impracticable for such purposes." The chamber's president, Charles Fox Bennett, urged Governor Henry Prescott to keep the remaining troops in the town forts. Property owners would have shed few tears when the Board of Ordnance abandoned the concentration scheme in the 1840s.

The Great Fire of June 9, 1846

The Great Fire of June 9, 1846, strained the garrison's firefighting abilities and placed its officers at the forefront of reconstruction politics. The fire started around 8:30 a.m. near the intersection of Queen and Duckworth (now New Gower) streets, and although military firefighters were on the scene within 20 minutes, lack of water for their engines left them powerless to prevent its spread.[28]

It was a warm day with a strong west by northwest wind that rapidly pushed the fire eastward and south to the Water Street business district, where it not only continued on its eastward course, but also managed to fork off to the westward.[29] In the latter direction military and civilian firefighters, aided by what for them was a favourable wind, eventually stopped the fire in front of the Newman premises at River Head. To

THE COMING OF THE FROST   95

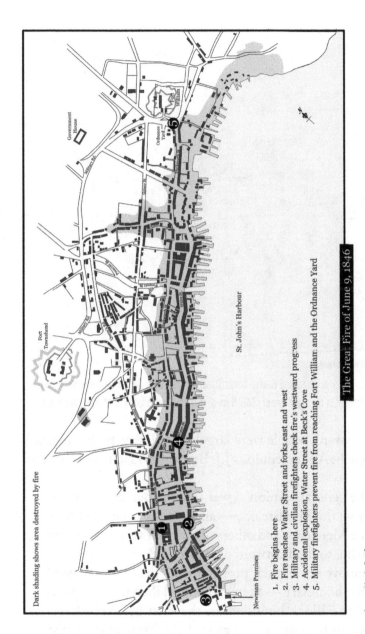

Source: Map by Don Parsons.
Figure 12: The Great Fire of June 9, 1846.

Source: *Rooms Provincial Archives, MG 24-3.*

Figure 13: Customs House and view of Water Street, October 1841. All the buildings shown here were destroyed in the Great Fire of 1846. Note soldiers milling about in front of the auction mart.

the eastward, people were largely indifferent to the inferno's approach. An incredulous J.J. Broomfield later recalled that:

> the general opinion ... was that the flames would not cross the Fire Breaks, — and so fully persuaded were the Merchants and others of this, that very few persons living to the Eastward of Warrens Cove attempted to remove any of their property until the fire had passed that boundary — then and not till then the occupants of the Block bounded on the East by Becks Cove began to remove — but still the Merchants in the next Block Eastward were not apprehensive of the

fire communicating with their range of Stone built Stores....[30]

Although the fire had already done major damage by the time it neared the Beck's Cove firebreak, the consensus afterward was that it likely would have stopped right there had it not been for a terrible accident. In an effort to expand the firebreak, Governor Harvey, not noted as a firefighter, ordered the Royal Artillery to blow up a wooden house on the south side of Water Street. The men who ignited the charge unfortunately mistimed it, and one of them was killed and another badly wounded when the powder exploded before they could exit the building. Some of the burning debris from the blast landed in oversized wooden vats behind Water Street that were being used to render seal fat into oil. This triggered a nightmarish explosion that sent a shower of flaming seal oil over neighbouring buildings. Wholesale panic ensued, and civilians who might have stayed to fight the fire instead flew to their homes to save what they could. In their absence, looters ran wild. Meanwhile, soldiers who had come down from Signal Hill had to turn around and go back in order to put out brush fires ignited by burning embers carried there by the wind, further reducing the manpower available to fight the fire in town.

Late in the day an exhausted party from the Royal Newfoundland Companies and the Royal Artillery led by Robe and Law made a desperate stand near the east end of Duckworth Street. They succeeded in diverting the fire from the Ordnance Yard and Fort William, and in the process probably saved St. Thomas's Garrison Church, the Commissariat and Royal Engineer establishments, and the residences of the Anglican bishop and several government officials.[31] Despite these and other heroic acts, the fire was not totally extinguished until mid-morning the next day, by which time it had claimed nearly three-quarters of the town and caused damages worth nearly £1 million.[i] Gone were the Anglican Church of St. John the Baptist, the courthouse and gaol, the Amateur Theatre, the Customs House, the Presentation Convent, both banks, all of the Water Street business district except for the now-orphaned Newman premises, the Ordnance Wharf, and the warehouses and wharves between Water Street and the harbour. Miraculously, there were only two fatalities, but 12,000 people out of a population of some 21,000 were suddenly homeless.

On June 10, Harvey convened a meeting of the town's "principal inhabitants" at Government House to begin reconstruction planning and relief administration. In addition to appointing a military patrol to prevent further looting,

---

[i] £888,356 to be precise. See C.R. Fay, *Life and Labour in Newfoundland* (Toronto: University of Toronto Press, 1956), 188.

THE COMING OF THE FROST   99

the meeting placed an embargo on shipping from the port, both to preserve essential supplies and to close a potential escape hatch for looters.[ii] To give teeth to the embargo, the Royal Newfoundland Companies' Lieutenant Hugh Chambers, who was Harvey's private secretary, stationed his yacht in The Narrows.[32]

The meeting struck a relief committee composed of merchants, politicians, clergymen, and, as ex-officio members, Law, Robe, Commanding Officer of the Royal Artillery Major H.R. Wright, Assistant Commissary General T.C. Weir, and Deputy Ordnance Storekeeper George Winter.[33] Robe and Surveyor General Joseph Noad were also appointed as commissioners to recommend a rebuilding plan to the legislature. On July 15, Robe and Noad submitted a report calling for a radical realignment of the town into gridded streets surrounding a central square; for straightening Water Street and widening both it and Duckworth Street to a minimum of 21.3 metres; and for adding more firebreaks.[34] The legislature ignored or amended most of the recommendations because of the potential cost of compensating individuals for property that would be lost in widening the streets, and because it would have meant shifting the Water Street business premises closer to the harbour, which the merchants were loath to do since it would have impinged on their warehouses and wharves.

On August 4 the legislature passed a rebuilding act that called for Water and Duckworth streets to be no more than 18.3 metres wide, thereby reducing the amount of land the government would have to acquire and sparing the mer-

---

[ii] There was more to the regiment's role than just policing. Its men also erected tents on Ordnance land west of Government House as temporary accommodations for the homeless. Before winter set in, these were replaced by wooden sheds on a section of the Fort Townshend parade ground. As fire victims rebuilt or found new living arrangements, these sheds, known as "the camps," were given over as housing for the town's poor. They continued to serve this role until the Poor Asylum opened in 1861.

chants from having to reconfigure their property.[35] The act did, however, provide for one more firebreak than the ten that the commissioners had recommended. It called for shortening Duckworth Street by ending it at the intersection with Gower Street; west of the intersection, Duckworth Street would become New Gower Street. Only stone or brick buildings could be erected on Water and Duckworth streets, but elsewhere wooden construction was permissible. The act's framers therefore sought to make Water and Duckworth streets a haven for the town's merchants and professionals, and to push the working class—and the fire hazard—north and west.[36] Achieving that vision would depend on revenues from an assessment to be levied on property owners, and on floating a £250,000 loan via the British government, with proceeds to be used for land acquisition and subsidizing the construction of stone and brick buildings. When London advised that it would not float the loan, the legislators found themselves back at square one. It was at this point that Robert Law took centre stage.

Despite his involvement in fighting the fire and launching the recovery effort, Sir John Harvey had no desire to see the process through, and had in fact long been angling for a new posting.[37] On September 1, jaws dropped as he hurriedly left St. John's to become governor of Nova Scotia, leaving others to clean up the mess he had been instrumental in creating.[38] Because his successor, Sir John Gaspard Le Marchant, did not arrive until April the following year, Law served during the interim as Administrator of the Colony, or effectively the acting governor. To him fell the weighty responsibility of supervising the relief effort and hammering out a compromise with the legislature over the rebuilding plan, tasks that became even more challenging after a destructive hurricane on September 19—called "the Great Gale" and acknowledged to be the worst in 30 years—a poor cod fishery, and a failed potato crop.

When the legislature reconvened on December 1, the

Great Fire dominated Law's opening address.[39] He regretted that not a single civilian fire company had been re-established since the fire, this despite the fact that the Phoenix Assurance Company had donated two new engines, currently in the military's care, for their use. He felt that the companies' reformation was a matter "of paramount importance." As for rebuilding the town, he cautioned that the colony's financial circumstances would not "admit of an extensive expenditure for alterations or improvements of an ornamental character." It would be difficult to imagine, however, that too many people were thinking about ornamentation at this time.

On January 14, 1847, the legislature passed a revised rebuilding act that kept most of the features of the original legislation, but with two important exceptions that reflected financial considerations. Stone or brick buildings would still be mandatory on Water Street, but on Duckworth Street they would be required on the south side only. In deference to the town's major property owners, a drastically reduced financing arrangement called for the government to float a £20,000 loan on its own credit, to be augmented by a 10 per cent duty on imports entering the port of St. John's, and not by the assessment envisaged in the original legislation. This was a victory for property owners, because even though many of them were merchants who would have to pay the new duty, that cost, unlike the assessment, could be passed on to their customers.

The administration of fire relief funds totalling £102,500 became highly contentious. The funds were earmarked for three main purposes: to provide fire victims with food, clothing, and shelter; to reimburse uninsured individuals for rebuilding their homes; and to pay passage money for those who wished to leave Newfoundland rather than stay and rebuild. Most of the money had been donated by the British and British North American governments, and Anglican congregations in Britain had raised £29,000 at Queen Victoria's request, an amount that came to be known as the Queen's Letter Fund. In November, Law recommended to the Colonial Secretary, Lord Grey, that as the uninsured had largely been compensated, no additional relief funds should be issued, since they were "demoralizing" to the recipients, a remark that, when word of it became public, caused Law to be excoriated in the press for "heartless swindling of the unfortunate."[40] He further recommended that some of the remaining money should be used to build a new Anglican cathedral, and that the balance should be reserved for the Colonial Office to be spent at its discretion. Grey, however, earmarked half of the Queen's Letter Fund for the new cathedral, even though it had not been raised for that purpose. His decision outraged the colony's other religious denominations, who felt that he was playing favourites with the Church of England, which of course he was. Catholic Bishop Michael Anthony Fleming protested that the former Anglican Church of St. John the Baptist "was not worth £200."[41] That may have been an exaggeration, but he made his point.

Aftermath of the Great Fire

After the fire, relief funds and a fierce public spirit produced numerous civic improvements, some of them of the "ornamental character" that Law had decried. New shops of brick or stone construction "with heavy slate roofs and more remarkable for solidity than beauty" sprang up along Water Street, which, together with Duckworth Street, was somewhat straightened.[42] Elsewhere some impressive public buildings and churches emerged from the ashes, and in a further sign of progress, a gas streetlight system that had been less than a year old when the fire struck was revived and extended.

Understandably, various measures were taken with fire protection in mind. Mere months before the fire, the Board

Source: Provincial Resource Library, Newfoundland and Labrador Collection, C70/PA190.

Figure 14: Colonial Building, 1851. Opened in 1850 to house the Newfoundland Legislature, the Colonial Building was one of several impressive structures erected in the aftermath of the Great Fire of 1846.

of Ordnance had granted permission to the St. John's Water Company to use George's Pond, on Signal Hill, as a town water supply. Spurred on by the fire, the company began tests in 1848, and the system became operational the following year.[43] It was complemented by four water cisterns at strategic locations around town, with a fifth being added in 1859.[44] Long before then, the seal oil vats that had played such a key role in the fire's spread had been moved to the harbour's largely unpopulated south side.[45]

Despite these outwardly progressive signs, all was not well. George's Pond proved to be too small to service even Water Street, and the town would lack a proper water supply until the Windsor Lake system was completed in 1862. (George's Pond was then retained as an auxiliary source.) By forcing the working class north and west of Duckworth Street, the government had only itself to blame for the emergence of Tarahan's Town, five blocks of combustible wooden tenements that were home to some 2,000 people, most of them poor. Also, immediately after the fire the legislature had repealed the 1833 fire companies' act and revived the voluntary system. Formed in 1847, the Phoenix Fire Brigade was first out of the gate; by 1860 it had been joined by the St. John's Water Company, Sons of Temperance, and Cathedral brigades. Funded by modest government grants and fitful private donations, the new brigades never amounted to much, once again leaving the military as the town's best hope against fire.[46]

There were sporadic fires after 1846, but no especially noteworthy ones until October 16, 1855, when the Tarahan's Town time bomb exploded. The fire raged for nearly three hours, consuming the entire neighbourhood and leaving its residents homeless yet again. That some of them were the wives of soldiers of the Royal Newfoundland Companies must have lent extra zeal to the men's efforts, because Edward Shea of the *Newfoundlander* wrote that they "never did more effective work on any such occasion that we remember."[47] This contrasted with the unseemly expressions of delight from the town's upper crust that a blight had been removed.[48]

The Tarahan's Town fire revealed another risk that the military incurred in its firefighting role. In an effort to keep the fire from reaching Prescott Street, military firefighters tore down the house of a dumbstruck John Chancey, who subsequently took legal action against Law, accusing him of trespass and seeking damages of £300.[49] The government, no doubt mindful of the military's crucial role, rushed to Law's defence, and none other than Premier Philip Francis Little, in his dual capacity as Attorney General, argued the case. Testifying before the Supreme Court on December 3, 1857, Law denied that he had given the order to pull the house down, claiming that he had been dining with Governor Darling at Government House when the alarm sounded, and that by the time he had reached the scene, the house was already being torn down. The orderly bugler and several soldiers who had been present also testified that Law never gave the order, although they never said who did. While the jury found in Chancey's favour, its members reduced the damages to £70, reflecting the court's instructions that if they were to award damages, they "must be regulated not by the real abstract value of the property, but by the value to be attached to it at the time, taking into consideration the jeopardy it was in and the perils by which it was surrounded." Based on pre-trial correspondence between Little and Colonial Secretary John Kent, the government probably paid Law's bill.[50]

On February 20, 1860, Law's successor as commanding officer, Major John James Grant, issued a new standing order making future military attendance at fires contingent on a magistrate's written request.[51] Because this upended the old practice by which military attendance was automatic, concerns arose within the community that military firefighters would now take longer to reach the scene. In the Assembly the opposition used the issue to press the government to create a permanent firefighting force funded by local assessment.[52] That effort, however, went nowhere.

The government's preference for volunteerism was typical of the times. Professional firefighters did not appear in the United States until the 1850s, and not until a decade later in British North America's larger centres.[53] Their spread thereafter was uneven, and volunteerism never completely disappeared. While St. John's had to wait until 1895 to get its first paid firefighters, that was only one year later than Halifax.[54] Regardless, the Royal Newfoundland Companies (and the Royal Artillery) were the backbone of firefighting during their time in St. John's, battling fires from Water Street to

Tarahan's Town, helping rich and poor alike, and performing selflessly under the most harrowing conditions.

CHAPTER 6
CIVIL COMMOTION

Politics and Society

Like firefighting, policing in British North America was so underdeveloped in the first half of the nineteenth century that the civil authorities "effectively transferred to the military the major responsibility for upholding public order."[1] In another time, this might not have mattered so much, but the period happened to be one of great political reform marked by the struggle to achieve responsible government. This struggle aroused passions that sometimes led to violence requiring military intervention. Newfoundland did not follow Upper and Lower Canada on the path to rebellion, but it had troubles enough of its own. Because much of its politically motivated violence occurred in Conception Bay, the Royal Newfoundland Companies maintained a detachment there on an intermittent basis between 1841 and 1855. The regiment's role in aiding the civil power culminated in a bloody riot in St. John's on May 13, 1861, in which Conception Bay influence was paramount. When the smoke cleared, politics and society would never be the same.

Although Newfoundland's achievement of representative

108   THE INVISIBLES

government[i] in 1832 was unanimously welcomed by the unlikely coalition that had forged it, harmony gave way to dis-
sension as the erstwhile partners faced the reality of coexisting
under the new system.[2] The main collaborators had included
middle-class professionals (lawyers, doctors, teachers, journal-
ists, contractors, shopkeepers, and such), most of whom were
Catholics or Protestant dissenters, and all of whom thought
an assembly was the best way to handle local problems. Members of the small, powerful, and overwhelmingly Protestant
mercantile elite feared that without an assembly they would
be taxed by a distant London to defray the costs of colonial
administration. The bulk of the Catholic community, which
was predominantly Irish and working class (mainly fishermen
and labourers), felt that representative government would
help it to achieve genuine equality in Newfoundland society.

Although Catholics accounted for slightly more than half
the colony's population of 73,705 in 1836, they were heavily
concentrated on the Avalon Peninsula, especially St. John's,
where they made up three-quarters of the town's 14,946
inhabitants. In Newfoundland as in Britain, Catholics had
long been second-class citizens.[3] The worst excesses of the
penal laws were over by the end of the eighteenth century, a
thaw that included the formal recognition (in 1799) of the
admission of Irishmen to the rank and file of the British
Army.[4] Led by Daniel O'Connell, Irish Catholics campaigned in the 1820s to remove the remaining legal restrictions,
among them the right to vote and to sit in the British Parliament. The campaign was distinguished by the active participation of the priesthood, signalling a break from the Irish
Catholic Church's traditional support for the status quo.[5] In
1829 Irish Catholics were rewarded when Parliament passed
the Catholic Emancipation Act, but in a perverse twist, the
Newfoundland Supreme Court ruled on a technicality that

---

[i] Government by elected members of a House of Assembly and a Crown-appointed Council.

the act did not apply to the colony. Alone within the British Empire, Newfoundland Catholics had to wait until 1832 to enjoy complete religious freedom, and even then, the struggle for equality was far from over.

The campaign for representative government, then, coincided with a time when Catholic rights dominated Newfoundland and British affairs alike, and when priests were becoming politically active. Unfortunately, instead of ushering in a new age of denominational harmony, emancipation triggered a Protestant backlash on both sides of the Atlantic. The Roman Catholic Church fed that backlash by embracing ultramontanism, a principle that exalted the church's authority over the state's, and whose inherent conservatism bucked the increasingly liberal trend of the times.[6] Newfoundland's ultramontane champion was the Franciscan priest and political animal Michael Anthony Fleming (born circa 1792), a native of Ireland who arrived in St. John's in 1823, and who after becoming bishop (vicar apostolic) in 1829 began remaking the local church along ultramontane lines.[7]

Ambitious, devout, and ruthless, Fleming—unlike his conciliatory predecessors—was not one for turning the other cheek.[8] When he clashed with Newfoundland's obdurate Protestant establishment,[ii] the shock waves affected the entire community, including the officers and men of the British Army.

The Poisoning

In the lead-up to the general election of November 1832 to choose the first 15-member House of Assembly, various factors gave establishment members pause. The 1831 cod fishery had been a poor one, and it was followed by a bitterly cold

---

[ii] By "establishment," I mean the governor and the coterie of appointed councillors and office-holders around him, including members of the judiciary.

Source: Frontispiece to M.F. Howley, Ecclesiastical History of Newfoundland (Boston: Doyle and Whittle, 1888).

Figure 15: Michael Anthony Fleming. A polarizing figure, Bishop Fleming loomed large over Newfoundland politics in the age of reform.

winter that added to the privations of fishing families. On August 18, 1832, a fire destroyed much of the Harbour Grace business district and left hundreds homeless; the price of cod that year was low; and in the fall the potato crop failed. Fearing social unrest, Governor Sir Thomas Cochrane drew the Colonial Office's attention to the feeble state of the Veterans and stressed "the absolute necessity of strengthening this Garrison before winter."[9] Those fears were shared by the Chamber of Commerce, which, also distrusting the Veterans, requested that a naval force be sent to St. John's "lest a spirit of dissatisfaction should shew itself during the coming winter when we may be without communications with Halifax and the neighbouring provinces."[10]

In June Chief Justice Richard Alexander Tucker approached the Commanding Royal Engineer, Lieutenant Colonel John Oldfield, to learn what military options existed in "the possible, but by no means probable contingency of civil commotion, arising from Famine, or other causes."[11] Revealing his own insecurities, Oldfield replied that if the troops were unable to keep order, they would do best to retire to the summit of Signal Hill, since it would be easier to defend that position than the town forts. In words that would have given Tucker cold comfort, Oldfield observed that nearly a quarter of the Veterans were currently in hospital and unlikely to be capable of "serious duty" during a major disturbance. Nor would Tucker have been happy to learn that the Signal Hill armoury, which lay outside the summit and held some 3,000 stand of arms, was "completely unprotected."

The election itself was relatively quiet, returning an Assembly in which Protestant and mercantile interests predominated. Nonetheless, certain developments occurred in St. John's that would poison the atmosphere for decades to come, justifying Cochrane's earlier prediction that, despite the prevailing surface calm between Catholics and Protestants, "a small spark would excite a flame not easily subdued."[12] A malignant feud erupted between Henry Winton, the English-born Con-gregationalist editor and publisher of the *Public Ledger*, and Bishop Fleming and Catholic candidate John Kent, an auction-eer and commission agent who was a native of Waterford and so close to Fleming that he would marry his sister Johanna in 1834.[13] Although Winton, like Fleming and Kent, had supported representative government, he began to have second thoughts as the election approached, and, like many Protestants in the immediate post-emancipation era, those thoughts were influenced by anti-Catholicism.

Winton's main complaint was priestly support for certain candidates, especially Kent. Perhaps if he had merely voiced his disapproval, nothing more would have happened, but he went much farther than that, describing Catholics in an infamous editorial as pawns in a priestly conspiracy designed to win control of the Assembly. While there is no doubt that Fleming and most of his priests were shamelessly political, Winton was wrong to tar all Catholics with the same brush. Factionalism was rife in the Catholic community, and, as in Ireland, priestly influence in Newfoundland politics was never as extensive as contemporary observers (and some modern-day historians) would have us believe.[14] As an Irish historian put it, the clergy "could lead their people only in the direction that they wanted to go."[15] There were also Protestants—albeit very few—in the anti-establishment camp, and they used Fleming for their purposes just as he used them for his. The Protestant establishment and the mercantile elite were, however, blind to such distinctions, and the war of words between Winton, Fleming, and Kent fanned the flames of denominational hatred.

The St. John's by-election of December 2, 1833, provided an early outlet for the bitterness sown in the general election, and its fallout brought the Veterans into a role they would never relinquish. The contest pitted Catholic shopkeeper Timothy Hogan against Scottish native Dr. William Carson, who, together with the Irish-born merchant Patrick Morris, had led the campaign for representative government. (During this period, in Newfoundland as elsewhere in British North America, there were competing interests but no formal political parties. Although conventional labels such as Liberals, Reformers, and Conservatives are problematic, this has not stopped historians from using them.)[16] Nominally Presbyterian, Carson was a fierce democrat whose hatred of entrenched, unelected privilege endeared him to Catholics and unnerved both the Protestant establishment and the sycophantic mercantile elite, whose leading members found their way onto Council.[17] Stung by defeat in the recent general election, Carson now diligently cultivated Fleming's support in order to advance his agenda. Another of his vehicles for doing so was the *Newfoundland Patriot*, a newspaper that he co-founded in July 1833 and briefly edited, and that quickly emerged as "the foremost champion of all the aggrieved within the colony."[18]

Carson's opponent, Timothy Hogan, belonged to a group of independent middle-class Catholics whose coziness with the Protestant establishment brought important government contracts their way. This made them anathema to Fleming, who sought to replace them with a new Catholic middle class that would be loyal to him.[19] His antipathy for Hogan and his kind was further influenced by their active lay role in the church—which he eventually crushed—and by Irish factionalism, Fleming and his coterie being Waterford men, and the independent Catholics, Wexford men. Scorned as "Orange Catholics" and "Mad Dogs,"[iii] these "Liberal Catholics" (as Fleming called them) would be the most visible casualties of Newfoundland's political warfare and Fleming's ultramontane purge. During that fall's by-election campaign Fleming openly backed Carson, while his priests, including

---

iii As noted by historian John FitzGerald, the term *Mad Dogs* originated in Ireland in the 1820s when it was used to describe Catholics who did not support O'Connell.

his chief lieutenant Father Edward Troy, threatened to withhold the sacraments from parishioners who did business with Hogan. Throngs of Carson supporters took to the streets, lending an edge of physical menace to the proceedings. Under financial pressure from the boycott, Hogan eventually withdrew his candidacy and publicly apologized to Fleming, enabling Carson to win unopposed.[20]

In the election's wake, Winton unleashed a barrage in the *Ledger* castigating Fleming and his priests for their political activism; they in turn added him to the list of reprobates whom they denounced from the pulpit. An informal campaign of violence and intimidation against Winton, which had begun with damage to his office on election day, now escalated. On Christmas Eve some mischief-makers armed with stones broke the windows of Winton's Water Street house, but this was merely a prelude to bigger things on Christmas Day, when growing numbers of people began to converge on the premises.[21] By late afternoon the magistrates realized that the paltry force at their disposal (seven police constables and five special constables)[iv] would soon be unable to stop further encroachments by an angry mob[v] that they now estimated to be close to a thousand people.[22] Accordingly, they sought military aid, presumably by submitting a written request to the officer commanding the troops, as specified by army regulations. As darkness descended some 80 Veterans commanded by Waterloo veteran Lieutenant Stephen Rice

---

[iv] Until 1853, the St. John's magistrates were responsible for all aspects of police administration, including hiring and firing. Outport magistrates retained these powers until the 1870s. On the evolution of the magistracy and the police, see Keith Mercer, *Rough Justice: Policing, Crime, and the Origins of the Royal Newfoundland Constabulary, 1729-1871* (St. John's: Flanker Press, forthcoming).

[v] Many historians use "crowd" instead of "mob" because the latter is thought to be pejorative, while the former confers moral standing. In the case of food riots and the like, this makes sense, but for present purposes I prefer "mob," defined by *The Compact Edition of the Oxford English Dictionary* as "a tumultuous crowd bent on, or liable to be incited to, acts of lawlessness and outrage," as indeed this one was.

arrived, some of whom took positions in front of the house while others cleared the street. After the mob dispersed, the bulk of the detachment withdrew to the courthouse, leaving a few men behind as sentries. No sooner had the detachment withdrawn, however, than the mob reassembled and began pelting the house with stones. After a sentry sounded the call to arms, the men at the courthouse returned and started to clear the street again. They were assisted by Edward Troy, who arrived around 9:00 p.m. and urged people to leave, which they gradually did.

Aiding the civil power was hardly new for the British soldier, either at home or abroad. It was practically the army's *raison d'être* in Ireland, and in British North America, resort to it at election time dated to 1785.[23] Much more recently—on May 21, 1832—British troops had fired on election rioters in Montreal, dropping three of them dead in their tracks.[24] It was a role that commanding officers universally detested, and for good reasons.[25] Training for it was pointless, since each situation brought its own unique circumstances; it put the men in harm's way; and officers and men could be tried in civil and military courts alike if they were thought to have used excessive force or, at the other extreme, to have neglected their duty.

Regardless of how officers felt, it was a role that the army had to perform owing to the Riot Act of 1714,[vi] which empowered magistrates to order groups of 12 or more people "being Unlawfully, Riotously, and Tumultuously Assembled together" to disperse, and to call in the army if they failed to do so in an hour.[26] The magistrates' role was therefore pivotal, but also fraught with complications. Although magistrates could be neglectful, they were more likely to be overly eager to involve the military, as army leaders complained they were in Ireland.[27] Magistrates often owned property that it was

---

[vi] I Geo. I, c. 5. Although passed in 1714, the act did not take effect until the next year.

116   THE INVISIBLES

in their own interests to protect, and in Newfoundland they were usually merchants and almost exclusively Protestants, predisposing them to fear the worst from mobs they presumed to be Catholic-dominated.

In their defence, the magistrates had good reason to doubt the adequacy of the police. In 1825, St. John's had only one high constable and eight constables, whose salaries were paid out of revenues from tavern licences.[28] Eight years later the newly constituted House of Assembly assumed financial responsibility for the force, but by 1839 the number of constables had shrunk to six, causing an English visitor to remark on what he perceived as "the entire want of all police."[29] Short of requesting military aid, the magistrates' only other recourse was, as at Christmas 1833, to designate special constables for temporary duty. These were untrained men recruited from the community's "respectable" ranks, and while they were likely to share the magistrates' biases, they were generally, and perhaps understandably, reluctant to serve.

In the aftermath of the Christmas Day bedlam at Winton's, Edward Shea of the *Newfoundlander*, a rare voice of moderation in a rising sea of shrillness, criticized the magistrates for requesting military aid in the first place, insisting that although a few individuals had shown "a disposition to be disorderly," most of the people at Winton's had been drawn there by curiosity rather than malice.[30] Although he also claimed that "the troops ... acted with the greatest prudence and forbearance," others saw things differently. A public meeting on December 27th adopted resolutions expressing indignation at the use of military force, and seeking redress for "several unoffending citizens" who allegedly had been bayonetted. The latter charge lacked all credibility.[31] Not only did it contradict Shea's account, but it was never legally pursued by a group—the reformers—whose members would rather litigate than eat. The meeting, incidentally, was chaired by William Carson, whose son-in-law had commanded the troops at Winton's on Christmas Day.

Cochrane and Fleming, meanwhile, had an apparently amicable meeting to discuss both the magistrates' request and the troops' deployment. It was nonetheless followed by a bewildering public exchange in which the two clashed over whether the governor had consented[vii] to using the troops.[32] (He had, although Fleming maintained he had not.) To no one's surprise, Cochrane's own investigation found that the magistrates had "exercised a legal, sound and necessary discretion" in making the request, and that the troops had "acted with great forbearance and moderation."[33] Colonial Office bureaucrats, who had short memories and a penchant for scapegoats, unfairly accused the governor of failing to warn them of the garrison's weakened state, and sent reinforcements in May.[34]

The events of Christmas Day were weighing on Cochrane's mind when he addressed a joint session of the legislature on January 30, 1834. While acknowledging that the military were legally bound to obey the magistrates when called upon, he pointed out that "His Majesty's Forces are not sent to the Colonies to perform Police duties; and that while they assist in protecting you from foreign foes, it is your province to guard against, and bring to punishment, your domestic enemies."[35] Accordingly, he recommended that a militia should be created to take the load off the troops. In reply, Council hoped that improvements would be made to the police instead, while touchy members of the Assembly were offended that Cochrane thought aid to the civil power necessary at all, "or that any portion of the people of this Island, however small, could be considered in the light of domestic enemies."[36]

[vii] While Cochrane's consent was not strictly necessary, it is not difficult to imagine that in a small garrison such as St. John's, the magistrates would have gone straight to him for approval, or that if they had gone to the commanding officer, the latter would have consulted Cochrane anyway.

In 1834 the Colonial Office persuaded the British government to lobby the Vatican to censure Fleming for his political activities, resulting in a reprimand but no loss of authority or position.[37] Believing as well that there was little hope of improvement while Cochrane remained in office, it replaced him with another Royal Navy veteran, Captain Henry Prescott, who arrived in St. John's on November 3, 1834. Prescott immediately tried to lower the temperature by withdrawing a libel suit that Cochrane had initiated against Troy after the priest had publicly accused him of bigotry and despotism.[38] Unmoved, the firebrand priest went right on instructing his flock to shun Mad Dog shopkeepers, threatening to excommunicate any that were caught doing business with them.[39]

By mid-May 1835, Prescott had become so alarmed by the intensity of Catholic rancour toward Winton that he mentioned it in a dispatch to the Colonial Office.[40] A mere five days later, a group of knife-wielding thugs, their faces concealed by paint, ambushed Winton on Saddle Hill between Carbonear and Harbour Grace, cropping (that is, cutting off) his left ear and removing parts of his right one. Since the cropping of humans and animals was a staple of Irish agrarian protest—as were shunning and boycotts—it is reasonable to assume that Winton's assailants had Irish Catholic backgrounds.[41] Around Conception Bay there were whispers that the perpetrator was Dr. Edward Molloy of Carbonear, but despite a sizeable reward no charges were ever laid.[42] Prescott blamed Troy and his fellow priests, arguing that even though they had not committed the atrocity, their words and actions had fostered a climate in which it was deemed acceptable.

The Neaven Funeral Riot

The 1836 general election brought renewed violence and resort to military aid, along with more indications that Conception Bay was a problem area that might need special attention. Rioting erupted in Harbour Grace on the first day of polling[viii] (November 1), when a throng including 400 men from Carbonear assaulted two of the candidates, merchants Thomas Ridley and Robert Prowse, and their supporters, inflicting some serious injuries in the process.[43] Ridley and Prowse dropped out of the race and their opponents were declared victorious, after which a group of concerned citizens failed to convince the governor that Harbour Grace should have its own army garrison.

In the capital the atmosphere was equally bitter, and some questionable behaviour earlier in the year by the acting commanding officer of the Veterans, (then) Major Robert Law, was a contributing factor. Ever since the use of troops at Winton's, the military had come under intense scrutiny by Carson's successor as editor of the *Patriot*, Harbour Grace native Robert John Parsons.[ix] A Presbyterian who converted to Anglicanism, the acid-tongued Parsons had become an anti-establishment darling after being jailed in May 1835 for an editorial mocking Chief Justice Henry John Boulton.[44] Although the Colonial Office later remitted his sentence, rumours that Parsons's supporters intended to tear down the courthouse during his incarceration had led to the stationing of military guards both there and at Boulton's home, inspiring Parsons to label the Veterans "the Boulton Infantry Regiment."[45]

On January 19, 1836, Parsons voiced surprise over the

---

viii Polling refers to the actual registering of the vote—which was given orally—in a polling book.

ix In 1840 Parsons would become the paper's sole owner.

recent demotion of Sergeant John Neaven of the Veterans, allegedly because he had allowed the sentry at Signal Hill to post guard inside the guardhouse during a blizzard.[46] Word of Neaven's demotion broke simultaneously with news that Private James Kilpatrick of the Veterans had died in one of Fort Townshend's infamous black holes while awaiting trial for drunkenness, an event that Parsons seized upon to renew his attacks on the military leadership. Neaven's case, however, was destined to be more significant.

On February 2, declaring that Neaven's sentence was disproportionate to his crime, Parsons wondered if it might not be related to a letter that Neaven had written to the *Patriot* on April 3, 1834.[47] In that stunning document, Neaven alleged that his wife had had an affair with the garrison commandant, Lieutenant Colonel William Sall, while serving as his housekeeper, and that Sall had made arrangements to convey her to Halifax aboard Governor Cochrane's yacht.[48] There is no question that Neaven's wife had been Sall's housekeeper, but the commandant, who was unmarried, scoffed at the charge, claiming he had simply fired her because of some other misconduct. For his troubles, Neaven was hauled before a garrison court martial and reduced to the rank of private, only to have his sentence remitted on compassionate grounds by the Major General Commanding in Halifax, Sir Colin Campbell. From that point forward, Neaven was, in Parsons's words, "a marked man."

John Neaven probably would have faded from history had he not died[x] in the Garrison Hospital on February 3, 1836, and had his funeral not put the military at odds with residents, and Law at loggerheads with Bishop Fleming. When the soldiers[xi] who were charged with the coffin

---

[x] According to Winton, Neaven died from delirium tremens; a strangely mawkish Parsons claimed he died of a broken heart.

[xi] The coffin would have been attended by a 10-man carrying party, a 12-man firing party, one fifer, and one drummer.

CIVIL COMMOTION   121

emerged from the hospital[xii] on February 6, they were swarmed by a crowd of Neaven's friends and sympathizers, estimated by Parsons to be "some thousands of persons," who commandeered the coffin and started down the lane toward Military Road.[49] As the irregular procession reached the foot of the lane, it bumped into Lieutenant John Grant of the Veterans, who had just come from Fort Townshend and who now ordered the soldiers to take back the coffin and to proceed westward along Military Road to the Catholic burial ground as originally planned. Some of the people begged Grant to turn eastward instead and to go down Cochrane Street in order to take the coffin through the heart of town, where, they said, Neaven's friends could pay their respects. After Grant refused, his men headed westward until they reached Kings Road, where the crowd pressed in, regained the coffin, and managed to carry it part way down the road before relinquishing it again after Grant ordered the firing party to fix bayonets. Instead of proceeding to the burial ground and potentially risking another confrontation, the soldiers now made for Fort Townshend, closely pursued by a handful of townsmen, the rest having scattered when the soldiers fixed their bayonets.

As the soldiers neared Fort Townshend they encountered Law, who had ridden out on his horse. Behind him at the gate he had drawn up an unspecified number of off-duty officers and men, all of them armed. Arriving almost simultaneously was Father James Murphy, who had earlier administered last rites to Neaven, and who had been at the burial ground awaiting the coffin's arrival. Murphy asked Law to let the people carry the coffin through town according to their earlier wishes; not only did Law refuse, but he expressed doubt about holding the funeral that day at all. Murphy replied that he would

---

[xii] Built in 1802, the hospital was located northwest of Government House at the end of a lane abutting Military Road. The lane would later evolve into Bannerman Road.

"guarantee the peaceable demeanour of the people" if Law would allow the funeral to go ahead, to which Law at last consented. He insisted, however, that the carrying and firing parties must stick to their original route, which they did in the company of the off-duty officers and men.

Three days later Prescott conveyed to the garrison commandant, a not disinterested William Sall, his gratitude for the "steadiness" of Lieutenant Grant and the "firmness and forbearance" of both Grant and Law. Sall then issued a garrison order containing the governor's words, which subsequently appeared in the press.[50] Parsons decried those words as "impolitic," denounced Law as "that pink of disciplinarians," and, in his own impolitic language, asserted that the people could have taken the garrison had they been inclined to do so.[51] Angered by Prescott's support for Law and Grant, and determined to correct Winton's account of the disturbance in the *Ledger*, Fleming sent a long, rambling letter to Prescott in which he demanded an investigation.[52] When this epistle appeared in the *Patriot* and, later, the *Ledger*, it provoked an equally self-important rejoinder from Law.[53] The exchange called to mind the one between the bishop and Cochrane at Christmas 1833, and was about as edifying.

By publicly contradicting Fleming's version of events, Law had broken the unwritten rule that army officers abroad should avoid local politics—although so long as the commandant sat on Council, that was going to be impossible in Newfoundland, a situation that Parsons rightly called "an anomaly."[54] (What the Colonial Office was thinking in creating this anomaly is anyone's guess.) In the process, Law had compromised his regiment's integrity and placed a target on his back. He nonetheless seemed to relish the situation, because on St. Patrick's Day, when a group of Mad Dogs broke from the Benevolent Irish Society—now controlled by Fleming supporters—and held a separate banquet, Law joined Prescott, Boulton, and Winton as honoured guests.

The St. John's election campaign kicked off on Sunday, October 23, when a group of Catholic priests, including Troy on horseback, led a parade of some 500 supporters of the reform trio Carson, Kent, and Morris.[55] (Fleming was overseas for the entire campaign lobbying Members of Parliament and Colonial Office bureaucrats for a grant of Ordnance land near Fort Townshend on which to build a cathedral.) Some people were so offended by this that Troy and Father Patrick Ward, the three candidates, and several supporters were subsequently charged with unlawful assembly. On November 10, troops were called out after a mob surrounded the mercantile candidates' committee room and pitched stones through the windows. Then, on the 13th, a commotion erupted during Sunday mass at the Catholic chapel when a Mad Dog congregant was forcibly removed on Troy's orders. Despite the presence of 140 special constables—Parsons called them "TORY special constables"—at the courthouse when the polls opened the following day, gangs including a Carbonear contingent were so intimidating that the magistrates requested military aid. The troops arrived in due course and stayed until nighttime, leading Parsons to assert that several people had been "pierced by their bayonets."[56]

As unlikely as it was that anyone was really bayonetted, the placement of cannons *outside* Fort Townshend's walls the very next morning was seen as an attempt to intimidate on behalf of the mercantile candidates. An unhinged Parsons blathered that the fort "was indubitably intended as a place of security for the troops in case the signal for massacre were given."[57] A contingent of troops was also back at the courthouse, and so was the mob, which had done such an effective job of instilling fear that most supporters of the mercantile candidates stayed away. It should be said here that the voting system was partly to blame for this sorry state of affairs. The electors, who were all men,[xiii] had to appear before a polling officer and publicly announce who they supported, making anonymity impossible.[xiv] The practice of scheduling voting at different times in different districts, and of spreading it over several weeks within each district, also facilitated mob recruitment and mobility, in this case from as far away as Carbonear.

Shortly after polling resumed, the mercantile candidates, who included the well-known Mad Dog, contractor Patrick Kough,[xv] followed their Harbour Grace brethren's example and withdrew from the contest. Troops nonetheless patrolled the town until late at night, so that the streets were, Parsons sneered, "again in possession of MARSHALL LAW." He reminded his readers that Law was now a member of Council —Sall was away on extended leave—which, he argued, "should be sufficient to show the danger of allowing such a man to have the command of troops in a time of contested election."

Together with the results from more peaceable districts, the upshot was a clear victory for the reform side.[xvi] The win, however, was short-lived. On the advice of Chief Justice Boulton and Attorney General James Simms, both of whom were members of Council, Prescott declared the results invalid because the election writs had not been properly sealed. Although the Law Officers of the Crown would later challenge that decision, it had the support of the Colonial Secretary, Lord Glenelg, who instructed Prescott to call a new election, one that was duly scheduled for June 1837. Anticipating violence, the governor asked Glenelg to authorize

---

[xiii] Newfoundland women first voted in the 1928 general election.

[xiv] The secret ballot would first be used in a Newfoundland general election in 1889.

[xv] Pronounced, and occasionally spelled, as "Keough."

[xvi] As others have pointed out, St. John's and Conception Bay were anomalies in the extent of their election violence. But they were also the two largest districts, accounting for over half the colony's population, and St. John's was the seat of government. What happened in these districts mattered.

CIVIL COMMOTION   125

an increase of the St. John's garrison[xvii] so that detachments could be sent to Harbour Grace and Carbonear during polling; he also requested that an extra naval vessel be added to the 1837 fishery patrol for possible deployment to keep order ashore.[58] Glenelg replied that the best he could do would be to arrange for naval and military support from Halifax if it became absolutely necessary. Given the amount of time it would take for this to happen, his answer was tantamount to a "No."

Motivated by fear, disgust, and class and ethnic snobbery, mercantile interests withdrew from the field and ceded the race to their opponents. This did not mean they were powerless, since they could still expect the governor and Council, on which they were represented, to check the Assembly. Ominously, Winton began to question whether Newfoundland deserved to have representative government, arguing that a return to rule by governor and Council would be preferable. This anti-democratic sentiment would escalate during the Assembly's ensuing war with Council, a war that culminated in the suspension of representative government in 1841. It was highlighted by battles over money bills, a successful campaign to remove Boulton from office, and numerous legal actions resulting in the incarceration of key establishment figures, including the Mad Dog, surgeon Edward Kielley, whose years-long legal odyssey began innocently enough when he and John Kent had words while passing in the street.[59] The list of people that the Assembly wanted to punish—including Law, who was meant to be the subject of an inquiry—was so long that there simply was not enough time to hunt them all down.[60]

Despite the Assembly's intolerant bent, it is important to remember that it had legitimate concerns, and that similar

---

[xvii] It will be remembered that the disposition of the troops was within the governor's authority provided he consulted the Colonial Office.

ones led to open rebellion in Upper and Lower Canada in 1837-38. Far from being radicals—although their enemies viewed them as such—British North American reformers merely wanted to adopt British cabinet government as their own. Under that system, the prime minister and the rest of the cabinet (or Executive Council) were chosen from and responsible to an elected body, hence "responsible government."[61] But like politicians the world over, the reformers also wanted power and all the benefits that came with it, jobs chief among them. Carson made no bones about this, arguing that a fair distribution of patronage would in and of itself calm the troubled waters.

While in London in 1838, Carson and his fellow assemblyman, the educator and Fleming protégé John Valentine Nugent, made a damning submission to the Colonial Office showing that Protestants occupied 93 per cent of government positions back home.[62] Against this and other evidence of the need for reform, the Assembly's foes continued to be deaf and blind. In a chilling petition to the Queen in December 1838, the Chamber of Commerce proved that anti-Catholicism and the related fiction of the Catholic monolith were alive and well.[63] Claiming that the priests had hijacked the Assembly, the would-be oligarchs of the business community held that the only possible way forward was rule by a governor and an enlarged, appointed Council (on which some chamber members undoubtedly expected to sit).

Finally motivated to make a peace offering, Prescott appointed Morris in March 1840 to the vacant Colonial Treasurer's position, making him the first Catholic to sit on Council. That this solitary gesture made little difference was borne out by the May-June by-election to fill Morris's vacant St. John's seat. The contest initially looked to be a non-event, given that mercantile interests failed to nominate a candidate, and that their opponents appeared to be united behind the Scottish Presbyterian James Douglas, a merchant and co-founder of the *Patriot*. Shortly before election day, at Nugent's urging and with Fleming's approval, the wealthy Catholic merchant Laurence O'Brien unexpectedly broke ranks and offered himself as a candidate.[64] The resulting schism among the reformers made for strange political bedfellows. Parsons, for one, now found himself on the same side as the Protestant mercantile elite, whose members had thrown their collective weight behind Douglas. Polling began on the 20th and was marked by the active participation of Catholic priests on O'Brien's behalf, although Edward Troy was conspicuously absent. Fleming had temporarily sent him to Merasheen Island, Placentia Bay, after the Foreign Office pressured Rome to remove him altogether.[65]

Numerous violent incidents against Douglas supporters on the 21st led the magistrates to seek military aid, but Prescott, who had taken over the approval process, refused.[66] He would relent on the 28th after several special constables, who had endured beatings, testified that without military protection "we cannot take upon ourselves to act our lives being evidently in danger," and after the magistrates themselves chimed in that "we find it utterly impossible to protect the Peace and tranquility of this Town owing to a riotous mob being assembled at the Committee Room of Mr. Douglas."[67] The troops' presence over the campaign's remaining days restored order, and in the end O'Brien narrowly prevailed. It was, however, a pyrrhic victory owing to the damage his candidacy inflicted on reform solidarity. That damage was compounded by the simultaneous emergence of the Newfoundland Natives' Society, which was non-denominational and thus a challenge to priestly influence.

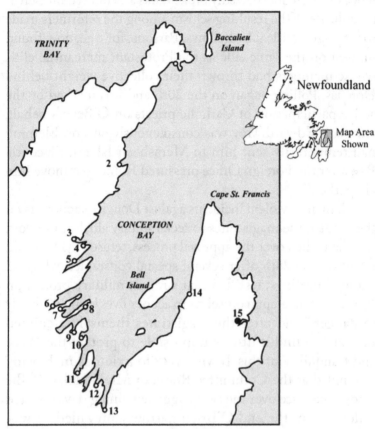

Figure 16: Conception Bay.

Source: Rooms Provincial Archives, A42-150.
Figure 17: "Water Street, Harbour Grace, N.F." The unofficial capital of Conception Bay, Harbour Grace for a time rivalled St. John's in economic importance.

Conception Bay

There was a second by-election in 1840, this one from November 9 to December 8, to fill a seat that had opened up in Conception Bay after the incumbent's death. By making the St. John's by-election look like a Sunday-school picnic, it played into the hands of the enemies of representative government and prompted renewed calls for a dedicated garrison in Harbour Grace.

On the surface at least, Conception Bay seemed peaceful enough. It was the oldest continuously inhabited region of European settlement in the colony, and was more populous, in the aggregate, than St. John's (28,026 people in 1845, versus 25,196), a lead it would not relinquish until the early 20th century. In the immediate aftermath of the Napoleonic Wars it dominated both the Labrador fishery and the seal hunt, and an affiliated shipbuilding industry further enhanced its reputation as "the first district in the island of

Newfoundland."[68] For a time, its two leading mercantile firms—Ridley and Company, and Punton and Munn—were the largest in the colony, and its economic and demographic clout was reflected in the House of Assembly, where its four seats were the most of any district.[xviii]

The only noteworthy community on the bay's eastern side was Portugal Cove, which was 14.5 kilometres by road from St. John's, and home to a government-financed packet-boat service that, in tandem with the road, offered the speediest means of transportation and communication between bay and capital.[69] (The distance between St. John's and Portugal Cove could be covered on foot in approximately four hours; with a favourable wind, the packet-boat could cross the bay in another four hours.)

The vast majority of the inhabitants were crammed into the area between Holyrood and Carbonear, a section that included the bay's unofficial capital, Harbour Grace. In 1839 Harbour Grace impressed the British geologist J.B. Jukes, who remarked that it "has altogether a more English and neat appearance than most places in Newfoundland. It contains, moreover, a very decent inn, which at this time even St. John's was destitute of."[70] During the 1830s Harbour Grace and Carbonear both had populations of over 4,000 people.

Appearances were deceiving. Unlike St. John's, Conception Bay was overly dependent on fishing and sealing and thus more vulnerable to reverses in those industries.[71] Prolonged downturns exposed the precarious lives of most fishing families, whose limited options included becoming further indebted to their merchant masters, accepting (after 1833) government relief, or emigrating. Even in good times, prosperity was not equally shared. During his years (1827-35) as a clerk with Slade, Elson, and Company of Carbonear, the English naturalist Philip Henry Gosse spoke well of the

---

[xviii] St. John's was next largest with three.

bay's second largest town, his only complaint being that there were too many Irishmen there.[72] Not long afterward, however, Jukes found that "as several mercantile establishments which formerly existed there have been broken up, it has, in parts, a forlorn and deserted air."[73] There was lots of life in Carbonear yet, but it paid a price for its exposed harbour and close proximity (5.6 kilometres) to Harbour Grace.

Some jealousy toward Harbour Grace was perhaps understandable, but the depth of it was breathtaking. Gravely invoking the spectre of insurrection, an anonymous Carbonear resident ranted in the *Weekly Herald and Conception-Bay Advertiser* that there would be hell to pay if the town continued to play second fiddle, for "Had not Switzerland her William Tell? And in more modern times, have we not seen the revolutions of France and St. Domingo?"[74] Unfortunately, bad blood seems to have come naturally to Carbonearites, who also disdained their neighbours on the North Shore, as the stretch between Carbonear and Bay de Verde was known.[75] Accordingly, while most Conception Bay residents hated St. John's, that unity was offset by intense localism. When religious, factional, and class differences were also thrown into the mix, it could be difficult to tell exactly what forces were at work during times of political or social unrest.

Unrest was a well-known quantity around the bay, as were resistance to authority and resort to violence. In 1819 a police officer attempting to repossess Cupids fisherman James Lundrigan's home turned tail after Lundrigan's wife threatened to shoot him.[76] Three years later another constable was actually fired upon while trying to execute a court order in nearby Brigus.[77] In 1826 the merchants and other self-styled "respectable inhabitants" of Harbour Grace complained to Governor Cochrane about the "dangerous state of the public peace" and petititioned, for the first time, for a separate military garrison.[78] Their fears gained credence after a series of violent acts in Carbonear and Harbour Grace in 1830-31,

Source: Rooms Provincial Archives, MG 24.34.18.

Figure 18: "New road made after the attack on Winton 1835/Saddle Hill." The brutal attack on Henry Winton was a sign of more violence to come in Conception Bay.

most of them aimed at merchants, but also, in one case, at people attending a house party. Henry Winton's maiming was not an isolated event, for on May 15, 1840, his employee Herman Lott was assaulted in identical fashion on Saddle Hill. (In 1841, to give travellers at least some degree of safety, the road over Saddle Hill was realigned and the woods on both sides were levelled.)[79]

Coming as this did during the St. John's by-election campaign, it had to have been politically motivated. It was a disturbing omen—as if any were needed—for the upcoming by-election.

The two candidates—Harbour Grace businessman James

Luke Prendergast and Carbonear sealing captain Edmund Hanrahan—were both Catholics, but Hanrahan had priestly support and Prendergast did not.[80] Much of the voting, including that at Harbour Grace, was completed without incident by mid-November, seemingly giving the lie to Prescott's previously stated concern about the likelihood of trouble. But Prendergast led by a mere eight votes when the scene shifted to the North Shore community of Western Bay, where voting was to take place December 1-3.[81] On the 30th of November, as 60 of his drum-playing, banner-waving Harbour Grace supporters attempted to pass through Carbonear en route to Western Bay, they were assaulted by a group of some 300 men. With only six constables at their disposal, the magistrates were unable to intervene, and afterward they wrote to Prescott requesting "a strong military force to assist ... in preserving

Source: Rooms Provincial Archives MG 24.34.8.

Figure 19: "N[orth] View of the Harbour Grace Court House Aug. 1841." Note soldiers and guardhouse on the left.

the peace."[82] On polling day, after the governor had turned a deaf ear to their request, a group of stick-wielding Hanrahan supporters prevented a contingent of Prendergast voters from entering the Western Bay polling place.

The stakes were therefore high when the focus shifted to Carbonear, where, as fate should have it, the election was scheduled to end over December 7 and 8. By that time Prescott had rejected yet another request for military aid for the dubious reason that it was too late in the year to send troops. If, as seems probable, he was hoping for trouble, he would not be disappointed. Writing from Carbonear on the 4th, returning officer Robert John Pinsent, who was also a magistrate, captured the mood of grim resignation that prevailed

there: "I feel that we shall stand on a volcano, but we must endure the result."[83]

Fighting erupted on the 8th, apparently because Hanrahan's people believed that Prendergast's lead was going to hold.[84] In the ensuing chaos, Pinsent closed the poll, triggering a larger brawl in which the Harbour Grace magistrate, merchant Thomas Ridley, suffered a fractured skull that nearly killed him. After the Harbour Grace men retreated to their own community with Hanrahan supporters nipping at their heels, the latter turned against their fellow townsmen who had had the audacity to vote for Prendergast.[85] One such was Nicholas Ash, whose house was besieged, and who shot and wounded several people—two women among them—before he and his family managed to escape, after which his assailants burned his house to the ground.

The next evening, after rumours reached Harbour Grace

that 200 armed Carbonearites were coming to torch the town, horrified citizens loaded their muskets and braced for the assault. Although it never came, magistrates Thomas Danson and John Stark feared that the threat "will yet be carried out, unless we are afforded military protection."[86] Carbonear, they informed Colonial Secretary James Crowdy, "is governed by the mob, and without the pale of the law. Ten warrants for riot and murderous assaults at the election are issued, but we cannot execute them without force." With that, Prescott miraculously dispatched the Veterans on the 10th, completely undermining his reasoning for not acting sooner. The speed with which the troops arrived suggests that they marched to Portugal Cove before boarding the brig *Margaret Parker*, which arrived at Harbour Grace on the 11th bearing 58 men for that town and 48 for Carbonear, all commanded for the time being by Major Law, and accompanied by Solicitor General H.A. Emerson.[87] In Harbour Grace the troops were quartered in the courthouse; the site of their Carbonear accommodations is unknown.[88]

Although the magistrates immediately began issuing warrants, the police were slow to execute them because so many people had fled to avoid arrest. In the end, however, more than a hundred were arrested for rioting, assault, and arson, including those who had burnt Nicholas Ash's house. According to Danson and Stark, "but for the presence of the Military not one of the offenders would have been apprehended."[89] If that seems like an exaggeration, it should be noted that only nine of those charged were brought to trial.[90] Many potential witnesses refused to testify, actual ones clearly perjured themselves, and juries on the whole were sympathetic.[91] Sentences ranged from 14 days to nine months imprisonment.

In a sign that his earlier inaction was likely deliberate, Prescott now wrote to the Colonial Secretary, Lord John Russell, recommending that the Veterans be increased to four companies so that one could be permanently stationed in Harbour Grace. Otherwise, he warned, "the colony must materially suffer, for it cannot be supposed that respectable people will continue to live in a neighbourhood where life and property can at any moment be jeopardized, and the utmost brutality be practised against them."[92] To no one's surprise, a meeting of the "respectable Inhabitants" of Carbonear convened on December 16, resulting in a memorial to Prescott seeking a permanent garrison for their town too.[93] That proposal was never seriously entertained, and Russell also rejected Prescott's request for a permanent Harbour Grace detachment, reminding him, à la Cochrane's address to the legislature in 1834, that "The proper and legitimate mode of preserving the public peace is by the organization of an effective militia, or police force" to be financed by the colony.[94] Undeterred, Prescott gave him a litany of reasons why a militia would be unworkable, and claimed without explanation that the Assembly would never agree to expand the police.[95] He again urged that the Veterans' detachment at Harbour Grace should be made permanent; in the meantime, and in the absence of instructions to the contrary, he would keep both of the Conception Bay detachments right where they were.

Despite their differences over the need for a permanent military presence at Harbour Grace, Prescott and Russell agreed on one thing: Bishop Fleming and his priests were responsible for the rioting. That explanation, which for Prescott had become a reflex, would later be challenged by Boulton's successor as chief justice, J.G.H. Bourne, who, as the legal proceedings wound down, reported that where the Carbonear election violence was concerned, "there was about as much in evidence to trace it to Local Jealousy, the rivalry of two neighbouring Towns, each desirous to return its own candidate," as to religious differences.[96] Bourne also concluded that the magistrates had greatly exaggerated the mob's size, which in his opinion probably consisted of a hundred people, a figure representing "a very small proportion of the thousands living

138   THE INVISIBLES

in and assembled at Carbonear at the time."

Unfortunately for democracy's course in Newfoundland, Bourne's dissenting opinion went against the anti-Catholic tide, then experiencing another of its periodic high points.[97] From the other side of the Atlantic Ocean, British evangelical Protestants screamed that "popery" was out of control in the colony, while the British press regurgitated material from that model of objectivity, the *Public Ledger*.[98] Nor did it help that the Colonial Office's most powerful bureaucrat, Under-secretary James Stephen, was an Evangelical Anglican who described Carbonear's voters as "a Body of men who approach the Savage much more than the Civilized State, and who are as little qualified for the discharge of such a duty as so many Malays would be."[99] Anti-Catholicism also suffused the many petitions the Colonial Office received from St. John's and Conception Bay merchants, and from British businessmen with Newfoundland ties, all proposing some combination of abolishing the legislature, implementing rule by governor and an enlarged Council, or appointing a commission of inquiry into the colony's affairs.

The question of whether troops should be permanently stationed in the bay had therefore become part of the larger issue of whether the allegedly undue influence of the Catholic Church had rendered Newfoundland unfit for representative government. Stephen, who despite his anti-Catholic bias recommended only that Carbonear's voters should be disen-franchised, was overruled. In March 1842 Colonial Secretary Lord Edward Stanley announced that representative government would not be restored,[xix] but would instead be replaced by an Amalgamated Legislature of 15 elected members and 10 appointees, to be led by the governor—this at a time when the other British North American colonies

---

[xix] The constitution had been suspended since April 26, 1841. The new one embodying the Amalgamated Legislature took effect on January 17, 1843.

were moving closer to responsible government.

The first governor under the new system was Prescott's immediate successor, Sir John Harvey, who had arrived in St. John's on September 16, 1841, and who before the month was out had visited Conception Bay to decide[xx] once and for all on the distribution of the troops there.[100] On October 8 he wrote to tell Russell that he had withdrawn all the men from Carbonear and had left 53 at Harbour Grace as a permanent detachment.[101] Carbonearites now had something else to moan about, but among the Harbour Grace merchants who won contracts to supply the detachment with provisions, there was much rejoicing. The only sour note was sounded by Magistrate Stark, who groused that the detachment's commanding officer, Peninsular War veteran Lieutenant William Mason, was "a thorough going Priests man."[102]

In an attempt to thwart mob influence, the December 1842 general election for the Amalgamated Legislature was the first to feature simultaneous polling.[103] The campaign's lone blemish was the dispatch of troops from Harbour Grace to Spaniard's Bay and Port de Grave, where, according to Danson and Stark, supporters of the "Radical party" had prevented "Conservative" voters from entering the polling places.[104] In the ensuing pushing and shoving, the Port de Grave merchant and justice of the peace, John Jacob, suffered an injured thumb, but that was the extent of the damage. Carbonear was peaceful, and at Harbour Grace the election "proceeded in perfect quietness and good order."

For various reasons, the tenor of public life was much improved during the Amalgamated Legislature phase. Temperance and nativist movements cut across religious lines, with nativism in particular attracting independent-minded, middle-class Catholics who were heirs to the Mad Dog

---

[xx] Presumably he had a mandate to do so, since governors could only order troop movements with London's permission.

tradition.[105] Enthusiasm for the British monarchy, which amounted to a "fetish" during Queen Victoria's reign, was also becoming widespread, with Harvey in particular cultivating it at every turn.[106] Fleming's preoccupation with financing his magnificent cathedral kept him out of the colony for long stretches of time, and also consumed most of his attention and prodigious energy, to the detriment of his health.[107] The most important factor, however, was Harvey's insistence on giving Catholics a greater share of government patronage, thereby confirming what Carson and Nugent had said in 1838. Carson, who passed away in February 1843, missed the gravy train; Nugent, who in 1844 became Newfoundland's first inspector of schools, was one of many who climbed aboard. Nugent's appointment was made possible by the legislature's most notable achievement: abandoning the dysfunctional education system that had been created in 1836, and replacing it with a church-controlled system in which educational funding was shared by separate Catholic and Protestant school boards.

Despite the shiny veneer, all was not well. Nugent's instructions forbade him to inspect Protestant schools unless invited to do so, and such invitations were rare.[108] Moreover, he held the position for only a year before a Protestant succeeded him. Protestants, who dominated the Amalgamated Legislature and still received the lion's share of patronage, were troubled by more than just Nugent's appointment. When, for example, Harvey made Patrick Doyle the first Catholic magistrate in St. John's, dozens of indignant Protestants petitioned against it. The new Church of England Bishop, the pretentious high-churchman Edward Feild, arrived in 1844 and added to the stink. Feild saw enemies around every corner: evangelicals in his own church, Catholics of course, and also Methodists, whose growing numbers included converts from Anglicanism.[109] With the help of his main ally in the legislature, lawyer Hugh Hoyles, Feild began a campaign to subdivide the Protestant education grant and to apportion it on a per capita basis—a change that, if implemented, would increase the Anglican share of the grant to some 70 per cent.[110] This alarmed Methodists, who worried that they would no longer be able to afford their own schools.

Feild also drew criticism when, in the wake of the Great Fire of June 9, 1846, half of the Queen's Letter Fund was reserved for a new Anglican cathedral. Fleming, who had spent so much time and energy fundraising for his own cathedral, grew as frosty toward Le Marchant as he had been warm toward Harvey.[111] (He conveniently forgot that the British government had gifted him 3.6 hectares of prime real estate on which to build his own cathedral and associated structures.) Fleming may have been exhausted and bitter, but his chosen successor, the Franciscan priest John Thomas Mullock, who breathed new life into Catholic politics, was not. Mullock, who became bishop when Fleming died in 1850, was blunter, louder, and more interfering than Fleming in his prime. Thus, despite outward signs of progress, the embers of hatred continued to flicker.

The Reckoning

The 1848 general election may have heralded representative government's return, but it was greeted with such apathy that fewer than half of eligible voters took part. This was only partly because of Harvey's conciliatory efforts, which according to Parsons had made it impossible to tell friend from foe in the legislature.[112] The Great Fire and the natural disasters of 1846 had been followed in 1847 by a typhus epidemic, another failed potato crop, and depressed fisheries in several major bays.[113] With the economy barely beginning to recover in 1848, there was little enthusiasm for politics, even if it did include talk of the Holy Grail itself, responsible government. That talk nonetheless grew louder after 1850, and as it did the old schisms reappeared, with Catholics supporting it and most

Protestants, including the business community, opposing it for fear that control of the Executive and Legislative Councils would produce a Catholic ascendancy.

Protestant misgivings were fuelled by Mullock's outspoken support for responsible government, and his public endorsement of the new leader of what many were now calling the Liberal party, lawyer Philip Francis Little.[114] (By the same token, members of the old mercantile party were increasingly being called Conservatives or Tories.) Although he had only arrived from Prince Edward Island in 1844, Little was elected to the Assembly in 1848 and in rapid succession became Fleming's executor and Mullock's confidante. Able though he was, luck played a role in his meteoric rise: Morris died in 1848, Nugent was defeated in the election, and Kent temporarily withdrew from politics following his appointment as Collector of Customs in 1849.

The November 1852 general election boosted Liberal fortunes by exposing a major fracture in Protestant unity. Conservative efforts to subdivide the Protestant education grant had driven the Methodists into Liberal arms, and with Methodists holding the balance of power in the Burin and Conception Bay electoral districts, the Liberals were able to form a majority government.[115] The only violence, such as it was, was again in Conception Bay, where the antics of 40 "ruffians" from Harbour Grace delayed polling by 24 hours in Bay Roberts.[116] Pinsent considered sending troops from the Harbour Grace detachment but seems to have thought better of it.

With their majority, the Liberals pushed for responsible government, which London approved in 1854, and which was consummated after the general election of May 1855. That contest returned another Liberal majority, again with Methodist support, and witnessed the unification of the Catholic middle class, albeit with some wariness among independent thinkers such as Ambrose Shea.[117] It was also a peaceful affair, even in Conception Bay, where Pinsent lamented that "we had no music, no colours, no fun."[118] Still, he conceded that "the serenity of the proceedings may justly be considered as immeasurably outweighing the lack of amusement."

Already on borrowed time, the Harbour Grace detachment of the Royal Newfoundland Companies was withdrawn to St. John's after the election.[119] As originally constituted, the detachment had proven to be too large: for most of its life it numbered between 20 and 30 men commanded by a lieutenant and relieved every two years by fresh faces from St. John's.[120] After a brief stay in the courthouse, the men were housed in a two-storey wooden barracks that had originally been built as a cholera hospital.[121] They were temporarily withdrawn to St. John's after the Great Fire of June 9, 1846, when the garrison there was stretched to the limit.[122] Their absence caused unease among the "respectable inhabitants" of Harbour Grace, who were ecstatic when they returned in December 1847. Upon their return they moved into new quarters in the courthouse, their old barracks having reverted to a hospital during their absence.[123] Because their occupation of the courthouse was incompatible with the business of the itinerant Northern Circuit Court, when court was in session they would temporarily shift back into their former quarters, whose use as a hospital was short-lived.[124]

Prescott's fear that the bay would descend into barbarism without a military presence was undoubtedly exaggerated. Other than fighting the occasional fire and putting in rare appearances when the police were not up to some task—such as keeping order during the 1853 Carbonear sealers' strike—the detachment's men had little to do except fight boredom and get into trouble.[125] Conception Bay could be volatile, but in good economic times, with someone like Harvey at the helm, and with priests and politicians minding their manners, it could be as civilized as the next place, maybe even more so; for serious crime in Newfoundland—Conception Bay included—was rare.[126]

Local merchants appear to have taken advantage of the detachment's presence to over-charge for provisions—either that, or flour really was 22 per cent more expensive in Harbour Grace than in the capital.[127] Either way, financial opportunities for the business community cannot be discounted as a factor in requests for an army detachment. Those requests were invariably supported by the bay's magistrates, most of whom were also merchants. But by 1854 the high cost of maintaining the detachment, together with the additional responsibilities borne by the regiment following the Royal Artillery's withdrawal, were causing pressure to bring the detachment back to St. John's for good.[128] When the regiment was reduced by a third of its strength in March 1855, that pressure became irresistible. To console senior government officials, Robert Law pointed to the existence of steamship service in Conception Bay and telegraphic communication between the bay and St. John's.[129] These modern conveniences, he said, meant that future requirements for aid to the civil power could be met by sending men rapidly from St. John's on the shortest possible notice. As further reassurance, he noted that during the entire eighteen months when the detachment's men were in St. John's after the Great Fire, there had not been a single problem. Nor, he might have added, had there been one during the recent election. Conception Bay, it seemed, had finally come of age.

Responsible government is usually seen as both a marker of political maturity and a formative step on the road to nationhood. In its wake there were indeed signs that the old divisions were yielding to a nascent Newfoundland nationhood. In 1857, when British negotiators signed a draft convention with France that would have reserved parts of the Newfoundland coast exclusively for French fishermen, legislators from both parties were so vehemently opposed that the British abandoned the convention and swore never to adjust Newfoundland's maritime rights and boundaries without its prior consent. Over time, this commitment assumed the character of a local "Magna Carta."[130] By cutting across political, religious, and class lines, anti-French sentiment was well on its way to becoming a pillar of Newfoundland nationalism. It would remain so until the First World War made it obsolete.

Another nationalistic building block—loyalty to the monarchy—reached an early pinnacle during the visit of the Prince of Wales (the future King Edward VII) to St. John's in July 1860, an event that provoked outpourings of affection by all denominations and classes.[131] The swarm of dignitaries who greeted the prince when he disembarked on the 23rd included Bishops Mullock and Feild, who were able to bury the hatchet for one day at least. The prince was accompanied by the Colonial Secretary, the Duke of Newcastle, who seems to have bent the royal ear with that office's anti-Catholic line.

Source: Frank Leslie's Illustrated Newspaper, Aug. 11, 1860, pg. 183.

Figure 20: "The Prince of Wales leaving St. John's, Newfoundland for Halifax, Nova Scotia."
The visit of the Prince of Wales in July 1860 demonstrated how devotion to the monarchy could overcome local differences. This illustration also provides the best contemporary depiction of Royal Newfoundland Companies, whose men can be seen flanking the prince's route.

This would explain why, when the prince later met separately with the bishops and their clergy, he told them it was his "constant prayer" that "the Inhabitants of this Colony may long live in the expression of an earnest faith, and, at the same time, in religious peace and harmony."[132]

Although Parsons, who was something of a prophet, had first used the word *nation* in 1840, awareness of Newfoundland as a nation was rare until the 1890s.[133] In addition to being virtually unknown in the 1850s, the concept was also tenuous, for despite the good wishes of the Prince of Wales, the forces of division were merely submerged, not drowned. As a condition for granting responsible government, the British had insisted that the number of Assembly seats must be increased, and legislators in both chambers spent years trying to distribute the agreed upon 30 seats in a way that would strike an acceptable denominational balance.[xxi] Unhappy with the result, the Conservatives, led by Hoyles, denounced responsible government as "a Roman Catholic plot."[134] The first House of Assembly under the new regime featured a Conservative opposition whose every member was Protestant—the party had campaigned on a slogan of "Protestant Union"—and the 1859 general election produced the same result.

The 1859 general election was also noteworthy for marking the return of electoral violence to Conception Bay, a district that now boasted seven seats. These had been apportioned in such a way that if people voted strictly according to their religious affiliations, the results could be predicted for all except one of the two Harbour Grace seats. Accordingly, that seat became "the pivot of Conception Bay politics."[135] Well before polling day (November 7), the Harbour Grace magistrates (and merchants) Harrison Ridley and John Munn had approached the government via Pinsent to seek mili-

---

[xxi] If not for this, Newfoundland almost certainly would have achieved responsible government before 1855.

CIVIL COMMOTION 147

tary assistance in sufficient numbers to "ensure the peace and independence of this District."[136] Although the Executive Council decided to recommend to Governor Sir Alexander Bannerman that he should grant the request,[xxii] the acting Colonial Secretary, who was unfamiliar with his duties, neglected to forward the recommendation.[137] As a result, no troops were present in Harbour Grace on polling day when a mob opposed to the candidacy of independent Catholic Robert Walsh invaded the polling station, seized the poll books (in which the votes were recorded), and went on a rampage breaking the windows of houses belonging to Walsh and his supporters.[138] Pinsent maintained that the mob would have done worse had not some priests convinced them to disperse, but the damage was done and Walsh, who feared for his life, withdrew from the contest.

Ridley, Munn, and John Stark used the incident to urge Bannerman to re-establish the Harbour Grace detachment. Seeing no conflict of interest in their overlapping judicial and commercial roles,[xxiii] they alleged that the detachment's creation in 1841 had been "attended with the most beneficial results by restoring confidence, and a large increase of Commercial and Industrial prosperity immediately followed."[139] Since its withdrawal, however, "the former scenes of riot and outrage have been renewed on many occasions, and particularly in the Autumn and Spring of each year when considerable numbers of foreign shipping are in our Port, and large numbers of strangers congregate here on their return from the Seal and Cod fisheries." These scenes of riot and outrage, they continued, "are fearfully aggravated during the frequent return of our Election contests"—there had been

---

[xxii] The Executive Council's involvement in the approval process was another change wrought by responsible government.

[xxiii] Ridley and Munn, that is. Stark was an officer of the Harbour Grace northern circuit court.

a grand total of one election since the detachment's with-drawal—"when excitement usually runs high, leaving life and property at the mercy of a lawless mob." They concluded by requesting that the detachment be re-established, it being their "firm conviction that the Subjects of Her Most Gracious Majesty cannot otherwise be protected, or enjoy their rights and privileges."

Disingenuous though they were, the magistrates found a sympathetic audience in Bannerman, although not in the government of Premier John Kent, who had become Liberal leader in 1858 after Little resigned to become a Supreme Court judge. Despite having been removed as governor of Prince Edward Island in 1854 because of his interfering ways, Bannerman still fancied himself de facto premier and had already concluded that Kent and his cabinet were "unfit to govern."[140] Grasping at a well-worn straw, he blamed the election-day disturbance on "the Catholic Priesthood assuming the power to prevent any one but their own nominee to come forward as a candidate at any Election."[141] He informed Newcastle that if he suspected for a minute that the Executive Council had deliberately failed to forward their recommendation regarding the use of troops, he would be "fully justified" in dismissing them. This statement is frequently misinterpreted as an expression of intent to dismiss Kent and his government.[142] While it was not that, it did reveal the governor's animus toward them, and was a bad sign given that the times required cool heads, not hot ones—and Bannerman's was boiling.

Bannerman relayed the magistrates' letter to London with a request for guidance, adding his opinion that 50 or 60 troops would be needed at Harbour Grace for the next election. Newcastle's reply sounded the familiar refrain that troops "are not stationed there to put down Civil disturbances, and they cannot be so employed except under circumstances of urgent necessity."[143] Still, he consented to a small detachment being posted at Harbour Grace come election time, "on the understanding that it is not to be used except in case of absolute necessity."

While awaiting Newcastle's reply, the governor appointed three commissioners to inquire into the violence. The two Protestant commissioners, St. John's magistrate Thomas Bennett and lawyer and justice of the peace Charles Simms, began by stating the obvious: that the five-man Harbour Grace police detachment was too small to have deterred the rioters.[144] They insinuated that all of the rioters were Catholics, noted their compliance when the priests intervened, and rather than recommend that the police force be enlarged, argued that the army detachment should be re-established. The third commissioner, Attorney General George James Hogsett, a Catholic, submitted a minority report that read like it came from another planet.[145] He faulted the magistrates for failing to swear in special constables, and charged that Ridley and Munn had spent election day not at the polling place but at their respective business premises, allegedly to ensure that these would not be damaged. Calling to mind Chief Justice Bourne's findings from 1841, Hogsett rejected the notion that the rioters were exclusively Catholic, nebulously claiming that "violence was resorted to by the partizans of all the candidates when it suited their purpose." His conclusion that the remedy lay in increasing the police presence in Harbour Grace rang hollow, given that as attorney general he was perfectly placed to do exactly that, but did not. It would take a change of government before the police force would begin to expand.

Never one to sit idly by, Premier Kent also condemned the magistrates, informing Bannerman that, as businessmen, they were "reported to have taken a leading interest in the late Election."[146] This was an important point, and one easily lost in the official obsession with priestly influence. Businessmen, including magistrates, exerted political pressure on their customers, and if those customers happened to be indebted fishermen, the pressure could be intense. There is incontrovertible evidence that merchants delivered votes to their preferred candidates, and Harbour Grace's nickname of "Munnsborough" was a blatant nod to the custom.[147] (John Munn, incidentally, had been an elected member of the Amalgamated Legislature and was appointed to the Legislative Council in 1855.) As for Ridley's and Munn's depiction of Harbour Grace's languishing post-1855 economy, Kent rebutted that the town had lately "made rapid advances in mercantile and general prosperity," and as evidence cited an increase in its customs' revenues from £3,600 in 1853 to £9,700 in 1859.

On the basis of the commissioners' reports, a select House of Assembly committee nullified the Harbour Grace election result, forcing a by-election on November 7, 1860. On October 27, in a virtual replay of the previous year, Pinsent sent the government a new request by Ridley and Munn for military aid.[148] Cabinet rubber-stamped it, and this time no one forgot to forward the requisite paper to Bannerman, who immediately arranged with Major John James Grant, Commanding Officer of the Royal Newfoundland Companies, to send a hundred men by steamer from Portugal Cove to Harbour Grace. The troops, however, never got out of St. John's. Supporters of Liberal candidate James Luke Prendergast, who this time had priestly support—he was known as "Mad Luke" because of his unpredictable allegiances—scooped the governor and everyone else by rioting on nomination day (November 1). This caused the opposing candidate, the Wesleyan Thomas Higgins, to withdraw, and handed victory[xxiv] to Prendergast.[149] Never at a loss for scapegoats, a livid Bannerman rebuked the magistrates for waiting too long to ask for help, a baffling claim given how quickly their

---

[xxiv] Although the House of Assembly would strike yet another select committee to examine this particular election violence, the committee had not reported when the House was abruptly dissolved on March 7, 1861.

request (and cabinet's approval) had reached him.

Bannerman would have his day. Liberal solidarity had been shaky ever since the launch of responsible government, based as it was on the support of Methodists and independent middle-class Catholics. Anything that might alienate either of those two groups, especially the more numerous Methodists, was likely to jeopardize Liberal rule. In June 1860 the edifice began to crumble when Mullock lambasted Kent's government in an open letter to the Catholics of the St. John's diocese.[150] In an effort to lift Newfoundlanders from, as he called it, the "state of darkness to which ages of bad government have reduced it," Mullock and his good friend Judge Little had taken it upon themselves to go to New York and negotiate terms for chartering a steamship to operate between St. John's and the outports. With the economy struggling and relief payments to unemployed fishermen mounting accordingly, Kent felt the contract was too expensive and decided not to honour it, thus prompting Mullock's explosive letter, in which he assailed Kent and his administration not only for rejecting the contract, but also for corruption in the distribution of poor-relief funds.

Kent's predicament worsened when a down cod fishery was compounded by a failed potato crop, creating still more demands for poor relief during the ensuing winter.[151] In January 1861, in an effort to appease Mullock, Kent offered to de-politicize the poor relief system by giving magistrates and clergymen a greater say in it. This, however, caused a revolt in government ranks, among whom one of the most outspoken critics was the member for Harbour Main, independent Catholic Patrick Nowlan.[xxv] Kent backtracked in order to maintain support in the House of Assembly, but lost Mullock again in the process. He was also facing a threat to his leadership

---

xxv   Immortalized as "Patsy Nolan" in Johnny Burke's song "The Kelligrews Soiree." I am indebted to Bob Cuff for bringing this connection to my attention.

from independent Catholic Ambrose Shea, and altogether it was probably true that "the strife in the party was so keen that there would have been a split even if this untoward event [Mullock's letter] had not happened."[152]

February brought signs that the pressure might be getting to the premier. On the 6th, Receiver General Thomas Glen introduced a bill calling for the payment of public accounts, including the salaries of the governor and the judiciary, in colonial currency instead of more valuable British sterling. Bannerman and the judges strenuously objected, and on the 25th, Glen withdrew the bill. Speaking in the House that same day, Kent accused Bannerman of conspiring with the judges and opposition leader Hoyles to defeat the bill. When the text of Kent's speech appeared in the press, Bannerman asked him to explain himself. Kent unwisely replied that he owed him no explanation, and on that gauzy pretext Bannerman dismissed his administration, but only after consulting Hoyles to see if the Conservatives were prepared to govern; as might be expected, Hoyles said that they were.[153] Bannerman then passed the baton to Hoyles, but on March 5 the Liberals, who still had a majority in the House, passed a no-confidence motion. Two days later Bannerman dissolved the Assembly and called a general election for May 2.

It did not take long for the governor's actions, which appalled the Colonial Office, to bring Mullock back into the Liberal fold. Alleging that a Protestant conspiracy was afoot, on March 21 he publicly asked Catholics to unite; unwilling to let Kent completely off the hook, he urged his charges to vote for candidates backed by their clergy.[154] This call to arms provoked an equally intemperate public outburst from Feild, who defended Bannerman, charged that Kent and the Liberals were unfit for office, and voiced support for Hoyles.[155] Between them, the leaders of the colony's two largest denominations succeeded in making an already volatile situation that much more explosive. The Liberals, however, had the most to lose, since Mullock's stridency alienated Methodists and independent Catholics alike, increasing the odds of a Conservative victory.

The election was uneventful in those districts where one denomination enjoyed a clear majority of the voters, as this made the outcomes foregone conclusions. With 14 Conservatives thus being elected by acclamation, the Liberals had to win all 16 remaining seats in order to retain their majority. Feelings ran high in the few seats that were up for grabs, but also, thanks to Mullock, in seats where independent Catholic candidates opposed church-endorsed ones. This put the spotlight on Conception Bay, and on April 22, Bannerman sent 103 men and officers of the Royal Newfoundland Companies to Harbour Grace, where a small steamer stood ready to take them elsewhere in the bay should that become necessary.[156] Since this contingent represented nearly half the regiment's strength, two of the St. John's volunteer companies were told to get ready to man the town forts should the remaining troops be called out to keep order there.[157]

There was only one incident in the capital, and it was serious enough. In the district of St. John's West the three Catholic Liberal candidates were opposed by the publican Pierce Barron, who was an independent Catholic, and the merchant Kenneth McLea, a Protestant and a Conservative. After a raucous nomination meeting on April 29, a mob besieged McLea's business premises (McLea and Sons), whose terrified occupants fired on their attackers, wounding several.[158] The simultaneous arrival of priests and troops averted further bloodshed, but McLea and Barron had gotten the message and withdrew from the race, allowing the three Catholic Liberals to win.[159]

Perhaps it was just as well that so many men had been sent to Harbour Grace, for on the morning of the 26th (nomination day) fighting erupted there between supporters of "Mad Luke" Prendergast (who had the backing of John Dalton, the Roman Catholic Bishop of the recently created Harbour Grace diocese) and those of the Conservative candidate, Protestant merchant Henry Moore, and the independent Liberal candidate, lawyer John Hayward, who was a Protestant.[160] Some helpful soul telegraphed word of the ruckus to Carbonear, and before long 400 of that town's finest appeared on the outskirts of Harbour Grace, bent on lending their muscle to Prendergast. Around noon Pinsent handed Captain Thomas Hanrahan a written request for military aid, and although troops rushed to the scene, the only way they could stop such a sizeable group from entering town was to fire on them, and to do that they needed a direct order from Pinsent. This he refused to give, because, as he later told Bannerman, he did not want anyone getting killed. Bannerman, whose powers as governor included the right to appoint or dismiss magistrates, suspended him when he learned what had happened.

The streets soon filled with rioters, most of whom went looking for property belonging to Moore and Hayward supporters. A petrified Hayward gathered up his family and hid in the building that the troops were using as a barracks.[161] Thomas Hanrahan recounted that "the mob moved about from one end of the Town to the other destroying property on the way, and on the approach of the Troops would move off through some bye street to a different part of the Town." With Pinsent still refusing to give the order to fire, there was not much else the troops could do, and the fury abated only after some priests appeared and implored the rioters to go home. Three days later Moore withdrew from the contest, and although this cleared the way for the Liberals to take both seats, the returning officer decided that he would let the House of Assembly determine, when it re-convened, whether Prendergast and Hayward should be allowed to claim them.

Similar circumstances brought different results in Carbonear. Early on the 25th, the incumbent, Catholic Liberal Edmund Hanrahan, personally led an attack on the house of a supporter of his Conservative rival, the planter and Methodist William Taylor. At Magistrate Joseph Ryan's request, Pinsent and 21 men of the Royal Newfoundland Companies, led again by Captain Hanrahan, left Harbour Grace on foot around 9:00 a.m.[162] When they arrived they found the streets empty except for a few harmless drunks, but when their presence became known a crowd began to form around them. After someone got near enough to knock Pinsent's hat off his head, Hanrahan proposed that the troops should return to Harbour Grace, "as their presence seemed to create rather than prevent disturbances." When Ryan agreed that "he did not see any necessity of the Troops remaining any longer," Pinsent ordered their withdrawal. The next day, while all hell was breaking loose in Harbour Grace, the violence resumed in Carbonear. Fearing for his life, Taylor withdrew and the returning officer declared Edmund Hanrahan elected.

The situation in the dual riding of Harbour Main was no less confused, but here the battle was squarely between rival Catholic factions.[163] Liberal candidates Charles Furey and Kent's Attorney General, George Hogsett, had received Bishop Dalton's public blessing, while their opponents, Thomas Byrne and the incumbent, Patrick Nowlan, were independent Catholic Liberals. On polling day a clash occurred at Cat's Cove (now Conception Harbour) when a group of Hogsett and Furey supporters from nearby Salmon Cove, led by the priest, Father Kyran Walsh, went there to register their votes.[164] Cat's Cove being a Nowlan and Byrne stronghold, their supporters had other plans. Armed and dangerous, they barricaded their village's entrance and opened fire as the outsiders drew near, killing one of them and wounding several others. The dead man, George Furey, was candidate Charles Furey's cousin. Afterward, the able-bodied members of the Salmon Cove contingent made their way to Harbour Main and voted there, even though the regulations required them to vote in Cat's Cove.

Much would depend on whether Harbour Main's returning officer and justice of the peace, Patrick Strapp, accepted the Salmon Cove votes. In order to ensure his safety and also to arrest[xxvi] those who had shot up the Salmon Cove delegation, 70 soldiers commanded by now Lieutenant Colonel Grant and accompanied by Charles Simms arrived at Harbour Main by steamer on May 4.[165] By then Strapp had already signed a certificate declaring Hogsett and Furey elected, albeit after both Hogsett and Walsh had separately visited and threatened him. Allegedly under pressure from Grant, Strapp now made out a second return declaring Nowlan and Byrne the victors. Afterwards, the troops returned to St. John's, leaving a 30-man detachment at Harbour Grace to watch over the forlorn landscape of post-election Conception Bay. Their presence failed to prevent assaults and verbal abuse against Protestant clergymen, and in general it was said of the bay at this time that "a Protestant could not safely walk the streets."[166] But the streets were also unsafe for some Roman Catholics, notably returning officer Strapp, who five days after the election had his house destroyed and his livestock killed by vengeful Hogsett and Furey supporters.[167]

The Conservatives, who were still the governing party, rejected the Harbour Main results on the reasonable ground that Strapp had signed the original election certificate under duress. This decision, together with the lack of a return from Harbour Grace, gave the Conservatives 14 seats to the Liberals' 12, enabling them to form a new, if temporary, majority government. When the House of Assembly convened on the afternoon of Monday, May 13, the atmosphere in St. John's was electric.

An estimated 2,000 people had gathered outside the Colonial Building and along adjacent parts of Military Road,

---

[xxvi] On December 3, 1861, four men were convicted and given sentences ranging from five to 12 months. All were released early at Bannerman's behest so they could go to the 1862 seal hunt.

CIVIL COMMOTION   157

among them substantial contingents from Harbour Grace and Harbour Main.[168] It was well known that Hogsett and Furey were going to try and take the disputed Harbour Main seats, and the crowd had come to show their support. After the two politicians did indeed take the seats, they were evicted by the police. This excited the crowd, who were briefly stilled when Magistrate Peter Carter read them the Riot Act. But they soon revived and now attempted to carry Hogsett back into the building on their shoulders, only to be stopped by soldiers and police stationed at the entrances.

Next, some of Hogsett's more exuberant supporters hoisted him aloft on a chair, and with their ersatz king on his ersatz throne, decamped west along Military Road, then turned south on Prescott Street en route to Water Street, hell-bent on mischief.[169] Around 5:00 p.m., when Bannerman left for Government House via Military Road, some of the remaining crowd stoned his carriage and probably would have done worse if troops had not been present. Soldiers also accompanied Hoyles and other government members to their homes when they left the building around 7:00 p.m.[170]

Not long after Bannerman had returned to Government House, Magistrates Carter and Thomas Bennett, who were still at the Colonial Building, were informed that a mob including women and children had looted the business premises of Michael Nowlan and William Kitchin,[xxvii] and was now running amok on Water Street.[171] Nowlan and Kitchin were relatives of the Harbour Main candidate, independent Catholic Patrick Nowlan,[xxviii] connections that left no doubt as to the riot's Conception Bay origins. The magistrates proceeded to Fort William, where shortly after 6:00 p.m. they hand-

---

xxvii Nowlan's premises were at 93 Water Street, now home to the King George V Building. Kitchin's were at 238 Water Street (now 240), on the northwest corner of Water Street and McBride's Hill. I am indebted to Bob Cuff for identifying these locations.

xxviii Michael Nowlan was Patrick Nowlan's uncle; Kitchin's wife was his aunt.

158   THE INVISIBLES

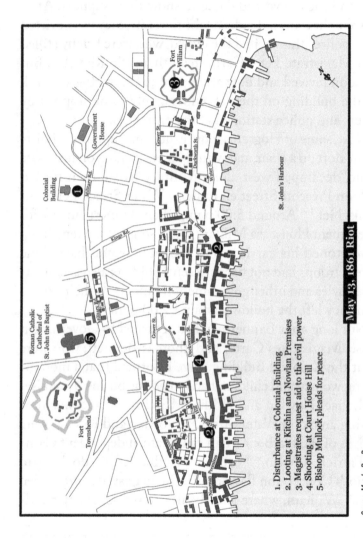

Source: *Map by Don Parsons.*
Figure 21: May 13, 1861, Riot.

ed Lieutenant Colonel Grant a written request for aid. On Grant's orders, Lieutenant Arthur Saunders Quill rounded up the available men at that post and sent word to Fort Townshend for reinforcements. Accompanied by Bennett, Quill (on horseback) and his men hurried down Kings Road toward Water Street, where they spun westward and were joined by the reinforcements from Fort Townshend. Quill and his force of approximately 80 men would have to contend with a mob of over 2,000 people, who by this time were concentrated in the west end near the Newman and Company premises.[172]

Soon after the troops reached the scene, a suddenly nervous Bennett told Quill that the men should pull back, since the crowd not only seemed to be agitated by their presence, but was growing larger by the minute. Quill agreed, and as his men retraced their steps with rioters in close pursuit, they came upon Lieutenant Colonel Grant, who had just descended McBride's Hill on horseback, and who, as the senior officer, now took command. Several priests were also present, including the regiment's Roman Catholic chaplain, Father Jeremiah O'Donnell. They now begged Grant to return the troops to barracks, to which he replied that they were there at the magistrates' request and could not leave unless Bennett ordered them to do so. For reasons known only to himself, Bennett, who only minutes earlier had asked Quill to withdraw his men, refused to order them back to barracks.

The troops halted under the courthouse, and although the crowd was eerily quiet, it pressed in on the redcoats until someone suddenly bolted toward Grant and tried to pull him off his horse. The attacker was collared and handed over to a police constable, who with a small troop escort tried to leave for the lock-up. The mob, now massive and fully alive, pelted the escort with whatever they could find—rocks, stones, bricks, gravel, even sticks of wood—and made moves to rescue the prisoner, causing Grant to send reinforcements at the charge. These, along with the escort, formed a circle around the prisoner at the foot of Court House Hill.[xxix] A section of troops then dislodged some rioters from the courthouse terrace, from where they had been raining down projectiles. With that, the main body of rioters swarmed up Court House Hill and reassembled at its top. Fearing for his men's safety, many of them having been injured, Grant ordered them to load their rifles. Believing, as he later told a coroner's inquest, that "energetic measures" were required, he asked Bennett if he should give the order to fire. In this he was following army regulations forbidding the officer commanding the troops to give such an order "unless distinctly required to do so by the Magistrate."[173] Bennett, by his own account, answered "whatever Sir is for the best," and while this was hardly a clear instruction, Grant took it as such.[174]

At this point, descriptions of events become even murkier. Grant testified that he heard a shot from atop Court House Hill, whereupon he ordered Quill to take five sections up the hill, leaving the sixth in possession of the terrace. The troops began their ascent under a hail of bricks and stones, Grant atop his white horse on one flank and Quill atop his black mount on the other. Part way up there was a crucial communication breakdown. Turning toward Quill, who could not hear him above the roar, Grant shouted "Let the leading section fire," meaning that Quill was to give the order. As Grant himself acknowledged, the word *fire* was not a command unless preceded by the words *ready, present*. Nonetheless, some of the men who heard him say it took it for a command and discharged their weapons; this was followed by isolated shots, at which point Grant and "several officers" ordered the men to cease firing.[175] When they did, three male rioters, one of them a youth, lay dead. Some 20 more had been wounded, including Father O'Donnell, ironically the chaplain

---

[xxix] As it was spelled at the time. In testimony before a coroner's inquest, it was also called Market House Hill, the confusion deriving from the fact that the building had a dual function, with the court occupying the floor above the market.

Source: Provincial Resource Library, Newfoundland and Labrador Collection, MN 616.

Figure 22: Court House and Market, 1851. This was the setting for the climactic scene on May 13, 1861, when the Royal Newfoundland Companies opened fire and killed three rioters.

to some of the very same men who had shot him.

Significantly, Quill later recounted that he "saw the flash and heard the report of a gun instantaneously with the firing on the part of the troops."[176] This differs both from Grant's account and from the testimony of civilian witnesses, none of whom could remember hearing *any* shot coming from the mob.[177] The conflicting testimony suggests that someone was mistaken, maybe even lying. It is also worth noting that in a clear dereliction of duty, Grant ignored the additional requirement in army regulations that people opposing the troops must be told "that in the event of the troops being ordered to fire, their fire will be effective." He was lucky that he never had to appear before a military court, where he might have paid a price for his conduct.

162   THE INVISIBLES

The blast from the troops having cleared the mob from atop Court House Hill, Grant brought his men back down to Water Street. There he was approached by Judge Little and the Catholic priest, Father Enrico Carfagnini, who implored him and Bennett to return the troops to barracks, and promised to use their influence to get the mob to disperse. Possibly in shock, Bennett would not budge, causing Little, as a superior court judge, to overrule him and to appeal directly to Grant, who finally gave the order.[178] Accompanied by Bennett and Little, the troops and their prisoner (the man who had tried to unhorse Grant) headed eastward along Water Street before turning up Prescott Street en route to Fort Townshend. They were harassed almost to the fort's gate, which may explain why, in a further disciplinary breakdown, some of the troops fired into cross-streets and lanes as they made their way to safety. Once inside the fort at approximately 8:30 p.m., they received medical attention for everything from cuts to contusions to broken bones. Among the injured was Grant, who had been "severely hurt by a blow from a stone on the head."[179]

While the troops were retreating, the bells of the Roman Catholic Cathedral began to peal, summoning the rioters to their own sanctuary. A crowd estimated by Mullock at 5,000 people eventually crammed into the building. Addressing them from the altar, he begged them to go home and to keep the peace, and exacted "a promise ... that, for the honour of the Divine Presence, they would obey his instructions, and endeavour to induce all within their influence to do the same."[180] Not everyone got the message. Later that night Feild was stoned as he made his way home, and someone burned down the stable of Judge Bryan Robinson, a Protestant and driving force behind the judiciary's opposition to the fateful currency bill that had helped to bring about Kent's downfall.[181] There were more fires over the next few nights, all targeting Protestants and Protestant symbols. Hoyles's summer cottage was destroyed, and the Anglican theological college would have been as well had not the flames been discovered early enough to be doused.

The next day Mullock met Bannerman at Government House, unnerving him with a ridiculous claim that 10,000 men armed with sealing guns were ready to lay siege to the town that very night. Betraying some fear himself, the bishop pledged that he and his priests would do their best to "keep the people quiet" if no troops were called out. A mortified Bannerman promised to try and keep them in barracks for the time being. Although he told the bishop that he was "never frightened," his subsequent actions belie the claim. On Grant's recommendation he agreed to withdraw the remaining 30 men from Harbour Grace, believing that they would be in grave danger if they stayed there.[182] The crowning proof, though, was his desperate request for reinforcements from Halifax, in which he pleaded that "no time [be] lost" in sending them, as Newfoundland was "different from other Colonies, many [people] having Seal Guns."[183] His prayers were answered on the 19th when eight officers and 214 men (one full company) of the 62nd Regiment arrived from command headquarters.

As soon as people recovered from the shock of the riot, they went looking for scapegoats, with the priests, the magistrates, and the troops taking much of the early blame.[184] A coroner's inquest of May 25-28, tasked with determining the cause of death of the youth Clifford and Messrs. Fitzpatrick and Hunt, went easy on the troops. Jurors were hamstrung by the refusal of Clifford's mother to allow surgeons to examine his body, and by the inability of witnesses to swear that Fitzpatrick "was killed by the Military."[185] This left Hunt, whose death the jurors attributed in measured tones to "the effects of a Bullet fired by the Military in the discharge of their duty in aiding and assisting the civil power in quelling a Riot." This foreshadowed the decision of a House of Assembly committee that absolved the military because they had been so blatantly provoked.[186]

Bannerman, who was hardly an innocent bystander, never thought to blame Grant, nor did the colonel for one minute think to blame himself. Nothing better captures his attitude than his comportment on the day after the riot, when he "walked up through the city alone with his cane and a little dog," seemingly without a care in the world, to testify before the coroner's inquest.[187] The governor instead targeted Hogsett, who along with two henchmen was brought before the Supreme Court in November and tried for inciting riot. But Chief Justice Francis Brady, who had gone so far as to deliver his charge to the jury, had to dismiss the case when one of the jurors became ill.[188] A proposed retrial seems never to have happened. Hogsett, meanwhile, returned the favour by helping to organize a petition to the Queen seeking Bannerman's dismissal. That document was weighted down by the ink of 8,000 signatures, including those of Bishops Mullock and Dalton and numerous priests.[189] Although nothing came of this either, justice of a kind did get served. In September a Magistrates' Court fined Hogsett and ordered him to pay costs for striking John Williams McCoubrey, owner of the *Times and General Commercial Gazette*, for no apparent reason.[190] Plainly not a man to be trifled with, McCoubrey did Bannerman and a great many others a favour by thrashing Hogsett with his cane.

From the other side of the ocean, Bannerman's actions drew a stinging rebuke from Newcastle. Although he did not object to the troops' deployment during the election, the Colonial Secretary declared that they were not in Newfoundland "for the purpose of quelling civil tumults arising out of the excesses of party spirit and religious rancour."[191] This had a familiar and by now decidedly hollow ring, but not so his conclusion that "it is impossible to permit the despatch of reinforcements from a neighbouring colony and their main-

CIVIL COMMOTION   165

tenance at St. John's as a Police Force to keep order between contending factions unless the Colony is willing to undertake the cost of such a proceeding." In the event, this last proviso caused Hoyles's government no trouble whatever, and in September, with an eye to the November 20 by-election to fill the two vacant Harbour Grace seats, it agreed to foot the bill to retain the 62nd.[192]

In late June a House of Assembly select committee concluded that Messrs. Nowlan and Byrne were the rightful winners of the Harbour Main seats. This left the Liberals and Conservatives with 14 seats apiece, although with independents such as Nowlan, Byrne, and Shea in the ranks, Liberal unity was tottering. Regardless, someone would need to win both Harbour Grace seats in order to form a majority. A Liberal victory would likely result in Bannerman's recall as governor, since Newcastle had already said that "success"— by which he meant a Conservative majority government— was the only possible way to justify his dismissal of Kent's administration.[193] A Liberal loss, on the other hand, would spell trouble for Kent's leadership and the party's future. For these and other reasons, when November rolled around, the pressure was immense.

Bannerman and Hoyles left no stone unturned to ensure that voters would be safe and the results a true reflection of the electorate's wishes. In October the governor received a petition from Harbour Grace requesting military aid.[194] It had been signed not only by Magistrates Ridley, Munn, and Joseph Peters (who had replaced Pinsent), but also by the Methodist and Presbyterian ministers. The likelihood of that petition being turned down was nil, and on November 12 approximately 100 men of the 62nd Regiment disembarked in Harbour Grace, where they were joined by HMS *Spiteful* and HMS *Hydra* and their crews, who had come from Halifax.[195] They arrived too late to prevent the murder by stoning of Harbour Grace police constable Jeremiah Dunn, who along with several other policemen was attacked in the streets on the night of October 22.[196] Although the martial presence contributed to a peaceful election, another influential factor was a pastoral letter by a chastened Mullock urging Catholics to keep the peace. At Sunday mass on the 17th, Bishop Dalton also counselled his flock against harassing the troops, who, he said, were merely following orders and were "more to be pitied than abused."[197] More characteristically, he reminded them that they "must return a member of their own religion."

Even if every Catholic in the district did as their bishop directed, the arithmetic was against them. The 1857 census showed that the district contained 3,390 Catholics, 5,490 Anglicans, and 1,187 Dissenters (mostly Methodists).[198] Protestants therefore outnumbered Catholics by a ratio of nearly two to one, and the election results more than bore this out. Of the 1,390 votes cast, Liberal chameleon James Prendergast received 432, the remainder being almost evenly divided between his Conservative opponents. It was a near-run thing, but Hoyles had his majority, Bannerman's job was secure, and the Liberals faced an uncertain future.

Dénouement

After the by-election Bannerman withdrew roughly half the men of the 62nd from Harbour Grace. In January, after the entire company was ordered back to Halifax, he reluctantly re-staffed the detachment with 27 officers and men of the Royal Newfoundland Companies, in whom he had lost faith.[199] He took solace in the assurance of the Major General Commanding in Halifax, Charles Hastings Doyle, that reinforcements would be sent again if needed, but his efforts to convince Newcastle to station troops permanently in Harbour Grace came to nothing, as did his bid to get the War Office to replace the Royal Newfoundland Companies with a regiment of the line.[200] The Harbour Grace troops returned to St. John's in March 1862 after the last of the Conception Bay sealers had sailed for the ice. Bannerman, who felt that the sealers needed watching, called them "the worst class of the population."[201]

Before the year was out the Royal Newfoundland Companies would be absorbed into the Royal Canadian Rifle Regiment, not because of anything Bannerman said or did, but because the die had already been cast. The Royal Canadian Rifles continued to aid the civil power, most notably during the 1869 general election, when confederation with Canada was the burning issue. One hundred forty-five men were distributed among the Conception Bay communities of Brigus, Bay Roberts, Port de Grave, and Spaniard's Bay, while HMS *Niobe* and its crew stood ready in Harbour Grace harbour.[202] This was the last time that British troops would be so used in Newfoundland.

In 1868 William Gladstone's Liberals had come to power in Britain on a platform of government retrenchment and army reorganization. With that, garrison reduction, which had been stalled by the American Civil War, resumed its inexorable course. The piecemeal withdrawal of the St. John's garrison began in 1869 and concluded on November 8, 1870, when the last contingent of the Royal Artillery departed for Bermuda aboard HMS *Tamar*. It did so over the objections of the House of Assembly, the Legislative Council, the Chamber of Commerce, and above all of Governor Sir Stephen Hill, whose hysterical fears of imminent societal collapse proved to be unfounded.[203]

For all of the nonsense that sometimes emanated from the Colonial Office, the use of troops to aid the civil power was standard procedure throughout the British Empire. In Britain itself, the period between the end of the Napoleonic Wars and the suppression of Chartism in 1848 was one of widespread working-class unrest, so much so that army pensioners had to be used to supplement regular troops in keeping order.[204] Despite police modernization throughout the United Kingdom, in 1891 the Secretary of State for War, Edward Stanhope, could still describe aid to the civil power as the army's main role there.[205] Election riots were common in British North America, especially Montreal, where in 1849 rioting over the Rebellion Losses Bill culminated in the burning of Parliament House. Even tiny Prince Edward Island had to endure the election-related Belfast Riot of March 1, 1847, which left four dead.[206] (Coincidentally, one of the candidates in that contest was John Little, who would follow his brother Philip to St. John's.) Tragic though the loss of life was on all such occasions, events in British North America were nothing like the bloody clashes that occurred between British troops, colonists, and the colonized during New Zealand's Maori Wars (1845-72), Australia's Eureka Rebellion (1854), the Indian Mutiny (1857), and Jamaica's Morant Bay Rising (1865).

If the violence of May 13, 1861, in St. John's was mild by comparison, its effects were nonetheless profound. Determined to bridge the gulf between Protestants and Catholics and to prevent further bloodshed, Premier Hugh Hoyles convinced Laurence O'Brien to join his cabinet. Three years later he sent Ambrose Shea (a Catholic) and Frederic Carter (a Protestant) to represent Newfoundland at the Quebec Conference to discuss the confederation of the British North American colonies.[207] Carter, who succeeded Hoyles as premier in 1865, took the next step by bringing not only Shea and his brother Edward into cabinet, but also John Kent, thereby creating Newfoundland's first "strong, pan-sectarian administration."[208] Accommodating middle-class Catholics did not entirely keep their bishops and priests out of politics, but they were seldom again as overtly involved as Fleming and Mullock had been. The main exceptions were their opposition to confederation with Canada in 1869 and 1948, an opposition they shared with the bulk of the business community they had previously despised.

By tacit agreement, most subsequent governments sought denominational balance not only in cabinet but in all patronage appointments, so that civil service positions, for example, came to be apportioned equally between Catholics, Methodists,[xxx] and Anglicans.[209] This approach found its most famous expression in the Education Act of 1874, which sub-divided the Protestant education grant according to population. Eventually joined by the Salvation Army and the Pentecostal Assemblies, the denominational education system would persist until 1998. Altogether, the denominational principle became so ingrained that it "acquired the status of a constitutional convention."[210] Hindsight tells us that it outlived its usefulness, and that by sustaining division it kept religious prejudice alive. But hindsight was unavailable to our ancestors, who chose this as the price to be paid to quiet the clergy and stem the violence. There were bumps along the way, most conspicuously during the Harbour Grace Affray of December 26, 1883,[xxxi] but by and large they succeeded.[211] On a handful of occasions after 1870 the Royal Navy answered requests by the Newfoundland government to aid the civil power, for the last time in 1932.[212] Other than in the aftermath of the Harbour Grace Affray, all were for reasons unrelated to sectarianism.

[xxx] United Church from 1925.

[xxxi] Five people were killed and some 15 wounded when members of the Orange Order attempted to parade through a Catholic neighbourhood of Harbour Grace.

CHAPTER 7

CONCLUSION

Legacy

The Royal Newfoundland Companies left a mark on their own times and later ones as well. Merchants, publicans, and farmers earned money from providing the regiment's men with food, drink, supplies, and services, while members of the working class found employment in the construction and maintenance of their barracks and other facilities. In February 1870, John Kent, now a legislative councillor, estimated that the garrison was worth £30,000 a year to the business community—this at a time when annual colonial revenues were approximately £163,000.[1] Although it is impossible to assign a value, the regiment's roles in firefighting, aiding the civil power, and operating the port signalling service took pressure off colonial finances. St. John's would survive the garrison's withdrawal, proving, as in other parts of British North America, that the garrison was not indispensable.[2] But it made welcome contributions to the economy, and there was literally a price to be paid when it left.

As we have seen, regimental officers were influential in the development of sports, music, theatre, libraries, and museums, enriching popular culture and public education. The presence of officers at social and sporting events, and the public appearances of the regimental band, lent colour to the city and reinforced its ties to the monarchy and the empire, as was the case wherever army regiments were stationed.[3] Whether St. John's had a stronger British connection by virtue of having had a garrison for so long is difficult to say, since other factors, including a fawning press, the celebration of Queen Victoria's Golden and Diamond Jubilees, and the unwavering anglophilia of the mercantile elite, were also influential. But long into the twentieth century there were people in St. John's who worshipped all things British, and the memory of the garrison may have played a role in sustaining such sentiment.

The regiment, or, more properly, the garrison, left more tangible reminders. In 1871 Fort Townshend became headquarters of the Newfoundland Constabulary, as the newly reconstituted police force was then known. Today the name "Fort Townshend" is still used to designate the headquarters of the Royal Newfoundland Constabulary, even though all

Source: Rooms Provincial Archives E 14-2.

Figure 23: "St. John's Station – looking northeast from housetop, west of Devon Row, before 1900." The Fort William railway station incorporated some of the old military infrastructure.

CONCLUSION 173

traces of the fort have disappeared except for some walls that were uncovered prior to construction of the adjacent Rooms complex in 2005. In the 1880s, elements of Fort William were incorporated into a railway station that was destroyed by fire on March 31, 1900. A hotel and its parking lot occupy the site today.

From 1874 until 1978, when it was replaced by the General Hospital component of the Health Sciences Centre, the former Garrison Hospital on Forest Road was the main hospital for St. John's. "The Old General," as it was later known, is now a municipal heritage structure. Two military barracks on Signal Hill were also used as hospitals following the garrison's withdrawal. The first, for patients with infectious diseases, burned down in 1892; the second, for the treatment of tuberculosis and infectious diseases, was destroyed by fire in 1920. Today the archaeological remains of both structures are part of Signal Hill National Historic Site of Canada.

Some would argue that the city's best preserved garrison building is Commissariat House, which contained the Assistant Commissary General's residence and offices, and is now a provincial historic site. Nearby, however, are St. Thomas's Anglican Church and Government House. From the latter the governor formerly reported to the Secretary of State for War and the Colonies, and did his bidding. These three buildings, together with Government House's still ample grounds, are an impressive reminder of a once extensive military cultural landscape.

The garrison also left its mark on the city's streets, most notably in the form of Military Road, built in the 1770s to link Forts William and Townshend, and Signal Hill Road, opened in the 1790s to enable the hill's development as a citadel, a pipe dream that was a long time dying. Parade Street, to the west of Fort Townshend, is a vestige of the old Fort Townshend parade ground, and Ordnance Street, opposite the former site of Fort William, conjures up the once extensive Ordnance Yard facilities there. Last but not least there is Garrison Hill, which many a man of the Royal Newfoundland Companies eagerly trod on his way downtown, only to reluctantly climb en route to Fort Townshend after too many rounds at the pub.

And what of the human legacy? The records suggest that only one of the regiment's commissioned officers retired in the colony. Captain William John Coen, who had commanded the Harbour Grace detachment, participated in the Crimean War (with the 49th Regiment), and served as Sir Alexander Bannerman's private secretary, became a magistrate in Grand Bank before being named Governor of the Newfoundland Penitentiary in 1874.[4] He held the position until his death in 1878, leaving behind a widow and a large family, some or all of whom seem to have eventually moved to Chicago.[5] Most of Coen's fellow officers returned home either to retire on half pay or to seek civilian employment, typically in law enforcement.[6] A few may have accepted offers of cheap land that were extended to retired army officers to encourage them to settle elsewhere in the empire. By 1843, Nova Scotia was the only British North American colony where this benefit was still available.[7]

Until late in the regiment's history, discharged members of the rank and file tended either to return home via the regimental depot in Chatham, England, or to emigrate to other British North American colonies. In an example that was typical for the time, of 21 men who were discharged in August 1848, 12 planned to return to depot, six to settle in Canada West (formerly Upper Canada), one in Halifax, and two in Newfoundland.[8] This pattern prevailed until the late 1850s, when the vast majority of discharged men elected to stay in Newfoundland, almost certainly because they had married locally. Among them were the incorrigible Private Joseph Prime, who was discharged in May 1857, and who stated that he intended to remain in St. John's; Sergeant Thomas Woods, discharged in October 1857 and bound for Portugal Cove; and Sergeant James Roil (or Royle), discharged in May 1858 and headed for Mosquito, Conception Bay.[9] Discharged at the same time as Roil and all planning to live in St. John's were Sergeant Luke Fallon and Privates John Chambers, Joseph Moore, John Nicol, and John Wilkinson. Eight of 11 men discharged in June 1859 remained in St. John's, as did eight of 12 in February 1860.[10]

Although there is no way of knowing how all of these men supported themselves and their families, some at least found jobs in law enforcement, which was as natural an option for the rank and file as it was for officers. Of Irish extraction, Luke Fallon was appointed high constable at Harbour Grace in 1861 and moved to Montreal sometime before his death in 1879.[11] Born in Elgin, Scotland, in 1816, John Nicol spent a few years as an asylum keeper in St. John's before joining the police force in 1865. He made sergeant two years later and died in 1882; his modern-day descendants include members of the Bursey family of St. John's.[12] A native of Linlithgow, Scotland, Sergeant Peter McBay was discharged in 1862, became high constable at Carbonear in 1863, and moved to St. John's to assume the rank of head constable in 1883.[13] He died there in 1911 at the grand old age of 88.

Patrick Myrick's Limp

On September 25, 1896, Patrick Myrick passed away in St. John's.[14] Born in 1821, he had spent most of his life in town before becoming a lightkeeper at Cape Race in 1874.[15] He was recognizable to all on account of his limp, an affliction traceable to May 13, 1861, when he took a bullet to his leg while attempting to help a fallen Father Jeremiah O'Donnell. Like all the dead and wounded on that fateful day, Myrick became a martyr, and a decade after his passing it was said that the "old Liberals of St. John's" still revered his memory.[16] Liberal nostalgia was perfectly understandable, because the same hail of bullets that shattered Myrick's leg also helped destroy the party. There would not be another Liberal government until 1893, and by that time the party had been changed beyond recognition, led as it was by an Anglican (Sir William Vallance Whiteway), and free as it was of priestly influence.[17] It is, however, an exaggeration to claim that Hoyles's ministry launched "a durable Protestant ascendancy," for it was a strange kind of ascendancy that guaranteed Catholics cabinet positions and a share of the spoils, and thus equality.[18] The shots that were fired on Court House Hill may not have been heard around the world, but they rang long and loud in Newfoundland.

ACKNOWLEDGEMENTS

My interest in the Royal Newfoundland Companies dates to about 1980, when, as a recently hired Parks Canada historian, I was asked to provide background material on the regiment for the Signal Hill Tattoo. I summarized my findings in an unedited manuscript that was rightfully buried in Parks Canada's *Microfiche Report Series*. The manuscript nonetheless generated useful feedback from Jim Hiller, now Emeritus Professor of History at Memorial University, and the late Cyril Byrne of St. Mary's University. Until I retired from Parks Canada in 2011, I continued to gather information on the regiment as a by-product of my ongoing research into the history of Signal Hill. Additional material came courtesy of Carol Whitfield, now retired but then the Chief Historian at Halifax Citadel National Historic Site of Canada.

After publication of my book *Cantwells' Way: A Natural History of the Cape Spear Lightstation* (2014), I finally gave the regiment my full attention, believing there was an interesting and important story to be told. I am grateful that the Historic Sites Association of Newfoundland and Labrador not only shared that belief, but also defrayed some of the book's publication costs. Rebecca Rose and James Langer, respectively President and Editor of Breakwater Books, recognized the need for a history of the Royal Newfoundland Companies and, most importantly, saw fit to publish it. They also assigned Jocelyne Thomas to edit the book, and her deft touch has made me look better than I am. Sincere thanks as well to Production Manager Rhonda Molloy for design and vigilance.

Joan Sullivan, Managing Editor of the *Newfoundland Quarterly*, allowed me to draw from my article on military firefighting which appeared in that journal in 1992. Longer ago than that, Fiona Day took me on a memorable tour of the old garrison church, St. Thomas's Anglican. Mark Ferguson of the Rooms Provincial Museum, together with Scott Andrews and, especially, Christopher Martin of Provincial Historic Sites, helped to identify the residence of the Collector of Customs in a sketch by Lieutenant Colonel John Oldfield of the Royal Engineers. Jennifer Reddy, Manager, Mistaken Point Cape Race Heritage Inc., went the extra distance to find out when Patrick Myrick joined the lightkeeping service at Cape Race. David Liverman of Cricket Newfoundland and Labrador opened my eyes to the history of cricket in the province. Genealogist Randy Whitten confirmed the marriage of William Carson's daughter Fanny to Lieutenant Stephen Rice of the Veterans, and with an assist from Ed Chafe identified the location of the old Roman Catholic burial ground, where the regiment's Sergeant John Neaven was laid to rest.

Colonel Alexander Steele of the Royal Highland Fusiliers Museum, Glasgow, supplied a photograph of Lieutenant General Robert Law, something I thought I would never find. Helen Ryan, Parish Administrator, St. Mary's Church of Ireland, Leixlip, discovered Law's baptism date and connected me with historian Suzanne Pegley, who shed light on his family's Irish background, as did University of Aberdeen historian Thomas Bartlett.

ACKNOWLEDGEMENTS 179

Melvin Baker of Memorial University fielded so many information requests that I have lost track of them. Suffice it to say that the man is practically indispensable. In addition to compiling the book's index, Joan Ritcey, retired Head of Memorial University's Centre for Newfoundland Studies, made helpful editorial suggestions and dug out important material on the denominational principle. I must also mention Joan's trailblazing efforts with the Centre's Digital Archives Initiative, without which I am not sure that I could have completed this book. Garry Shutlack and his stellar team at the Nova Scotia Archives facilitated my access to that institution's collection of British military records, among which there is much about Newfoundland. Melanie Tucker and Sandra Ronayne of the Rooms Provincial Archives patiently and expertly handled my requests for documentary and visual material. Alanna Wicks of the City of St. John's Archives impressed me with her knowledge of Lieutenant Colonel John Oldfield's work, and with her exemplary service. Another guardian of the province's visual history, John Griffin of the Provincial Resource Library, also performed yeoman service. Jean Pierre and Elizabeth Andrieux helped to facilitate a research trip to St. John's by means of their unparalleled hospitality.

My old boss and mentor at Parks Canada, the late Bill Naftel, supported my work on the regiment and offered occasional research assistance. Retired Parks Canada military curator Wayne Moug volunteered his services to help artist Carl McIntyre create the illustration of a Royal Newfoundland Companies' soldier found in these pages. Don Parsons, Interpretation Specialist with Parks Canada's Newfoundland East Field Unit, somehow made time to create maps of Conception Bay, the Great Fire of June 9, 1846, and the riot of May 13, 1861. Our conversations and emails about the maps were as enjoyable as they were educational. The indefatigable Allen Penney, retired Professor of Architecture at the former

Technical University of Nova Scotia (now part of Dalhousie University), redrew plans of selected military facilities from originals that were difficult to read and impossible to reproduce. As usual, his are better than the originals.

Historian Cameron Pulsifer, now retired from the Canadian War Museum, read drafts of the book's early chapters and kept me on the straight and narrow. David Facey-Crowther, retired Professor of History at Memorial University, did the same for the chapter on aid to the civil power. Bob Cuff, historian and writer at Gerald Penney Associates Limited, not only answered numerous information requests with speed and insight, but also read and commented on most of the manuscript in draft form. His input has been pivotal. By the time the entire revised manuscript got to Peter Neary, Emeritus Professor of History at Western University, it was much improved. Peter nonetheless proceeded to make it tighter still, and stopped me from driving off some hidden cliffs. These fine people are blameless for any remaining faults, which, I regret to say, are solely my responsibility.

APPENDIX I

COMPOSITION OF THE ROYAL NEWFOUNDLAND COMPANIES, 1845

Lieutenant Colonel (1)
Captains (3)
Lieutenants (7)
Ensigns (3)
Sergeants (22)
Corporals (15)
Drummers (6)
Privates (271)

Note: One lieutenant also served as regimental adjutant and another as regimental paymaster.

Sources: H.G. Hart, *The New Army List, for 1845* (London: John Murray, 1845), p. 261; The National Archives [Great Britain]: Public Record Office, War Office 27 (Inspection Returns), Vol. 345, "Inspection Return of the Royal Newfoundland Companies," Aug. 5, 1845.

APPENDIX 2

COMMANDING OFFICERS OF THE ROYAL NEWFOUNDLAND (VETERAN) COMPANIES

1824-31: Colonel[i] Thomas Kirwan Burke
1831-41: Lieutenant Colonel[ii] William Sall
1841-59: Lieutenant Colonel Robert Law
1859-62: Lieutenant Colonel[iii] John James Grant

Whoever was most senior of the commanding officers of the regiment, the Royal Artillery, or the Royal Engineers was deemed to be the garrison commandant, a position whose benefits included extra pay and allowances, a clerk, special living quarters in Fort William, and personal garden space. Whenever the commanding officer of the Royal Newfoundland Companies (or the Veterans) became the commandant, he was replaced in the regiment by an acting commanding officer. The above list does not reflect such acting appointments, nor does it reflect acting appointments that occurred when commanding officers were away on official or personal business. William Sall, for example, was gone for the better

---

[i] Brevet rank, attained in 1830. Burke's substantive rank was major.

[ii] Brevet rank, attained in 1830. Sall's substantive rank was captain.

[iii] Brevet rank, attained in 1861. Grant's substantive rank was major.

part of 1836-38, during which Robert Law saw time as both commanding officer and commandant; when he was the commandant, the next ranking officer below him commanded the regiment.

APPENDIX 3

PLANS OF SELECTED MILITARY FACILITIES, 1861

The following plans of Fort Townshend, Fort William, the Garrison Hospital, and the Ordnance Yard in 1861 were redrawn by Allen Penney from originals in the City of St. John's Archives drawn by Captain T.A.L. Murray of the Royal Engineers. They have been selected to convey a sense of the range of military facilities in old St. John's. I have omitted Signal Hill, having extensively covered it in my book *The Lookout: A History of Signal Hill* (St. John's: Creative Publishers, 2011). I saw no reason to include military property on the south side of the harbour, which consisted of Fort Amherst—properly a battery, not a fort—and over 500 hectares of rock and scrub. It is well to remember that until the garrison's withdrawal in 1870, the War Department (and, until 1855, the Board of Ordnance) was the town's largest property owner.

3.1 Fort Townshend

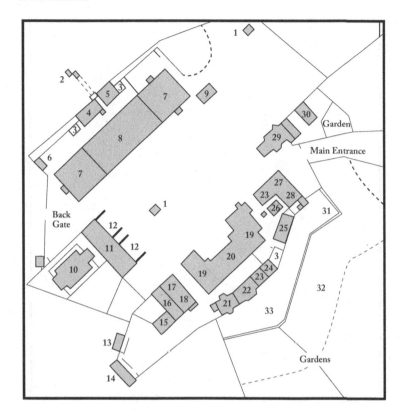

1	Well	19	Officers' Quarters
2	Women's Privies	20	Regimental Sergeant Major
3	Ash Pit		Commissariat Issuer
4	Washhouse		Regimental Orderly Room
5	Cookhouse		Garrison Doctor
6	Officers' Privy	21	Staff Sergeant's Quarters
7	Officers' Quarters	22	Cookhouse
8	Soldiers' Quarters	23	Cells
9	Regimental Magazine	24	Stable
10	Old Magazine in Ruins	25	Coachhouse
11	Commissariat Store	26	Carriage Shed
12	Ball Court	27	Guard Room
13	Soldiers' Privy	28	Quartermaster's Store
14	Privy	29	Staff Sergeant's Quarters
15	Major's Stables	30	Stable
16	Engine Workshop	31	Flag Station
17	Engine House	32	Remains of Old Ditch
18	Provision Store	33	Terreplein of Old Grand Battery

3.2 Fort William

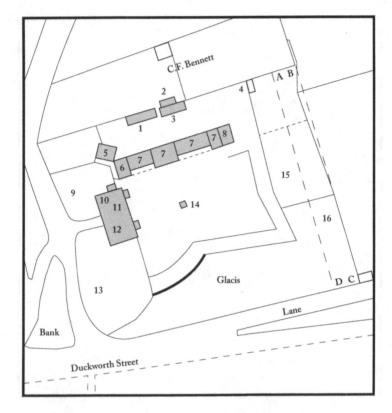

1	Stables etc.	9	Clerk of Works' Garden
2	Washhouse	10	Clerk or Works' Quarters
3	Cookhouse	11	Guardroom and Cells
4	Privies	12	Commandant's Quarters
5	Magazine used as Coal Shed	13	Commandant's Garden
6	Officers' Quarters	14	Well and Pump
7	Soldiers' Quarters	15	Garden
8	Gunroom	16	Strip of land ABCD granted to Anglican Bishop of Newfoundland in 1843

3.3 Garrison Hospital

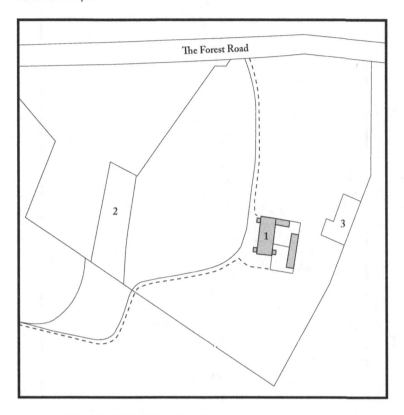

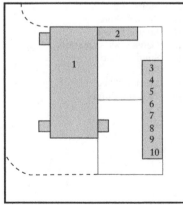

Map
1 Hospital
2 Medical Officer's Garden
3 Hospital Sergeant's Garden

Detail
1 Hospital
2 Privies
3 Deadhouse
4 Washhouse
5 Coal
6 Ashes
7 Privy
8 Coal
9 Stable
10 Coachhouse

3.4 Ordnance Yard

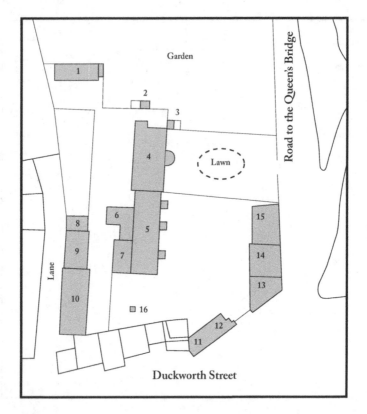

1	Stables etc.	9	Store
2	Privy	10	Barrack Store
3	Privy	11	Engine House
4	Storekeeper's Quarters	12	Gatekeeper's Quarters
5	Store Clerk's Quarters and Military Store Office etc.	13	Smith's Shop
6	Part of Office	14	Store
7	Store Clerk's Quarters	15	Carriage Shed
8	Forge Shed	16	Well and Pump

ENDNOTES

INTRODUCTION

1   *St. John's Public Ledger and Newfoundland General Advertiser* (hereafter *Ledger*), June 12, 1866, 3.

2   See Desmond Morton, *A Military History of Canada*, 5th ed. (Toronto: McClelland and Stewart, 2007), 73, in which Morton says that the British garrisons in North America were "[s]cattered from Halifax [Nova Scotia] to Fort Malden [Ontario]."

3   Since 2016 that engagement has been the centrepiece of a permanent exhibit at the Rooms Provincial Museum, an exhibit that unfortunately is long on sentiment and short on understanding. See my "'Beaumont-Hamel and the Trail of the Caribou: Newfoundlanders and Labradorians at War and at Home 1914-1949.' Permanent Exhibition, The Rooms Provincial Museum, St. John's, NL, 1 July 2016-Ongoing," *Newfoundland and Labrador Studies* 31, no. 2 (2016): 367-72.

4   For Placentia, see Jean-Pierre Proulx, "Placentia: 1713-1811," *History and Archaeology 26* (Ottawa: Parks Canada, 1979), 113-93. The longest-serving unit, Phillips's 40th Regiment of Foot, was stationed at Placentia from 1717 to 1764. The Royal Newfoundland Companies had the second-longest tenure (1824 to 1862).

5   Keith Mercer, "The Murder of Lieutenant Lawry: A Case Study of British Naval Impressment in Newfoundland, 1794," *Newfoundland and Labrador Studies* 21, no. 2 (2006): 261-66.

6   Jerry Bannister, *The Rule of the Admirals: Law, Custom, and Naval Government in Newfoundland, 1699-1832* (Toronto: University of Toronto Press, 2003), 109-14.

7   Olaf U. Janzen, "Newfoundland and British Maritime Strategy during the American Revolution" (Ph. D., Queen's University, 1983), 184.

8   C.P. Stacey, "Halifax as an International Strategic Factor, 1749-1949," *Canadian Historical Association Annual Report* 28, no. 1 (1949): 49-50.

9   John J. Mannion, "Introduction," in *The Peopling of Newfoundland: Essays in Historical Geography*, ed. John J. Mannion (St. John's: Memorial University of Newfoundland, 1977), 13.

10   Jeff A. Webb, "William Knox and the 18th-Century Newfoundland Fishery," *Acadiensis* 54, no. 1 (2015): 118.

11   Robertson Davies, *Fifth Business* (1970; repr., Toronto: Penguin Canada, 2005), v. Davies

190   THE INVISIBLES

later confessed that he invented the concept, but it is no less useful because of that. See Robertson Davies, *For Your Eyes Alone: Letters 1976-1995*, ed. Judith Skelton Grant (Toronto: McClelland and Stewart, 1999), 43.

CHAPTER I
THE LABYRINTH

[1]   The best monograph on army administration remains J.S. Omond, *Parliament and the Army 1642-1904* (Cambridge: Cambridge University Press, 1933). For a superb concise account, see Carol M. Whitfield, "Tommy Atkins: The British Soldier in Canada, 1759-1870," *History and Archaeology* 56 (Ottawa: Parks Canada, 1981), 7-42. For a summary that treats most of the period covered by this book, see Hew Strachan, *Wellington's Legacy: The Reform of the British Army 1830-54* (Manchester: Manchester University Press, 1984), 229-62. Although its focus might seem narrow, John Sweetman, *War and Administration: The Significance of the Crimean War for the British Army* (Edinburgh: Scottish Academic Press, 1984) is indispensable.

[2]   Ministry of Defence, *The Old War Office Building: A History* (London: Ministry of Defence, n.d.), 5.

[3]   Henry L. Hall, *The Colonial Office: A History* (London: Longmans, Green and Company, 1937), 87-91.

[4]   Hall, *The Colonial Office*, 49.

[5]   Ronald Hyam, *Britain's Imperial Century, 1815-1914: A Study of Empire and Expansion*, 3rd ed. (Houndmills, Basingstoke: Palgrave Macmillan, 2002), 5-6.

[6]   As noted in Sweetman, *War and Administration*, 2-7.

[7]   Donald Breeze Mendham Huffer, "The Infantry Officers of the Line of the British Army 1815-1868" (Ph. D., University of Birmingham, 1995), 277.

[8]   Elinor Kyte Senior, *British Regulars in Montreal: An Imperial Garrison, 1832-1854* (Montreal: McGill-Queen's University Press, 1981), 215.

9   The National Archives of the United Kingdom (hereafter TNA): Public Record Office (hereafter PRO), War Office 30 (hereafter WO 30) (War Office, Predecessors and Associated Departments, Miscellaneous Papers), Vol. 86, fol. 13, Law to Bazalgette, Nov. 6, 1848.

[10]   Nova Scotia Archives (hereafter NSA), Manuscript Group 12 (hereafter MG 12) (Great Britain: Army, Headquarters General Orders), Vol. 42, May 30, 1849.

[11]   NSA, MG 12, Vol. 42, June 28, 1849.

[12]   NSA, MG 12, Vol. 43, Jan. 8, 1852.

[13]   NSA, MG 12, Vol. 47, Aug. 14, 1856.

[14]   *Newfoundlander*, May 9, 1861, 3.

[15]   Phillip A. Buckner, *The Transition to Responsible Government: British Policy in British North America, 1815-1850* (Westport, CT: Greenwood Press, 1985), 51; J.C. Beaglehole, "The Royal Instructions to Colonial Governors 1783-1854: A Study in British Colonial Policy" (Ph. D., University of London, 1929), 420.

[16]   F.A. O'Dea, "Government House," *Canadian Antiques Collector* 10, no. 2 (1975): 49.

[17]   Patrick O'Flaherty, *Old Newfoundland: A History to 1843* (St. John's: Long Beach Press, 1999), 141.

[18]   April 24 to June 9, 1857.

[19]   The Rooms Provincial Archives (hereafter RPA), GN2.2 (Incoming Correspondence, Office of the Colonial Secretary fonds), Oldfield to Crowdy, Nov. 24, 1834; TNA:PRO, War Office 1 (hereafter WO 1) (In-Letters and Papers), Vol. 549, pp. 813-23, "Report of the Committee appointed by the Lords Commissioners of Her Majesty's Treasury...," Aug. 7, 1851.

[20]   Richard Henry Bonnycastle, *Newfoundland in 1842: A Sequel to "The Canadas in 1841"*

ENDNOTES **191**

(London: Henry Colburn, 1842), 2:95.

21 RPA, GN2.2, Yorke to Officer Commanding the Troops, Newfoundland, Jan. 25, 1855.

22 Memorial University of Newfoundland, Centre for Newfoundland Studies Archives, MF-280, "Memoranda on Newfoundland during a residence from October 25, 1830 to October 12, 1835," by Lieutenant Colonel John Oldfield.

23 H. G. Hart, *The New Army List, for 1845* (London: John Murray, 1845), 261.

24 On agents' myriad roles, see Huffer, "The Infantry Officers of the Line," 332-66.

CHAPTER 2

THE RISE AND FALL OF THE ROYAL NEWFOUNDLAND COMPANIES

1 On this subject, see Peter Neary, "The French and American Shore Questions as Factors in Newfoundland History," in *Newfoundland in the Nineteenth and Twentieth Centuries: Essays in Interpretation*, eds. James Hiller and Peter Neary (Toronto: University of Toronto Press, 1981), 95-123.

2 Peter Burroughs, "An Unreformed Army? 1815-1868," in *The Oxford History of the British Army*, eds. David G. Chandler and Ian Beckett (1994; repr., Oxford: Oxford University Press, 2003), 167; A.S. White, "Garrison, Reserve and Veteran Battalions and Companies," *Journal of the Society for Army Historical Research* (hereafter *JSAHR*) 38, no. 156 (1960): 166-67.

3 Michael Mann, *The Veterans* (Wilby: Michael Russell, 1997), 25-26.

4 In 1797, when the army set an infantry private's pay at one shilling, a private in the Invalids actually made one and a quarter pence more. See J.W. Fortescue, *A History of the British Army* (London: Macmillan, 1906), 4, 2:935.

5 Whitfield, "Tommy Atkins," 68.

6 Numbers are from Harold E. Raugh, Jr., *The Victorians at War 1815-1914: An Encyclopedia of British Military History* (Santa Barbara, CA: ABC-CLIO, 2004), xiv; Strachan, *Wellington's Legacy*, 68; J.W. Fortescue, *A History of the British Army* (London: Macmillan, 1923), 11:436. Hardinge was Secretary at War between 1828 and 1830.

7 Strachan, *Wellington's Legacy*, 68-69; Fortescue, *History of the British Army*, 11:437; Charles M. Clode, *The Military Forces of the Crown; Their Administration and Government* (London: John Murray, 1869), 2:289, 593-94; J.K. Johnson, "The Chelsea Pensioners in Upper Canada," *Ontario History* 53, no. 4 (1961): 2-3; Paul Cowan, "'Please, write we are starving now'," *Dorchester Review* 6, no. 2 (2016): 65-68.

8 Johnson, "The Chelsea Pensioners in Upper Canada," 1.

9 TNA:PRO, War Office 17 (hereafter WO 17) (Monthly Returns), Vol. 2252, fols. 85-91, Nov. 25, 1824, and fols. 93-98, Dec. 25, 1824.

10 TNA:PRO, Colonial Office 194 (hereafter CO 194) (Colonial Office and Predecessors: Newfoundland Original Correspondence), Vol. 74, fols. 97-102, Cochrane to Bathurst, Jan. 29, 1827.

11 Great Britain. House of Commons. *Sessional Papers*, 1839, Vol. 16, "Statistical Reports on the Sickness, Mortality, & Invaliding among the Troops in the United Kingdom, the Mediterranean, and British America; Prepared from the Records of the Army Medical Department and War Office Returns," 296.

12 On the Australian experience, see R.H. Montague, "The Royal Veterans in Australia," *Journal of the Royal Australian Historical Society* 68, no. 3 (1982): 238-46.

13 TNA:PRO, War Office 3 (hereafter WO 3) (Office of the Commander-in-Chief: Out-letters), Vol. 253, pp. 333-36, "Memorandum respecting the Newfoundland Veteran Companies," May 25, 1827; TNA:PRO, CO 194/83, fol. 248, "Duty State of the Troops Newfoundland," enclosure in Cochrane to Maitland, Sept. 13, 1832.

14 RPA, GN2.2, Macdonald to Greenwell, June 28, 1833.

15 NSA, MG 12, Vol. 32, March 20, 1840.

16 TNA:PRO, WO 17/2270, fols. 44-53, May 1, 1842.

17 Bonnycastle, *Newfoundland in 1842*, 96.

18 Kenneth Bourne, *Britain and the Balance of Power in North America 1815-1908* (London: Longmans, 1967), 120-23.

19 Library and Archives Canada (hereafter LAC), R3607-0-6-E (Gustavus Nicolls Papers), F 23, "Report … Relative to the State of the Fortifications and Public Buildings at St. John's, Newfoundland, and upon the System of Defense on that Station," Aug. 25, 1827.

20 D.W. Prowse, *A History of Newfoundland from the English, Colonial, and Foreign Records* (London: Macmillan, 1895), 425. Government House was completed in June 1831. See O'Dea, "Government House," 50.

21 TNA:PRO, War Office 55 (hereafter WO 55) (Ordnance Office and War Office: Miscellaneous Entry Books and Papers), Vol. 868, fols. 328-29, Byham to Bryce, Dec. 16, 1831.

22 James E. Candow, *The Lookout: A History of Signal Hill* (St. John's: Creative Publishers, 2011), 101-04.

23 RPA, GN2.2, Rendell to Crowdy, Apr. 5, 1841; TNA:PRO, WO 55/878, fols. 368-72, Bonnycastle to Mulcaster, Apr. 26, 1842.

24 TNA:PRO, CO 194/82, fols. 149-53, "Report on the present State of the Fortifications in this Island," Dec. 22, 1831; RPA, GN2.2, Byham to Respective Officers, July 14, 1834.

25 RPA, GN2.2, Oldfield to Mulcaster, June 11, 1835.

26 RPA, GN2.2, Oldfield to Cochrane, Jan. 21, 1834.

27 Patrick O'Flaherty, *Lost Country: The Rise and Fall of Newfoundland, 1843-1933* (St. John's: Long Beach Press, 2005), 73-74; Hyam, *Britain's Imperial Century*, 49.

28 C.P. Stacey, *Canada and the British Army 1846-1871* (Toronto: University of Toronto Press, 1963), 39.

29 Burroughs, "An Unreformed Army? 1815-1868," 164.

30 Burroughs, "An Unreformed Army? 1815-1868," 176-77.

31 TNA:PRO, CO 194/147, fols. 250-54, "The Memorial of the Legislative Council of Newfoundland," Apr. 6, 1856, enclosure in Darling to Labouchere, Apr. 30, 1856.

32 Douglas G. Anglin, *The St. Pierre and Miquelon 'Affaire" of 1941: A Study in Diplomacy in the North Atlantic Quadrangle* (Toronto: University of Toronto Press, 1966), 8.

33 TNA:PRO, CO 194/147, fols. 248-49, Labouchere to Darling, July 10, 1856.

34 Gertrude E. Gunn, *The Political History of Newfoundland 1832-1864* (Toronto: University of Toronto Press, 1966), 101-02.

35 TNA:PRO, CO 194/156, fols. 165-67, Bannerman to Newcastle, Aug. 30, 1859.

36 The standard work is Ian F.W. Beckett, *Riflemen Form: A Study of the Rifle Volunteer Movement 1859-1908* (Aldershot: The Ogilby Trusts, 1982). For the Newfoundland experience, see Elizabeth Brown, "Citizen Soldiers: Political Pawns: The Newfoundland Volunteer Companies 1860-1870" (B. A., Memorial University of Newfoundland, 1998).

37 Newfoundland and Labrador (House of Assembly), *Journal of the House of Assembly* (hereafter *JHA*), 1865, Appendix, "Nominal Return of the Volunteer Force of Newfoundland, January 1865," 758-758N.

38 LAC, RG 8, C Series (British military and naval records), Vol. 369, pp. 11-12, Forster to Under-Secretary of State for War, Sept. 30, 1862.

39 RPA, GB7.4 (British War Office collection. British Army records [St. John's, NL]) Garrison order, Nov. 15 and Nov. 19, 1862.

40 RPA, GB7.4, General order, Nov. 19, 1862.

41 RPA, GB7.4, Detachment order, Jan. 29, 1863.

CHAPTER 3
THE SCUM OF THE EARTH

[1] Edward M. Spiers, *The Army and Society 1815-1914* (London: Longman, 1980), 44-52; Strachan, *Wellington's Legacy*, 53-54. Army historians have traditionally subscribed to the belief that rural depopulation was a function of the Great Famine. It is now clear, however, that Ireland's population growth rate had been slowing since 1821. See R.F. Foster, *Modern Ireland 1600-1972* (1988; repr., London: Penguin Books, 1989), 331-32.

[2] Robert Woods, *The Demography of Victorian England and Wales* (Cambridge: Cambridge University Press, 2000), 369.

[3] David Ascoli, *A Companion to the British Army 1660-1983* (London: Harrap, 1983), 10.

[4] Cameron Pulsifer, "Beyond the Queen's Shilling: Reflections on the Pay of Other Ranks in the Victorian British Army," *JSAHR* 80, no. 324 (2002): 327.

[5] The army averages in this paragraph and the next two are from Spiers, *The Army and Society*, 46-51. Figures for England include Wales.

[6] TNA:PRO, War Office 97 (hereafter WO 97) (Royal Hospital Chelsea: Soldiers' Service Documents), Vols. 1164-70.

[7] TNA:PRO, WO 17/2289, fol. 51, "Distribution of the Troops serving in Newfoundland," May 1, 1861.

[8] TNA:PRO, WO 30/86, fol. 53, "Return of the different persuasions of the Troops serving in Newfoundland," Feb. 25, 1851.

[9] H. De Watteville, *The British Soldier: His Daily Life from Tudor to Modern Times* (London: J.M. Dent and Sons, 1954), 81.

[10] John P. Greene, *Between Damnation and Starvation: Priests and Merchants in Newfoundland Politics, 1745-1855* (Montreal and Kingston: McGill-Queen's University Press, 1999), 125.

[11] TNA:PRO, CO 194/147, fols. 258-63, Law to Darling, Apr. 29, 1856.

[12] Myna Trustram, *Women of the Regiment: Marriage and the Victorian Army* (Cambridge: Cambridge University Press, 1984), 55.

[13] Robert Law, *Regimental Standing Orders for the Guidance of the Royal Newfoundland Companies* (St. John's: Henry Winton, 1850), 54-55.

[14] TNA:PRO, CO 194/83, fol. 248, "Duty State of the Troops Newfoundland," enclosure in Cochrane to Maitland, Sept. 13, 1832; RPA, GN2.2, Sall to Crowdy, July 10, 1833, and Law to Crowdy, May 17, 1855.

[15] RPA, GN2.2, Law to Crowdy, May 17, 1855.

[16] Law, *Regimental Standing Orders*, 13.

[17] TNA:PRO, WO 3/169, pp. 391-92, Torrens to Deputy Secretary at War, Jan. 23, 1826.

[18] TNA:PRO, WO 55/871, fols. 302-04, Oldfield to Pilkington, June 14, 1832.

[19] NSA, MG 12, Vol. 32, July 10, 1839 and March 20, 1840.

[20] G. Tylden, "The Royal Canadian Rifle Regiment, 1840-1870," *Journal of the Society for Army Historical Research* (hereafter JSAHR) 34, no. 138 (1956):59.

[21] LAC, R3607-0-6-E, F 23, "Report ... Relative to the State of the Fortifications and Public Buildings at St. John's, Newfoundland, and upon the System of Defense on that Station," Aug. 25, 1827.

[22] TNA:PRO, WO 55/868, fols. 328-29, Byham to Bryce, Dec. 16, 1831.

[23] RPA, GN2.2, Sall to Cochrane, Oct. 12, 1832.

[24] TNA:PRO, WO 55/870, Oldfield to Cochrane, March 20, 1833.

[25] TNA:PRO, WO 55/2802, fol. 9, "Plan of Soldiers Barracks, South, Signal Hill," May 11, 1841.

[26] Strachan, *Wellington's Legacy*, 60.

[27] Law, *Regimental Standing Orders*, 12; Trustram, *Women of the Regiment*, 70-72; Veronica Bamfield, *On the Strength: The Story of the British Army Wife* (London and Tonbridge: Charles

Knight, 1974), 22; Carol M. Whitfield, "Tommy Atkins' Family," *Bulletin of the Association for Preservation of Technology* 5, no. 4 (1973): 67.

[28]   John Laffin, *Tommy Atkins: The Story of the English Soldier* (London: Cassell, 1966), 123.

[29]   Trustram, *Women of the Regiment*, 95. See also Annabel Venning, *Following the Drum: The Lives of Army Wives and Daughters, Past and Present* (London: Headline Book Publishing, 2005), 63.

[30]   TNA:PRO, WO 55/872, fols. 226-27, Byham to Mulcaster, Aug. 26, 1835.

[31]   RPA, GN2.2, Burke to Cochrane, Nov. 12, 1830 (with enclosures).

[32]   RPA, GB 7.4, General Order, May 12, 1848.

[33]   City of St. John's Archives (hereafter CSJA), Map A 009.2, "Plan of W.D. Lands at Fort William," June 4, 1861, and Map A 009.5, "Plan of Fort Townshend and War Dept. Land adjacent," Nov. 26, 1861.

[34]   TNA:PRO, CO 194/116, fols. 282-86, Harvey to Somerset, Jan. 14, 1842.

[35]   *Newfoundlander*, Jan. 20, 1842, 3.

[36]   TNA:PRO, WO 55/878, fols. 383-86, Bonnycastle to Mulcaster, March 22, 1843.

[37]   TNA:PRO, WO 55/879, fols. 528-29, Robe to Mulcaster, May 9, 1845.

[38]   TNA:PRO, WO 55/2988, fol. 12, "A Statement of the Barracks at St. John's Newfoundland…," Aug. 20, 1851.

[39]   TNA:PRO, WO 30/86, fols. 89-90, Law to Respective Officers, Newfoundland, March 28, 1855, and fol. 95, Law to Respective Officers, Newfoundland, July 18, 1855 (letter not sent, but entered for reference purposes).

[40]   Venning, *Following the Drum*, 64.

[41]   TNA:PRO, CO 194/147, fols. 258-63, Law to Darling, Apr. 29, 1856; RPA, GB 7.4, Law to Synge, July 14, 1858.

[42]   RPA, GB 7.4, A, Quill to Acting Barrack Master, Oct. 5, 1858.

[43]   Trustram, *Women of the Regiment*, 11-13; Clare Gibson, *Army Childhood: British Army Children's Lives and Times* (Oxford: Shire Publications, 2012), 8.

[44]   RPA, GB7.4, Regimental Order, Nov. 19, 1852.

[45]   Trustram, *Women of the Regiment*, 36.

[46]   RPA, GB7.4, Regimental Order, Nov. 19, 1852. Although this order rescinded night passes, this presupposes they existed beforehand.

[47]   RPA, GN2.2, "Report of the Police Magistrates of St. John's on the state of the Town," March 9, 1850.

[48]   RPA, GB7.4, Law to Carter, Jan. 7, 1854.

[49]   RPA, GB7.4, Law to Carter, Jan. 7, 1854.

[50]   TNA:PRO, WO 55/869, Oldfield to Tucker, June 11, 1832.

[51]   *St. John's Patriot and Terra-Nova Herald* (hereafter *Patriot*), Jan. 2, 1847, 2.

[52]   RPA, GN2.2, Simms to Crowdy, March 13, 1843.

[53]   RPA, GN2.2, Danson and Power to Crowdy, May 14, 1842.

[54]   RPA, GN2.2, Law to Crowdy, June 3, 1842.

[55]   RPA, GN2.2, Law to Crowdy, June 8, 1842.

[56]   Spiers, *The Army and Society*, 58-59; Burroughs, "An Unreformed Army? 1815-1868," 172-73.

[57]   TNA:PRO, WO 1/549, pp. 813-23, "Report of the Committee appointed by the Lords Commissioners of Her Majesty's Treasury…," Aug. 7, 1851.

[58]   See, for example, *Newfoundlander*, May 24, 1858, 3.

[59]   Peter Barnes, "An Anatomy of Medical Practice: An Examination of the Health, Diseases, and Medical Practices of the St. John's Garrison, 1861" (B. A., Memorial University of Newfoundland, 2001), 20.

[60]   Trustram, *Women of the Regiment*, 40.

[61]   Robert MacKinnon, "The Agricultural Fringe of St. John's, 1750-1945" in *Four Centuries and the City: Perspectives on the Historical Geography of St. John's*, ed. Alan G. Macpherson

ENDNOTES **195**

(St. John's: Memorial University of Newfoundland, 2005), 55-58; and by the same author, "The Growth of Commercial Agriculture around St. John's, 1800-1935: A Study of Local Trade in Response to Urban Demand" (M. A., Memorial University of Newfoundland, 1981), 20-21.

62   TNA:PRO, War Office 44 (hereafter WO 44) (Ordnance Office and War Office: Correspondence), Vol. 163, fols. 415-16, Extract of Garrison Orders, March 28, 1832; RPA, GN2.2, Walker to Colonial Secretary, July 3, 1839; TNA:PRO, WO 55/877, fols. 618-23, Bonnycastle to Mulcaster, Dec. 22, 1842; TNA:PRO, WO 30/86, Jenkins to Law, May 2, 1850; CSJA, RG6/2/2, "Plan of W.D. Lands at Fort William," June 4, 1861, and "Plan of Fort Townshend and War Dept. Land adjacent," Nov. 26, 1861.

63   TNA:PRO, WO 55/2988, fol. 7, "A Statement of the Ordnance Lands at St. John's Newfoundland...," Aug. 20, 1851.

64   C.R. Binney, "An Account of an Extraordinary Instance of Rapid Decay of Girders in the Storehouses at St. John's, Newfoundland," *Professional Papers of the Royal Engineers, New Series*, 7 (1858), 135.

65   Law, *Regimental Standing Orders*, 13, 60.

66   Frances L. Stewart, "Mess Calls from Signal Hill, Newfoundland," *Northeast Historical Archaeology* 14 (1985): 65-66.

67   See, for example, *Newfoundlander*, Dec. 2, 1842, 3.

68   *Newfoundlander*, Dec. 7, 1848, 3.

69   Spiers, *The Army and Society*, 53. This was the rate for men stationed abroad; at home it was up to ten pence.

70   Great Britain. House of Commons. *Sessional Papers*, 1839, Vol. 16, "Statistical Reports on the Sickness, Mortality, & Invaliding among the Troops in the United Kingdom, the Mediterranean, and British America; Prepared from the Records of the Army Medical Department and War Office Returns," 296; Great Britain. Army Medical Department. *Statistical, Sanitary, and Medical Reports for the Year 1859* (London: Her Majesty's Stationery Office, 1861), 63.

71   TNA:PRO, CO 194/147, fols. 258-63, Law to Darling, Apr. 29, 1856.

72   TNA:PRO, WO 1/551, pp. 443-46, "Memorandum for Mr. Talbot," Nov. 2, 1854.

73   Law, *Regimental Standing Orders*, 47-49.

74   Law, *Regimental Standing Orders*, 47, 56; Great Britain. Army. *The Queen's Regulations and Orders for the Army* (London: Her Majesty's Stationery Office, 1859), 303.

75   Candow, *The Lookout*, 110.

76   RPA, GB7.4, General order, June 23, 1856. In his book *A Seaport Legacy: The Story of St. John's, Newfoundland* (Erin, ON: Press Porcepic, 1976), 2:575, Paul O'Neill misinterprets this general order by claiming that the incidents in question were occurring in St. John's.

77   Law, *Regimental Standing Orders*, 47-48.

78   RPA, GN2.2, Harris to Burke, Apr. 22, 1831, and Law to Crowdy, May 17, 1855.

79   TNA:PRO, CO 194/74, fol. 105, "Royal Newfd. Veteran Companies, Duty State, 25th January 1827."

80   Mary Durnford ed., *Family Recollections of Lieut. General Elias Walker Durnford, a Colonel Commandant of the Corps of Royal Engineers* (Montreal: John Lovell, 1863), 68.

81   TNA:PRO, CO 194/83, fol. 249, "Detail of duty required at St. John's Newfoundd.," Sept. 10, 1832.

82   LAC, RG 8, C Series, Vol. 369, p. 162, "Details of guards furnished by the Troops serving in Newfoundland," May 20, 1861. For an example of security concerns, see RPA, GN2.2, Grand Jury presentment, Oct. 24, 1859.

83   Law, *Regimental Standing Orders*, 52-53.

84   TNA:PRO, WO 17/2286, fol. 25, "Detail of the duties furnished by the Troops," March 1, 1858.

85   TNA:PRO, CO 194/74, fol. 105, "Royal Newfd. Veteran Companies, Duty State, 25th

January 1827"; RPA, GN2.2, Weiburg to Crowdy, Mar. 25, 1839; RPA, GB7.4, Regimental order, Aug. 8, 1853; Law, *Regimental Standing Orders*, 45.

[86]   TNA:PRO, WO 17/2286, fol. 25, "Detail of the duties furnished by the Troops," March 1, 1858.

[87]   TNA:PRO, CO 194/147, fols. 84-86, "Report upon the State of the Fortifications at St. John's, Newfoundland," Oct. 21, 1808.

[88]   TNA:PRO, WO 30/86, fol. 112, Law to Darling, Nov. 12, 1855; RPA, GB7.4, Law to Kirby, July 21, 1856.

[89]   In the parlance of the day, Quill's occupation was "gentleman." See NSA, MG 12, Vol. 43, General order, Dec. 11, 1851.

[90]   RPA, GB7.4, Law to Percy, Halifax, Nov. 25, 1858.

[91]   RPA, GB7.4, Regimental orders of June 20, 1866 and June 10, 1867; RPA, GN2.2, Long to Surveyor General, Aug. 2, 1890.

[92]   RPA, GB7.4, Grant to Percy, Sept. 12, 1860; NSA, MG 12, Vol. 54, General order, March 18, 1861.

[93]   *Ledger*, Sept. 30, 1862, 2.

[94]   *Ledger*, Oct. 3, 1862, 2.

[95]   TNA:PRO, WO 30/86, fol. 67, Law to Vernon, Aug. 21, 1852.

[96]   TNA:PRO, WO 17/2284, fol. 34, "Distribution of the Troops serving in Newfoundland," Apr. 1, 1856; TNA:PRO, WO 30/86, fols. 111-12, Law to Respective Officers, Aug. 23, 1856.

[97]   TNA:PRO, WO 17/2286, fol. 25, "Detail of the duties furnished by the Troops," March 1, 1858; TNA:PRO, CO 194/156, fols. 169-72, Law to Bannerman, Aug. 23, 1859.

[98]   TNA:PRO, WO 30/86, fols. 68-69, Law to Vernon, Oct. 26, 1852; RPA, GB7.4, Regimental standing order, Jan. 18, 1859.

[99]   Candow, *The Lookout*, 107-14.

[100]   David A. Webber, *Skinner's Fencibles: The Royal Newfoundland Regiment 1795-1802* (St. John's: Newfoundland Naval and Military Museum, 1964), 63-64.

[101]   Fiona Day, "The Old Garrison Church: St. Thomas', St. John's, Newfoundland," *Journal of the Royal Army Chaplains' Department* 28, no. 8 (1987): 6.

[102]   Law, *Regimental Standing Orders*, 45.

[103]   *Ledger*, Aug. 5, 1836, 2.

[104]   See R.W. Bennett, "Military Law in 1839," *JSAHR* 48, no. 196 (1970): 225-41; Alan Ramsay Skelley, *The Victorian Army at Home: The Recruitment and Terms and Conditions of the British Regular, 1859-1899* (London: Croom Helm, 1977), 128-41.

[105]   Peter Burroughs, "Crime and Punishment in the British Army, 1815-1870," *English Historical Review* 100, no. 396 (1985): 557.

[106]   Bennett, "Military Law in 1839," 236.

[107]   See, for example, RPA, GB7.4, General order, May 9, 1856.

[108]   RPA, GB7.4, Law to Holdsworth, Aug. 3, 1855; General Order, July 30, 1856; Law to Percy, Sept. 28, 1858. There had been isolated examples of this problem before 1855, but afterward it became routine.

[109]   On the mutiny, see Candow, *The Lookout*, 82-83.

[110]   Proulx, "Placentia: 1713-1811," 131.

[111]   Spiers, *The Army and Society*, 62-63.

[112]   Burroughs, "Crime and Punishment in the British Army," 560. On the eighteenth-century origins of transportation and hulks, see Randall McGowen, "The Well-Ordered Prison: England, 1780-1865," in *The Oxford History of the Prison: The Practice of Punishment in Western Society*, eds. Norval Morris and David J. Rothman (Oxford: Oxford University Press, 1995), 84-85.

[113]   For Bermuda, see TNA:PRO, CO 194/88, fols. 118-20, Cochrane to Spring-Rice, Aug. 1834. For England, see NSA, MG 12, Vol. 36, June 17, 1843.

ENDNOTES   197

[114] Seán McConville, "The Victorian Prison: England, 1865-1965," in *The Oxford History of the Prison*, 132-33.

[115] Phillip J. Hilton, "'Branded D on the Left Side': A Study of Former Soldiers and Marines Transported to Van Diemen's Land: 1804-1854" (Ph. D., University of Tasmania, 2010), 105.

[116] TNA:PRO, WO 30/86, fol. 70, Law to Brady, Dec. 11, 1852.

[117] Melvin Baker and James E. Candow, "Signal Hill Gaol 1846-1859," *Newfoundland Quarterly* 85, no. 4 (1990): 20-23.

[118] RPA, GN2.2, Garrett to Crowdy, Feb. 3, 1838.

[119] TNA:PRO, WO 55/879, fols. 545-46, "Replies to the Queries of the War Office circular...," Sept. 25, 1845.

[120] Webber, *Skinner's Fencibles*, 43; *Patriot*, Jan. 19, 1836, 3.

[121] Strachan, *Wellington's Legacy*, 83-84; Burroughs, "Crime and Punishment in the British Army," 564.

[122] For the garrison provost cells, see TNA:PRO, WO 30/86, fols. 19-20, Jenkins to Acting Barrack Master, Apr. 27, 1849; RPA, GB7.4, Law to Bridge, June 30, 1855. On the use of English civil prisons, see RPA, GB7.4, General Orders of Oct. 6, 1856 and June 27, 1862; NSA, MG 12, Vol. 55, Oct. 7, 1861.

[123] Whitfield, "Tommy Atkins," 82.

[124] Burroughs, "Crime and Punishment in the British Army," 565.

[125] I have found only one record of a Royal Newfoundland Companies' convict being confined in the Melville Island district military prison, and he may have been awaiting transportation to England. See NSA, MG 12, Vol. 55, Oct. 2 and Oct. 7, 1861.

[126] Hilton, "'Branded D on the Left Side,'" 103.

[127] Skelley, *The Victorian Army*, 149.

[128] DeWatteville, *The British Soldier*, 114-16.

[129] *Patriot*, May 26, 1841, 3.

[130] Law, *Regimental Standing Orders*, 25.

[131] Whitfield, "Tommy Atkins," 44.

[132] TNA:PRO, CO 194/147, fols. 258-63, Law to Darling, Apr. 29, 1856.

[133] TNA:PRO, CO194/147, fols. 258-63, Law to Darling, Apr. 29, 1856.

[134] TNA:PRO, WO 55/870, fols. 266-70, Oldfield to Cochrane, March 20, 1833.

[135] TNA:PRO, WO 55/868, fols. 423-24, Oldfield to Bryce, Nov. 28, 1831; TNA:PRO, WO 55/872, fols. 213-14, Byham to Mulcaster, Feb. 20, 1835.

[136] Peter Bailey, *Leisure and Class in Victorian England: Rational Recreation and the Contest for Control, 1830-1885* (London: Routledge and Kegan Paul, 1978), 9.

[137] NSA, MG 12, Vol. 32, Feb. 5, 1840.

[138] RPA, GN2.2, "Regulations of the Garrison Library St. Johns Newfoundland," ca. Oct. 31, 1832.

[139] Bayard Taylor, *At Home and Abroad: A Sketch-book of Life, Scenery and Men* (New York: G.P. Putnam, 1862), 255-56. Taylor mistakenly identified Fort Townshend as Fort Frederick.

[140] Skelley, *The Victorian Army*, 87.

[141] NSA, MG 12, Vol. 45, March 21, 1853.

[142] A.C.T. White, *The Story of Army Education 1643-1963* (London: George G. Harrap, 1963), 18-19; Gibson, *Army Childhood*, 37-38.

[143] RPA, GN2.2, Blackman to Sall, May 8, 1840.

[144] On the acceptance of Roman Catholic chaplains, see Michael Snape, *The Royal Army Chaplains' Department: Clergy Under Fire* (Woodbridge: Boydell Press, 2008), 157-58. For O'Donnell's appointment, see TNA:PRO, WO 17/2289, fols. 1-2, Jan. 1, 1861.

[145] N.T. St. John Williams, *Tommy Atkins' Children: The Story of the Education of the Army's Children 1675-1970* (London: Her Majesty's Stationery Office, 1971), 66.

198   THE INVISIBLES

146 RPA, GB7.4, Saunders to Cathcart, Jan. 1, 1854.

147 RPA, GB7.4, Law to Weatherall, Jan. 1, 1857.

148 RPA, GB7.4, Regimental Order, Nov. 19, 1852.

149 TNA:PRO, CO194/147, fols. 258-63, Law to Darling, Apr. 29, 1856.

150 *Statistical, Sanitary, and Medical Reports for the Year 1859*, 65.

151 TNA:PRO, WO 30/86, fol. 34, Law to Macdonald, Feb. 28, 1850.

152 Whitfield, "Tommy Atkins," 143.

153 TNA:PRO, CO194/147, fols. 258-63, Law to Darling, Apr. 29, 1856.

154 TNA:PRO, War Office 27 (hereafter WO 27) (Inspection Returns), Vol. 345, Harvey to Dickson, Aug. 28, 1845.

155 TNA:PRO, WO 30/86, fol. 44, Law to Bazalgette, July 1, 1850.

156 RPA, GB7.4, Law to Weatherall, Feb. 21, 1857.

157 RPA, GB7.4, Law to Fordyce, Nov. 11, 1857.

158 NSA, MG 12, Vol. 50, Jan. 4, 1858.

159 RPA, GB7.4, Law to Percy, May 26, 1858.

160 RPA, GB7.4, Law to Percy, Sept. 28, 1858. For the earliest instance of this request, see RPA, GB7.4, Law to Holdsworth, July 25, 1856.

161 Unless otherwise noted, this account is based on depositions contained in RPA, GN2.2, Carter, Doyle, and Bennett to Crowdy, March 9, 1850.

162 TNA:PRO, WO 30/86, fol. 33, Law to Carter, Dec. 11, 1849.

163 RPA, GN2.2, "Report of the Police Magistrates of St. John's on the state of the Town," March 9, 1850.

CHAPTER 4

BALLROOMS AND BATTLEFIELDS

1 Huffer, "The Infantry Officers of the Line," 7-9, 117-19; Strachan, *Wellington's Legacy*, 110. For evidence that the myth refuses to die, see Raugh, *The Victorians at War*, 250.

2 Philip Mason, *The English Gentleman: The Rise and Fall of an Ideal* (New York: William Morrow and Company, 1982), 1.

3 Huffer, "The Infantry Officers of the Line," 8.

4 Spiers, *The Army and Society*, 11.

5 Huffer, "The Infantry Officers of the Line," 20-21.

6 I have assembled Law's service history from various sources, but primarily the *Army List* for the respective years.

7 Richard Holmes, *Redcoat: The British Soldier in the Age of Horse and Musket* (2001; repr., London: HarperCollins, 2002), 283.

8 Gwyn Harries-Jenkins, *The Army in Victorian Society* (London: Routledge and Kegan Paul, 1977), 85-87; Huffer, "The Infantry Officers of the Line," 36.

9 RPA, GN2.30 (Department of the Colonial Secretary, Blue Books), Blue Book, 1844, 86-91.

10 Strachan, *Wellington's Legacy*, 113-14.

11 TNA:PRO, WO27/422, Inspection Return, Royal Newfoundland Companies, 25 June 1852.

12 Mason, *The English Gentleman*, 12.

13 J.H. Stocqueler, *The British Officer: His Positions, Duties, Emoluments, and Privileges* (London: Smith, Elder, 1851), 2.

14 For Law's Irish background, the best source is H.L.L. Denny, "Lawe of Leixlip," *Journal of the Co. Kildare Archaeological Society and Surrounding Districts*, 6 (1909-1911), 230-39.

15 Denny, "Lawe of Leixlip," 232. On corruption in the eighteenth-century Irish army, see Thomas Bartlett, "Army and Society in Eighteenth-century Ireland," in *Kings in Conflict: The Revolutionary War in Ireland and its Aftermath 1689-1750*, ed. W.A. Maguire (Belfast:

ENDNOTES   **199**

The Blackstaff Press, 1990), 175-79; Alan J. Guy, "The Irish military establishment, 1660-1776," in *Military History of Ireland*, 220; Ireland. House of Commons. *Journals 1739-1749*, 758-89, Report of the Public Accounts Committee, Jan. 14, 1745.

[16]   John Colgan, "Leixlip Around 1798," Leixlip History, accessed Jan. 29, 2018, http://www.kildare.ie/leixliphistory/archives/leixlip-around-1798/.

[17]   TNA:PRO, War Office 25 (hereafter WO 25) (War Office and Predecessors: Secretary-at-War, Secretary of State for War, and Related Bodies, Registers, Vol. 805, fol. 217, "Statement of the Services of Captain Robert Law...," Dec. 31, 1829; *Newfoundlander*, July 18, 1844, 3.

[18]   *Newfoundlander*, Oct. 25, 1838, 2.

[19]   De Watteville, *The British Soldier*, 170; Spiers, *The Army and Society*, 22.

[20]   RPA, GB7.4, General order, Dec. 24, 1856; Huffer, "The Infantry Officers of the Line," 172.

[21]   Huffer, "The Infantry Officers of the Line," 145.

[22]   *Newfoundlander*, Oct. 5, 1857, 3.

[23]   *Newfoundlander*, Feb. 8, 1858, 3; *Newfoundlander*, Jan. 13, 1862, 3.

[24]   RPA, GB7.4, Quill to Mitchell, Apr. 2, 1857.

[25]   RPA, GB7.4, Quill to Mitchell, June 27, 1858.

[26]   NSA, MG 12, Vol. 54, Jan. 16, 1860.

[27]   TNA:PRO, WO55/868, Oldfield to Bryce, Nov. 28, 1831.

[28]   Huffer, "The Infantry Officers of the Line," 187.

[29]   *Newfoundlander*, Feb. 18, 1830, 3.

[30]   *Times and General Commercial Gazette* (hereafter *Times*), Aug. 16, 1845, 2.

[31]   *Newfoundlander*, Aug. 21, 1845, 2.

[32]   RPA, GB7.4, Law to Weatherall, May 6, 1857.

[33]   TNA:PRO, WO30/86, Law to Acting Colonial Secretary, Oct. 25, 1851.

[34]   Strachan, *Wellington's Legacy*, 112. On living costs, see *Newfoundlander*, March 20, 1845, 2.

[35]   *Newfoundlander*, March 20, 1845, 2.

[36]   Bonnycastle, *Newfoundland in 1842*, 147.

[37]   For examples of this, see *Ledger*, Aug. 25, 1831, 3, and *Newfoundlander*, May 28, 1846, 2.

[38]   R.B. McCrea, *Lost Amid the Fogs: Sketches of Life in Newfoundland, England's Ancient Colony* (London: Sampson Low, Son, and Marston, 1869), 272-79.

[39]   *Newfoundlander*, March 20, 1845, 1.

[40]   Bonnycastle, *Newfoundland in 1842*, 146.

[41]   RPA, GB7.4, General order, Sept. 3, 1856.

[42]   See, for example, *Newfoundlander*, Oct. 8, 1829, 3, noting the marriage of Margaret Georgiana Vigoureux, daughter of Commanding Royal Engineer Lieutenant Colonel Henry M. Vigoureux, to Lieutenant Colonel William Gordon of HMS *Tyne*.

[43]   *Ledger*, Oct. 31, 1828, 2.

[44]   *Newfoundlander*, March 22, 1855, 2.

[45]   A.H. McLintock, *The Establishment of Constitutional Government in Newfoundland, 1783-1832: A Study in Retarded Colonisation* (London: Longmans, Green, 1941), 16; Stuart R. Godfrey, *Human Rights and Social Policy in Newfoundland 1832-1982: Search for a Just Society* (St. John's: Harry Cuff, 1985), 8.

[46]   *Newfoundlander*, Jan. 20, 1842, 1-2.

[47]   *Newfoundlander*, June 22, 1843, 2.

[48]   The best regional study is Martin Hewitt, "Science as Spectacle: Popular Scientific Culture in Saint John, New Brunswick, 1830-1850," *Acadiensis* 18, no. 1 (1988): 91-119.

[49]   For a classic study, see Bailey, *Leisure and Class in Victorian England*.

[50]   *Newfoundlander*, March 3, 1853, 1.

[51]   *Newfoundlander*, March 27, 1851, 2, and March 11, 1852, 2.

52   Louise Whiteway, "The Athenaeum Movement: St. John's Athenaeum (1861-1898)," *Dalhousie Review* 50, no. 4 (1971): 543-43; John Maunder, "The Newfoundland Museum: Origins and Development," accessed Feb. 15, 2018, http://www.therooms.ca/the-new-foundland-museum-origin-and-development.

53   Diane B. Malone, "A Survey of Early Military Theatre in America," *Theatre Survey* 16, no. 1 (1975): 56-57.

54   Yashdip S. Bains, *English Canadian Theatre, 1765-1826* (New York: Peter Lang, 1998): 25-27. For a summary that unfortunately neglects Newfoundland, see Natalie Rewa, "Garrison Theatre," in *The Oxford Companion to Canadian Theatre*, eds. Eugene Benson and L.W. Conolly (Toronto: Oxford University Press, 1989), 222-24. For Halifax, interested readers must sift through Alex Boutilier's appalling *The Citadel on Stage: British Military Theatre, Sports and Recreation in Colonial Halifax* (Halifax: SVP Productions, 2015).

55   I have found no evidence to support a claim that the garrison theatricals in St. John's originated in the eighteenth century. For that flight of fancy, see Denyse Lynde, "Amateur Theatrical Tradition," accessed Feb. 25, 2018, http://www.heritage.nf.ca/articles/arts/amateur-theatre.php.

56   Martin Banham ed., *The Cambridge Guide to Theatre* (Cambridge: Cambridge University Press, 1992), 146-47; Phillip McCann, *Island in an Empire: Education, Religion, and Social Life in Newfoundland, 1800-1855* (St. John's: Boulder Publications, 2016), 131-32; *Royal Gazette and Newfoundland Advertiser* (hereafter *Royal Gazette*), March 25, 1817, 2.

57   Bains, *English Canadian Theatre*, 19.

58   *Newfoundlander*, Nov. 7, 1833, 3.

59   *Newfoundlander*, Nov. 14, 1833, 2.

60   J.B. Jukes, *Excursions in and about Newfoundland during the Years 1839 and 1840* (London: James Murray, 1842), 1:221.

61   Bonnycastle, *Newfoundland in 1842*, 117.

62   Bains, *English Canadian Theatre*, 108.

63   Courier, Apr. 13, 1853, 3.

64   *Newfoundlander*, Jan. 30, 1854, 2.

65   *Newfoundlander*, Feb. 2, 1854, 2; Leslie O'Dell, "Amateurs of the Regiment, 1815-1870," in *Early Stages: Theatre in Ontario 1800-1914*, ed. Ann Saddlemyer (Toronto: University of Toronto Press, 1990), 62.

66   Robertson Davies, "The Nineteenth-Century Repertoire," in *Early Stages*, 90.

67   *Newfoundlander*, Apr. 24, 1854, 3.

68   *Newfoundlander*, May 22, 1854, 2.

69   RPA, GB7.4, Law to Weatherall, May 6, 1857.

70   TNA:PRO, WO 30/86, fol. 88, Law to Weatherall, Feb. 7, 1855; NSA, MG 12, Vol. 49, Oct. 10, 1856.

71   *Ledger*, Nov. 8, 1864, 3.

72   Anthony Makepeace-Warne ed., *Brassey's Companion to the British Army* (London: Brassey's, 1995), 35, 126; Trevor Herbert and Helen Barlow, *Music and the British Military in the Long Nineteenth Century* (Oxford: Oxford University Press, 2013), 1.

73   *Newfoundlander*, Apr. 30, 1829, 2.

74   RPA, GB7.4, Quill to Messrs. H. Distin and Co., March 4, 1856.

75   Herbert and Barlow, *Music & the British Military*, 91.

76   Law, *Regimental Standing Orders*, 39-40, 66.

77   RPA, GN2.2, Carter, Doyle, and Bennett to Crowdy, Oct. 19, 1850.

78   Herbert and Barlow, *Music & the British Military*, 78.

79   Philip Tocque, *Newfoundland: as it was, and as it is in 1877* (Toronto: John B. Magurn, 1878), 75.

80   Charles Royster, *The Destructive War: William Tecumseh Sherman, Stonewall Jackson, and the Americans* (1991; repr., New York: Vintage Books, 1993), 391. See also Herbert and Barlow, *Music & the British Military*, 217-18.

ENDNOTES 201

[81] *Newfoundland Express*, Aug. 2, 1860, 2.

[82] *Newfoundland Express*, March 24, 1860, 2.

[83] J.H. Plumb, "The Commercialization of Leisure in Eighteenth-century England," in *The Birth of a Consumer Society: The Commercialization of Eighteenth-Century England*, ed. Neil McKendrick, John Brewer and J.H. Plumb (Bloomington: Indiana University Press, 1982), 282.

[84] For an overview of the British North American experience—albeit with only passing reference to Newfoundland—see Peter Lindsay, "The Impact of the Military Garrisons on the Development of Sport in British North America," *Canadian Journal of History of Sport and Physical Education* 1, no. 1 (1970): 33-44.

[85] R.W. Dunfield, *The Atlantic Salmon in the History of North America* (Ottawa: Department of Fisheries and Oceans, 1985), 112-13; Edward Chappell, *Voyage of His Majesty's Ship Rosamond to Newfoundland and the Southern Coast of Labrador* (London: J. Mawman, 1818), 68-72; NSA, MG 12, Vol. 50, General order, Sept. 14, 1857.

[86] *Ledger*, June 21, 1836, 2; *Newfoundlander*, Oct. 27, 1831, 3.

[87] Alan Metcalfe, *Canada Learns to Play: The Emergence of Organized Sport, 1807-1914* (Toronto: McClelland and Stewart, 1987), 16.

[88] "History," Cricket Newfoundland and Labrador, accessed March 4 2018, http://www. canadacricket.com/nlcricket/?page_id=4. See also *Ledger*, Sept. 11, 1827, 2.

[89] *Newfoundlander*, Sept. 21, 1843, 2.

[90] Joseph R. Smallwood and Robert D.W. Pitt, eds., *Encyclopedia of Newfoundland and Labrador* (St. John's: Newfoundland Book Publishers (1967) Ltd., 1981), 1: s.v. "Cricket."

[91] Cyril F. Poole and Robert Cuff, eds., *Encyclopedia of Newfoundland and Labrador* (St. John's: Harry Cuff, 1994), 5: s.v. "Sports."

[92] Mason, *The English Gentleman*, 12.

[93] Wray Vamplew, *The Turf: A Social and Economic History of Horse Racing* (London: Allen Lane, 1976), 131.

[94] McCann, *Island in an Empire*, 200.

[95] *Newfoundlander*, Oct. 17, 1827, 3.

[96] *Ledger*, Sept. 23, 1828, 2.

[97] *Newfoundlander*, Aug. 7, 1845, 4.

[98] *Ledger*, Oct. 16, 1828, 3, and Oct. 17, 1828, 2.

[99] Mason, *The English Gentleman*, 68, 87-91.

[100] Robert Moss, "The Last Duel in Newfoundland," in *The Book of Newfoundland*, ed. Joseph R. Smallwood and James R. Thoms (St. John's: Newfoundland Book Publishers [1967] Limited, 1967), 4:450-53.

[101] M.J. O'Mara, "The Last Duel in Newfoundland," *The Cadet* 6, no. 2 (1919): 22.

[102] TNA:PRO, WO 25/2242, Casualty Returns, March 25-April 24, 1826.

[103] See, for example, the address by the Benevolent Irish Society, in the *Newfoundlander*, May 16, 1859, 2.

CHAPTER 5

THE COMING OF THE FROST

[1] RPA, Manuscript Group 543 (hereafter MG 543) (Phoenix Assurance Company), Jones to Wilson, June 6, 1809.

[2] RPA, MG 543, Broomfield to Richter, Oct. 25, 1845.

[3] John C. Weaver and Peter DeLottinville, "The Conflagration and the City: Disaster and Progress in British North America during the Nineteenth Century," *Social History/ Histoire sociale* 13, no. 26 (1980): 420.

[4] William Glascock, *Naval Sketch-Book: Or, The Service Afloat and Ashore...* (London: Henry Colburn and Richard Bentley, 1831), 1:131.

5   Donal M. Baird, *The Story of Firefighting in Canada* (Erin, ON: Boston Mills Press, 1986), 97-98.

6   B.E.S. Rudachyk, "The Most Tyrannous of Masters: Fire in Halifax, Nova Scotia, 1830-1850," (M. A., Dalhousie University, 1984), 44.

7   *Royal Gazette*, July 7, 1835, 1; Weaver and DeLottinville, "The Conflagration and the City," 428.

8   Baird, *Firefighting in Canada*, 16.

9   RPA, GB7.4, Saunders to Tunbridge, March 16, 1854.

10   RPA, GN2.2, General Order, Sept. 27, 1845.

11   Jukes, *Excursions*, 8.

12   *Newfoundlander*, Dec. 30, 1847, 3; *Royal Gazette*, Oct. 24, 1843, 3.

13   Law, *Regimental Standing Orders*, 18.

14   *Royal Gazette*, Oct. 24, 1843, 3; *JHA* 1857, Appendix, "Evidence before the Select Committee appointed to inquire into the best means of preventing the spread of Fire in the Town of St. John's," 499.

15   *Royal Gazette*, Oct. 24, 1843, 3.

16   *Newfoundlander*, Aug. 2, 1855, 3.

17   Rudachyk, "Fire in Halifax," 154, n. 1.

18   RPA, MG 543, Jones to Wilson, June 6, 1809.

19   See James E. Candow, *Cantwells' Way: A Natural History of the Cape Spear Lightstation* (Halifax and Winnipeg: Fernwood Publishing, 2014), 20-22.

20   Frederick W. Rowe, *A History of Newfoundland and Labrador* (Toronto: McGraw-Hill Ryerson, 1980), 235; Melvin Baker, *Aspects of Nineteenth Century St. John's Municipal History* (St. John's: Harry Cuff, 1982), 31.

21   Newfoundland 1833, 3 Wm. IV, c. 3.

22   TNA:PRO, WO 30/86, fol. 63, Law to Acting Colonial Secretary, Dec. 9, 1851.

23   *Newfoundlander*, Oct. 17, 1839, 2.

24   RPA, GN2.2, Law to Darling, n.d., but circa March 1856.

25   *Ledger*, Sept. 11, 1835, 2.

26   *Ledger*, Sept. 22, 1835, 2.

27   RPA, GN2.2, Bennett to Prescott, Oct. 5, 1835.

28   The main published accounts of the fire are Melvin Baker, "The Great St. John's Fire of 1846," *Newfoundland Quarterly* 59, no. 1 (1983): 31-34; and O'Neill, *A Seaport Legacy*, 628-31. Baker and O'Neill both contend that the fire began in a George Street cabinetmaker's shop, a claim that is contradicted by a period map showing the fire's extent and point of origin. See Great Britain. House of Commons. "Map of St. John's, Nfld. showing extent of fire of 1846" (London: Standage and Company, 1851). I thank Don Parsons for bringing this feature of the map to my attention.

29   TNA:PRO, CO 194/125, fols. 289-92, "Extract from a report made by Major Robe Commanding Royal Engineers St. Johns Newfoundland, to the Inspector General of Fortifications," June 10, 1846.

30   RPA, MG 543, Broomfield to Richter, Aug. 3, 1846.

31   TNA:PRO, CO 194/125, fol. 293, General order, June 10, 1846.

32   Tocque, *Newfoundland*, 70.

33   Irish University Press, *British Parliamentary Papers* (Shannon: Irish University Press, 1971), 19: 279. I am grateful to Melvin Baker for this reference.

34   The report was published in the *Newfoundlander*, July 20, 1846, 2.

35   Newfoundland 1846, 9 and 10 Victoria, c. 4.

36   Melvin Baker, "The Government of St. John's, Newfoundland 1800-1921" (Ph. D., University of Western Ontario, 1980), 63-64.

37   O'Flaherty, *Lost Country*, 18.

38   Phillip Buckner, "Harvey, Sir John," in *Dictionary of Canadian Biography*, vol. 8, University

ENDNOTES   203

of Toronto/Université Laval, 2003, accessed March 14, 2017, http://www.biographi.ca/en/
bio/harvey_john_8E.html. Buckner mistakenly says that Harvey left St. John's in August.

39   *British Parliamentary Papers*, 330.

40   *Patriot*, June 28, 1847, 2-3.

41   TNA:PRO, CO 194/127, fols. 286-87, Feild to Grey, June 25, 1847.

42   Taylor, *At Home and Abroad*, 254.

43   Melvin Baker, "The Politics of Assessment: The Water Question in St. John's, 1844-1864," *Acadiensis* 12, no. 1 (1982): 64.

44   RPA, GN2.2, Douglas to Crowdy, Feb. 12, 1851. I am grateful to Bob Cuff for this reference.

45   Samuel George Archibald, *Some Account of the Seal Fishery in Newfoundland and the Mode of Preparing Seal Ol...* (Edinburgh: Murray and Gibb, 1852), 6.

46   Baker, *Aspects of Nineteenth Century St. John's Municipal History*, 33-34.

47   *Newfoundlander*, Oct. 18, 1855, 2.

48   O'Neill, *A Seaport Legacy*, 631-32.

49   Unless otherwise noted, this section is based on information contained in E.P. Morris, ed., *Decisions of the Supreme Court of Newfoundland 1854-1864* (St. John's: Queen's Printer, 1900), 4:153-55.

50   RPA, GN2.2, Little to Kent, Nov. 4, 1856.

51   *Newfoundland Express*, March 3, 1860, 3.

52   *Newfoundland Express*, March 24, 1860, 2.

53   Amy S. Greenberg, *Cause for Alarm: The Volunteer Fire Department in the Nineteenth-Century City* (Princeton: Princeton University Press, 1998), 11-12; Baird, *Firefighting in Canada*, 75.

54   Mike Parker, *The Smoke-Eaters: A History of Firefighting in Nova Scotia c.1750-1950* (Halifax: Nimbus Publishing, 2002), xxvii.

CHAPTER 6

CIVIL COMMOTION

1   David Facey-Crowther, "The British Army and Aid to the Civil Power in British North America, 1832-1871," *JSAHR* 93, no. 376 (2015): 311.

2   This ground has been well covered, but see especially O'Flaherty, *Old Newfoundland*, 129-51, and Bannister, *The Rule of the Admirals*, 258-79.

3   For Britain, see Linda Colley, *Britons: Forging the Nation 1707-1837*, 2nd ed. (New Haven: Yale University Press, 2005), 18-25.

4   Peter Karsten, "Irish Soldiers in the British Army, 1792-1922: Suborned or Subordinate?," *Journal of Social History* 17, no. 1 (1983): 36.

5   J.H. Whyte, "The Influence of the Catholic Clergy on Elections in Nineteenth-Century Ireland," *English Historical Review* 75, no. 295 (1960): 239-40.

6   John Wolffe, *The Protestant Crusade in Great Britain 1829-1860* (Oxford: Clarendon Press, 1991), 1-2; and, by the same author, "North Atlantic Anti-Catholicism in the Nineteenth Century: A Comparative Overview," in *European Anti-Catholicism in a Comparative and Transnational Perspective*, eds. Yvonne Maria Werner and Jonas Harvard (Amsterdam: Rodopi, 2013), 30-32.

7   Raymond J. Lahey, "Fleming, Michael Anthony," in *Dictionary of Canadian Biography*, vol. 7, University of Toronto/Université Laval, 2003, accessed May 3, 2018, http://www.biographi.ca/en/bio/fleming_michael_anthony_7E.html.

8   For an overview of Fleming's predecessors, see Cyril Byrne, "Introduction," in *Gentlemen-Bishops and Faction Fighters: The Letters of Bishops O'Donel, Lambert, Scallan and Other Missionaries*, ed. Cyril Byrne (St. John's: Jesperson Press, 1984), 1-32.

9   TNA:PRO, CO 194/83, fols. 245-47, Cochrane to Maitland, Sept. 13, 1832.

204 THE INVISIBLES

[10] RPA, GN2.2, Memorial of Chamber of Commerce, Oct. 12, 1832.

[11] TNA:PRO, WO 55/869, fols. 422-26, Oldfield to Tucker, June 11, 1832.

[12] TNA:PRO, CO 194/74, fols. 131-37, Cochrane to Bathurst, May 1, 1827.

[13] This ground, too, is well covered, but see especially O'Flaherty, *Old Newfoundland*, 149-51.

[14] Although the literature for Ireland is voluminous, an excellent starting point is S.J. Connolly, *Priests and People in Pre-Famine Ireland 1780-1845* (New York: St. Martin's Press, 1982). For Newfoundland, useful correctives include John FitzGerald, "Conflict and Culture in Irish-Newfoundland Roman Catholicism, 1829-1850" (Ph. D., University of Ottawa, 1997), and Phillip McCann, "Bishop Fleming and the Politicization of the Irish Roman Catholics in Newfoundland, 1830-1850," in *Religion and Identity: The Experience of Irish and Scottish Catholics in Atlantic Canada*, eds. Terrence Murphy and Cyril J. Byrne (St. John's: Jesperson Press, 1987), 88-89.

[15] Whyte, "The Influence of the Catholic Clergy," 249.

[16] On the development of political parties in Upper Canada, see Buckner, *Transition to Responsible Government*, 72-77. For examples of the the misuse of party names in Newfoundland during this period, see Sean T. Cadigan, *Newfoundland and Labrador: A History* (Toronto: University of Toronto Press, 2009), 110-11, and McCann, "Bishop Fleming and the Politicization of the Irish Roman Catholics in Newfoundland," 90.

[17] Patrick O'Flaherty, "Carson, William," in *Dictionary of Canadian Biography*, vol. 7, University of Toronto/Université Laval, 2003, accessed May 3, 2018, http://www.biographi.ca/en/bio/carson_william_7E.html.

[18] Greene, *Between Damnation and Starvation*, 81.

[19] FitzGerald, "Conflict and Culture," 61-67, 127; O'Flaherty, *Old Newfoundland*, 158.

[20] O'Flaherty, *Old Newfoundland*, 154-55.

[21] *Ledger*, Dec. 27, 1833, 2-3; *Newfoundlander*, Dec. 26, 1833, 2.

[22] RPA, GN2.2, Brown, Blaikie, and Carter to Crowdy, Jan. 2, 1834.

[23] Virginia Crossman, "The Army and Law and Order in the Nineteenth Century," in *Military History of Ireland*, 358; Facey-Crowther, "Aid to the Civil Power in British North America," 312.

[24] Senior, *British Regulars in Montreal*, 20.

[25] Leon Radzinowicz, *A History of English Criminal Law and its Administration from 1750* (London: Stevens and Sons, 1968), 4:125-30; Huffer, "The Infantry Officers of the Line," 220; Spiers, *The Army and Society*, 77-83.

[26] Facey-Crowther, "Aid to the Civil Power in British North America," 314-15,

[27] Crossman, "The Army and Law and Order," 358.

[28] Arthur Fox, *The Newfoundland Constabulary* (St. John's: Robinson Blackmore, 1971), 22-23.

[29] Jukes, *Excursions*, 6.

[30] *Newfoundlander*, Dec. 26, 1833, 2.

[31] Unfortunately, this has not stopped historians from accepting it at face value. For examples of some who have, see FitzGerald, "Conflict and Culture," 147; Greene, *Between Damnation and Starvation*, 85; and Lahey, "Fleming, Michael Anthony."

[32] Gunn, *Political History of Newfoundland*, 20-21.

[33] TNA:PRO, CO 194/87, fols. 124-27, Crowdy to Carson, Jan. 8, 1834.

[34] TNA:PRO, CO 194/88, fols. 15-17, "Explanatory observations to accompany the Blue Book for the year 1833," enclosure in Cochrane to Stanley, July 8, 1834.

[35] *Royal Gazette*, Feb. 4, 1834, 3.

[36] *Royal Gazette*, Feb. 11, 1834, 3.

[37] This episode is well covered in FitzGerald, "Conflict and Culture," 166-73.

[38] Phyllis Creighton, "Troy, Edward," in *Dictionary of Canadian Biography*, vol. 10, University of Toronto/Université Laval, 2003, accessed May 9, 2018, http://www.biographi.ca/en/bio/troy_edward_10E.html.

ENDNOTES 205

39 RPA, GN2.2, McLean Little to Prescott, March 21, 1835.

40 Patrick O'Flaherty, "Winton, Henry David," in *Dictionary of Canadian Biography*, vol. 8, University of Toronto/Université Laval, 2003, accessed May 9, 2018, http://www.biographi. ca/en/bio/winton_henry_david_8E.html.

41 See, for example, James S. Donnelly, Jr., "The Whiteboy Movement, 1761-5," *Irish Historical Studies* 21, no. 81 (1978): 35.

42 Edmund Gosse, *The Life of Philip Henry Gosse F.R.S.* (London: Kegan Paul, Trench, Trübner, 1890), 81-82.

43 O'Flaherty, *Old Newfoundland*, 168-70.

44 Leslie Harris, "Parsons, Robert John," in *Dictionary of Canadian Biography*, vol. 11, University of Toronto/Université Laval, 2003, accessed May 11, 2018, http://www. biographi.ca/en/bio/parsons_robert_john_11E.html.

45 *Patriot*, June 16, 1835, 2.

46 *Patriot*, Jan. 19, 1836, 3.

47 *Patriot*, Feb. 9, 1836, 3.

48 Neaven's letter and William Carsons's comments on it can also be found in TNA:PRO, CO 194/88, fols. 89-92, enclosure in Cochrane to Spring Rice, Aug. 14, 1834.

49 Unless otherwise indicated, this account of the Neaven funeral disturbance is based on *Ledger*, Feb. 9, 1836, 3 Feb. 26, 1836, 3, and *Patriot*, Feb. 9, 1836, 3.

50 *Ledger*, Feb. 16, 1836, 3.

51 *Patriot*, Feb. 16, 1836, 2-3.

52 *Patriot*, Feb. 23, 1836, 2; *Ledger*, Feb. 26, 1836, 1.

53 *Ledger*, Feb. 26, 1836, 3 and March 1, 1836, 3.

54 *Patriot*, Nov. 19, 1836, 3. On the importance of impartiality in civil-military relations, at least in Ireland, see Crossman, "The Army and Law and Order," 376.

55 Greene, *Between Damnation and Starvation*, 113-17.

56 *Patriot*, Nov. 19, 1836, 3.

57 *Patriot*, Dec. 3, 1836, 2.

58 Gunn, *Political History of Newfoundland*, 34-36.

59 Patrick O'Flaherty, "Kielley, Edward," in *Dictionary of Canadian Biography*, vol. 8, University of Toronto/Université Laval, 2003, accessed May 29, 2018, http://www. biographi.ca/en/bio/kielley_edward_8E.html.

60 *Patriot*, Nov. 19, 1836, 3.

61 Buckner, *Transition to Responsible Government*, 5.

62 Greene, *Between Damnation and Starvation*, 170-72.

63 Gunn, *Political History of Newfoundland*, 56.

64 Although the best account of the by-election is Greene, *Between Damnation and Starvation*, 158-60, he is mistaken on the timing of the troops' deployment.

65 Creighton, "Troy, Edward."

66 RPA, GN2.2, Carter and Simms to Crowdy, May 21, 1840.

67 RPA, GN2.2, William Weston Carter et al. to Carter and Simms, May 27, 1840, and Carter and Simms to Crowdy, May 27, 1840.

68 Lewis Amadeus Anspach, *A History of the Island of Newfoundland*... (London: Sherwood, Gilbert, and Piper, 1827), 297-98.

69 Thomas Talbot, *Newfoundland; Or, a Letter to a Friend in Ireland in relation to the Condition and Circumstances of the Island of Newfoundland*... (London: Sampson Low, Marston, Searle, and Rivington, 1882), 6.

70 Jukes, *Excursions*, 34-35.

71 Greene, *Between Damnation and Starvation*, 182-83.

72 Gosse, *The Life of Philip Henry Gosse*, 33.

73 Jukes, *Excursions*, 53.

74 *Weekly Herald and Conception-Bay Advertiser* (Harbour Grace), Aug. 27, 1845, quoted

in Shannon Ryan, *The Ice Hunters: A History of Newfoundland Sealing to 1914* (St. John's: Breakwater, 1994), 133.

[75] Patrick O'Flaherty, *Paddy Boy: Growing up Irish in a Newfoundland Outport* (Lawrencetown, NS: Pottersfield Press, 2015), 5-6.

[76] Patrick O'Flaherty, "Lundrigan, James," in *Dictionary of Canadian Biography*, vol. 6, University of Toronto/Université Laval, 2003, accessed May 26, 2018, http://www.biographi.ca/en/bio/lundrigan_james_6E.html.

[77] O'Flaherty, *Old Newfoundland*, 132-46.

[78] TNA:PRO, CO 194, fols. 103-04, "Memorial of Inhabitants of Harbor Grace, for an Effective Police and Military Force," Dec. 29, 1826. O'Flaherty mistakenly dates the petition to 1827. See his *Old Newfoundland*, 145-46.

[79] RPA, GN2.2, Danson and Stark to Crowdy, Apr. 23, 1841.

[80] FitzGerald, "Conflict and Culture," 338-39; O'Flaherty, *Old Newfoundland*, 193-94; and David Dawe, *Riots and Religion in Newfoundland: The Clash between Protestants and Catholics in the Early Settlement of Newfoundland* (St. John's: Flanker Press, 2011), 159-67.

[81] TNA:PRO, CO 194/109, fol. 287, Danson to Crowdy, Nov. 14, 1840.

[82] TNA:PRO, CO 194/109, fols. 287-88, Danson and Stark to Crowdy, Nov. 30, 1840.

[83] TNA:PRO, CO 194/109, fols. 324-28, Pinsent to Crowdy, Dec. 4, 1840. I am indebted to Bob Cuff for biographical information on Pinsent.

[84] O'Flaherty, *Old Newfoundland*, 193. There is no evidence to support Greene's contention that Hanrahan "was coasting to inevitable victory when the election was suspended." If that were true, there would have been no reason for his supporters to start rioting. See his *Between Damnation and Starvation*, 184.

[85] Talbot, *Newfoundland*, 35-36.

[86] TNA:PRO, CO 194/109, fol. 343, Danson and Stark to Crowdy, Dec. 10, 1840.

[87] TNA:PRO, WO 17/2269, "Distribution of the Troops serving in Newfoundland," Jan. 1, 1841; Dawe, *Riots and Religion*, 166.

[88] TNA:PRO, WO 55/875, fol. 607, Sall to Bonnycastle, Dec. 23, 1840.

[89] RPA, GN2.2, Danson and Stark to Crowdy, Feb. 13, 1841.

[90] RPA, GN2.2, Bourne to Sall, June 5, 1841.

[91] Peter J. Roberts, "The Harbour Grace Elections 1832-1861" (M. A., University of New Brunswick, 1969), 69.

[92] TNA:PRO, CO 194/109, fol. 330, Prescott to Russell, Dec. 10, 1840.

[93] RPA, GN2.2, Pack and Power to Crowdy, Dec. 16, 1840.

[94] TNA:PRO, CO 194/109, Russell to Prescott, Jan. 14, 1841.

[95] TNA:PRO, CO 194/111, fol. 152, Prescott to Russell, March 3, 1841.

[96] RPA, GN2.2, Bourne to Sall, June 5, 1841.

[97] Wolffe, *The Protestant Crusade*, 198.

[98] McCann, "Bishop Fleming and the Politicization of the Irish Roman Catholics in Newfoundland," 91-93.

[99] TNA:PRO, CO 194/109, fol. 216, Stephen to Vernon-Smith, Jan. 7, 1841.

[100] TNA:PRO, CO 194/112, fols. 268-69, Harvey to Russell, Sept. 27, 1841.

[101] TNA:PRO, CO 194/112, fols. 331-33, Harvey to Russell, Oct. 8, 1841.

[102] RPA, GN2.2, Stark to Crowdy, Apr. 8, 1841.

[103] Roberts, "The Harbour Grace Elections," 76.

[104] RPA, GN2.2, Danson and Stark to Crowdy, Dec. 20, 1842.

[105] O'Flaherty, *Lost Country*, 16-17.

[106] Piers Brendon, *The Decline and Fall of the British Empire 1781-1997* (2007; repr., London: Vintage Books, 2008), 138; McCann, *Island in an Empire*, 298-300.

[107] McCann, "Bishop Fleming and the Politicization of the Irish Roman Catholics in Newfoundland," 94.

[108] William B. Hamilton, "Society and Schools in Newfoundland," in *Canadian Education:*

ENDNOTES **207**

A History, eds. J. Donald Wilson et al. (Scarborough, ON: Prentice-Hall of Canada, 1970), 138.

[109] Calvin Hollett, *Beating against the Wind: Popular Opposition to Bishop Feild and Tractarianism in Newfoundland and Labrador, 1844-1876* (Montreal and Kingston: McGill-Queen's University Press, 2016), 293-94.

[110] John P. Greene, "The Influence of Religion in the Politics of Newfoundland, 1850-1861" (M. A., Memorial University of Newfoundland, 1970), 19.

[111] O'Flaherty, *Lost Country*, 24-25.

[112] Greene, *Between Damnation and Starvation*, 196.

[113] O'Flaherty, *Lost Country*, 22-23.

[114] J.K. Hiller, "Little, Philip Francis," in *Dictionary of Canadian Biography*, vol. 12, University of Toronto/Université Laval, 2003 , accessed July 6, 2018. http://www.biographi.ca/en/bio/little_philip_francis_12E.html.

[115] Greene, "The Influence of Religion in the Politics of Newfoundland," 15-16.

[116] RPA, GN2.2, Pinsent to Law, Nov. 16, 1852.

[117] J.K. Hiller, "Shea, Sir Ambrose," in *Dictionary of Canadian Biography*, vol. 13, University of Toronto/Université Laval, 2003, accessed July 26, 2018, http://www.biographi.ca/en/bio/shea_ambrose_13E.html.

[118] RPA, GN2.2, Pinsent to Crowdy, May 8, 1855.

[119] RPA, GN2.2, Law to Crowdy, May 17,1855.

[120] TNA:PRO, WO 30/86, fol. 64, Law to Bazalgette, Dec. 31, 1851.

[121] TNA:PRO, CO 194/168, fols. 75-77, Murray to Law, March 3, 1862.

[122] TNA:PRO, CO 194/168, fols. 69-72, Bannerman to Grant, Feb. 18, 1862.

[123] RPA, GN2.2, Law to Crowdy, Dec. 6, 1847.

[124] RPA, GN2.2, Danson et al. to Crowdy, March 21, 1848 and March 29, 1848.

[125] On firefighting, see for example RPA, GN2.2, Danson and Pinsent to Crowdy, Feb. 7, 1850. On the sealers' strike, see RPA, GN2.2, Ryan to Crowdy, March 7, 1853.

[126] More than one contemporary noted the rarity of serious crime in the colony. See, for example, *Newfoundlander*, Feb. 25, 1861, 3.

[127] RPA, GN2.2, Saunders to Robinson, Apr. 24, 1854.

[128] RPA, GN2.2, Saunders to Robinson, Apr. 24, 1854.

[129] RPA, GN2.2, Law to Crowdy, May 17,1855.

[130] A.M. Fraser, "The French Shore," in *Newfoundland: Economic, Diplomatic, and Strategic Studies*, ed. R.A. MacKay (Toronto: Oxford University Press, 1946), 284.

[131] The mood is writ large in Robert Cellem, *Visit of His Royal Highness the Prince of Wales to the British North American Provinces and the United States in the Year 1860* (Toronto: Henry Rowsell, 1861), 17-47.

[132] *JHA*, 1862, 10, proceedings of Jan. 28, 1862.

[133] O'Flaherty, *Lost Country*, 167.

[134] Greene, *Between Damnation and Starvation*, 249.

[135] Roberts, "The Harbour Grace Elections," 101.

[136] TNA:PRO, CO 194/166, Ridley and Munn to Pinsent, Oct. 27, 1860.

[137] TNA:PRO, CO 194/161, Bannerman to Newcastle, Jan. 16, 1860.

[138] RPA, GN2.2, Pinsent to Shea, Nov. 11, 1859.

[139] TNA:PRO, CO 194/161, fols. 45-46, Ridley, Munn, and Stark to Bannerman, Jan. 6, 1860.

[140] Edward C. Moulton and Ian Ross Robertson, "Bannerman, Sir Alexander," in *Dictionary of Canadian Biography*, vol. 9, University of Toronto/Université Laval, 2003, accessed July 26, 2018, http://www.biographi.ca/en/bio/bannerman_alexander_9E.html.

[141] TNA:PRO, CO 194/161, fols. 41-44, Bannerman to Newcastle, Jan. 16, 1860.

[142] For prominent examples, see Moulton and Robertson, "Bannerman, Sir Alexander"; Gunn, *Political History of Newfoundland*, 152; O'Flaherty, *Lost Country*, 86.

143 TNA:PRO, CO 194/161, fols. 84-86, Newcastle to Bannerman, Feb. 23, 1860.

144 TNA:PRO, CO 194/161, fols. 51-53, Bennett and Simms to Bannerman, Dec. 29, 1859.

145 TNA:PRO, CO 194/161, fols. 53-55, Hogsett to Bannerman, Dec. 29, 1859.

146 TNA:PRO, CO 194/161, fols. 79-82, Kent to Bannerman, Jan. 16, 1860.

147 Elizabeth A. Wells, "Munn, John (1807-79)," in *Dictionary of Canadian Biography*, vol. 10, University of Toronto/Université Laval, 2003, accessed July 30, 2018, http://www.biographi.ca/en/bio/munn_john_1807_79_10E.html; James Hiller, "James Murray and the 1882 Newfoundland General Election," *Newfoundland and Labrador Studies* 33, no. 1 (2018): 238-39, 250-51.

148 TNA:PRO, CO 194/166, fols. 148-49, Pinsent to Kent [?], Oct. 27, 1860.

149 *Ledger*, Nov. 2, 1860, 2.

150 Hiller, "Little, Philip Francis." For the text of Mullock's letter, see Prowse, *History of Newfoundland*, 486-87, n. 1.

151 O'Flaherty, *Lost Country*, 88.

152 Prowse, *History of Newfoundland*, 488.

153 E.C. Moulton, "Constitutional Crisis and Civil Strife in Newfoundland, February to November 1861," *Canadian Historical Review* 48, no. 3 (1967): 258.

154 Frederick Jones, "Bishops in Politics: Roman Catholic v Protestant in Newfoundland, 1860-2," *Canadian Historical Review* 55, no. 4 (1974): 414-15.

155 Frederick Jones, *Edward Feild: Bishop of Newfoundland, 1844-1876* (St. John's: Newfoundland Historical Society, 1976), 26-27.

156 TNA:PRO, CO 194/165, Bannerman to Grant, Apr. 20, 1861; TNA:PRO, CO 194/165, fols. 203-04, Bannerman to Newcastle, Apr. 23, 1861.

157 *Ledger*, Apr. 30, 1861, 2.

158 Moulton, "Constitutional Crisis and Civil Strife," 263. I have flipped a coin and gone with Moulton's description of this episode, which differs substantially from Winton's, in which he claimed that the mob entered the premises and badly beat McLea. See *Ledger*, Apr. 30, 1861, 2.

159 Dawe, *Riots and Religion*, 192.

160 LAC, RG 8, C Series, Vol. 369, pp. 182-84, Hanrahan to Grant, May 5, 1861; TNA:PRO, CO 194/165, fols. 216-20, Bannerman to Newcastle, May 8, 1861.

161 Dawe, *Riots and Religion*, 190.

162 LAC, RG 8, C Series, Vol. 369, pp. 182-84, Hanrahan to Grant, May 5, 1861.

163 Moulton, "Constitutional Crisis and Civil Strife," 263-65.

164 Greene, "The Influence of Religion in the Politics of Newfoundland," 144; Roberts, "The Harbour Grace Elections," 134-38.

165 LAC, RG 8, C Series, Vol. 369, pp. 179a-181, Bannerman to Grant, May 4, 1861.

166 O'Flaherty, *Lost Country*, 91.

167 *Ledger*, May 21, 1861, 2.

168 TNA:PRO, CO 194/166, fols. 32-36, Testimony of John James Grant, May 15, 1861; LAC, RG 8, C Series, Vol. 369, pp. 153-61, Fordyce to Trollope, May 20, 1861; Tocque, *Newfoundland*, 52.

169 Memorial University of Newfoundland. Archives and Special Collections, MF-270 (D.W. Prowse Scrapbook 1900-1902), undated letter to the editor of the *Harbour Grace Standard* by "R.N.C."

170 LAC, RG 8, C Series, Vol. 369, pp. 176-78, Hanrahan to Grant, May 19, 1861.

171 *St. John's Telegraph*, May 22, 1861, 2; TNA:PRO, CO 194/166, fols. 28-32, Testimony of Thomas Bennett, May 15, 1861; Prowse, *History of Newfoundland*, 489.

172 I have estimated the troop size from Quill's testimony that there were six sections of men, each of which contained "about 14 men." See TNA:PRO, CO 194/166, fols. 37-42, Testimony of Arthur Saunders Quill, May 16, 1861.

ENDNOTES   209

173   *The Queen's Regulations and Orders for the Army*, 203.
174   TNA:PRO, CO 194/166, fols. 28-32, Testimony of Thomas Bennett, May 15, 1861.
175   LAC, RG 8, C Series, Vol. 369, pp. 168-72, Grant to Fordyce, May 19, 1861.
176   TNA:PRO, CO 194/166, fols. 37-42, Testimony of Arthur Saunders Quill, May 16, 1861.
177   See, for example, TNA:PRO, CO 194/166, fols. 15-16, Testimony of James Lawlor.
178   *Newfoundlander*, May 16, 1861, 2.
179   LAC, RG 8, C Series, Vol. 369, pp. 153-61, Fordyce to Trollope, May 20, 1861.
180   *Newfoundlander*, May 16, 1861, 2.
181   TNA:PRO, CO 194/165, fols. 260-63, Bannerman to Newcastle, May 17, 1861.
182   TNA:PRO, CO 194/165, fols. 279-80, Bannerman to Newcastle, May 17, 1861.
183   LAC, RG 8, C Series, Vol. 369, p. 157, Bannerman to Trollope, May 14, 1861.
184   *Newfoundland Express*, May 14, 1861, 2; *Telegraph*, May 22, 1861, 2; *Ledger*, May 25, 1861, 2; *Patriot*, May 27, 1861, 1.
185   TNA:PRO, CO 194/166, fols. 5-7, Bannerman to Newcastle, July 2, 1861, with enclosures.
186   Dawe, *Riots and Religion*, 211-12.
187   Prowse, *History of Newfoundland*, 490.
188   *Telegraph*, Nov. 13, 1861, 3.
189   *Patriot*, July 29, 1861, 2.
190   *Telegraph*, Sept. 11, 1861, 2.
191   TNA:PRO, CO 194/165, fols. 243-47, Newcastle to Bannerman, May 31, 1861.
192   TNA:PRO, CO 194/166, fols. 303-05, Bannerman to Newcastle, Sept. 10, 1861.
193   Moulton, "Constitutional Crisis and Civil Strife," 260; Gunn, *Political History of Newfoundland*, 160-61.
194   TNA:PRO, CO 194/166, fols. 391-92, Petition of Magistrates and Citizens of Harbour Grace, Oct. 16, 1861.
195   TNA:PRO, CO 194/166, fols. 443-45, Grant to Bannerman, Nov. 23, 1861, and fols. 446-48, Bannerman to Milne, Nov. 27, 1861.
196   *Telegraph*, Nov. 6, 1861, 3.
197   TNA:PRO, CO 194/166, fols. 441-42, Mesham to Grant, Nov. 18, 1861.
198   Gunn, *Political History of Newfoundland*, 208.
199   TNA:PRO, CO 194/166, fols. 443-45, Grant to Bannerman, Nov. 23, 1861; TAN: PRO, CO 194/168, fols. 4-5, Bannerman to Newcastle, Jan. 2, 1862.
200   TNA:PRO, CO 194/168, fols. 588-90, Lugard to Elliot, May 27, 1862, and fols. 77-78, Newcastle to Bannerman, May 10, 1862.
201   TNA:PRO, CO 194/168, Bannerman to Newcastle, Feb. 27, 1862.
202   LAC, RG 8, C Series, Vol. 1766, pp. 247-55, Mitchell to Fort Adjutant, Nov. 18, 1869; TNA:PRO, CO 194/180, fol. 5, Pasley to Wellesley, Jan. 3, 1870.
203   Candow, *The Lookout*, 122; C.P. Stacey, "The Withdrawal of the Imperial Garrison from Newfoundland, 1870," *Canadian Historical Review* 17, no. 2 (1936): 153-56; W. David MacWhirter, "A Political History of Newfoundland, 1865-1874" (M.A., Memorial University of Newfoundland, 1963), 65-78.
204   See F.C. Mather, *Public Order in the Age of the Chartists* (1959; repr., Manchester: Manchester University Press, 1966).
205   Correlli Barnett, *Britain and Her Army 1509-1970* (London: Allen Lane The Penguin Press, 1970), 353.
206   H.T. Holman, "The Belfast Riot," *The Island Magazine* 14 (1983): 6.
207   Frederick Jones, "Hoyles, Sir Hugh William," in *Dictionary of Canadian Biography*, vol. 11, University of Toronto/Université Laval, 2003, accessed October 4, 2018, http://www.biographi.ca/en/bio/hoyles_hugh_william_11E.html.
208   James Hiller, "Confederation Defeated: The Newfoundland Election of 1869," in *Newfoundland in the Nineteenth and Twentieth Centuries*, 70.

210 THE INVISIBLES

[209] J.G. Channing, *The Effects of Transition to Confederation on Public Administration in Newfoundland* (Toronto: Institute of Public Administration of Canada, 1982), 5. I am grateful to Joan Ritcey for this reference.

[210] S.J.R. Noel, *Politics in Newfoundland* (Toronto: University of Toronto Press, 1971), 24.

[211] TNA:PRO, CO 194/207, fols. 192-93, Glover to Derby, Dec. 30, 1884; Hiller, "History of Newfoundland, 1874-1901," 110-16.

[212] On 1932, see Noel, *Politics in Newfoundland*, 197-202.

CHAPTER 7

CONCLUSION

[1] *Newfoundlander*, March 1, 1870, 1; *JHA* 1870, Appendix, "Estimates and Public Accounts," 12A.

[2] John Philp, "The Economic and Social Effects of the British Garrisons in the Development of Western Upper Canada," *Ontario History* 41, no. 1 (1949): 48.

[3] E.M. Spiers, "Army Organisation and Society in the Nineteenth Century," in *A Military History of Ireland*, eds. Thomas Bartlett and Keith Jeffery (Cambridge: Cambridge University Press, 1996), 342; Richard A. Preston, "The British Influence of RMC," in *To Preserve and Defend: Essays on Kingston in the Nineteenth Century*, ed. Gerald Tulchinsky (Montreal and London: McGill-Queen's University Press, 1976), 120.

[4] *Royal Gazette Extraordinary*, Jan. 30, 1874, 1; *Royal Gazette*, Nov. 26, 1878, 3.

[5] *Daily News*, May 25, 1906, 1.

[6] Huffer, "The Infantry Officers of the Line," 465.

[7] LAC, RG 8, C Series, Vol. 1829, pp. 11-12, "Information for the use of Military and Naval Officers Purposing to Settle in the British Colonies," enclosure in Horse Guards Memorandum, Sept. 14, 1843.

[8] See, for example, TNA:PRO, WO 30/86, fols. 5-6, Law to Bazalgette, Aug. 1, 1848.

[9] RPA, GB7.4, Law to Fordyce, May 26, 1857; Law to Weatherall, Oct. 26, 1857; Law to Benn (?), May 26, 1858.

[10] RPA, GB7.4, Law to Weatherall, June 6, 1859; Grant to Weatherall, Feb. 29, 1860.

[11] *Dictionary of Newfoundland and Labrador Biography*, eds. Robert H. Cuff, Melvin Baker, and Robert D.W. Pitt (St. John's: Harry Cuff, 1990), s.v. "Fallon, Luke."

[12] Douglas L. Bursey, telephone conversation with author, Feb. 18, 1991.

[13] TNA:PRO, WO 97, Vol. 1168, "MacBay [sic], Peter; *Dictionary of Newfoundland and Labrador Biography*, s.v. "McBay, Peter"; *Daily News*, June 20, 1911, 6.

[14] "Vital Records, Register of Deaths, Book 2, 1896, St. John's City District, 437-43." Newfoundland's Grand Banks website, accessed Oct. 8, 2018, http://www.ngb.chebucto.org/Vstats/death-reg-bk-2-1896-437-443-sjc.shtmlhttp://www.ngb.chebucto.org.

[15] Jennifer Reddy, e-mail message to author, Oct. 12, 2018.

[16] *Evening Telegram*, Jan. 17, 1906, 3.

[17] Hiller, "A History of Newfoundland, 1874-1901," 19.

[18] Patrick O'Flaherty, "The Newfoundland Irish," *Newfoundland Quarterly* 86, no. 1 (1990): 22.

BIBLIOGRAPHY

PRINTED MATERIAL

Anglin, Douglas G. *The St. Pierre and Miquelon "Affaire" of 1941: A Study in Diplomacy in the North Atlantic Quadrangle.* Toronto: University of Toronto Press, 1966.

Anspach, Lewis Amadeus. *A History of the Island of Newfoundland....* London: Sherwood, Gilbert, and Piper, 1827.

Archibald, Samuel George. *Some Account of the Seal Fishery in Newfoundland and the Mode of Preparing Seal Oil....* Edinburgh: Murray and Gibb, 1852.

Ascoli, David. *A Companion to the British Army 1660-1983.* London: Harrap, 1983.

Bailey, Peter. *Leisure and Class in Victorian England: Rational Recreation and the Contest for Control, 1830-1885.* London: Routledge and Kegan Paul, 1978.

Bains, Yashdip H. *English Canadian Theatre, 1765-1826.* New York: Peter Lang, 1998.

Baird, Donal M. *The Story of Firefighting in Canada.* Erin, ON: Boston Mills Press, 1986.

Baker, Melvin. *Aspects of Nineteenth Century St. John's Municipal History.* St. John's: Harry Cuff, 1982.

———. "The Government of St. John's, Newfoundland 1800-

1921." Ph.D., University of Western Ontario, 1980.

———. "The Great St. John's Fire of 1846." *Newfoundland Quarterly* 59, no. 1 (1983): 31-34.

———. "The Politics of Assessment: The Water Question in St. John's, 1844-1864." *Acadiensis* 12, no. 1 (1982): 59-72.

Baker, Melvin, and James E. Candow. "Signal Hill Gaol 1846-1859." *Newfoundland Quarterly* 85, no. 4 (1990): 20-23.

Bamfield, Veronica. *On the Strength: The Story of the British Army Wife*. Tonbridge, UK: Charles Knight, 1974.

Banham, Martin, ed. *The Cambridge Guide to Theatre*. Cambridge: Cambridge University Press, 1992.

Bannister, Jerry. *The Rule of the Admirals: Law, Custom, and Naval Government in Newfoundland, 1699-1831*. Toronto: University of Toronto Press, 2003.

Barnes, Peter. "An Anatomy of Medical Practice: An Examination of the Health, Diseases, and Medical Practices of the St. John's Garrison, 1861." B.A., Memorial University of Newfoundland, 2001.

Barnett, Corelli. *Britain and Her Army 1509-1970*. London: Allen Lane, 1970.

Bartlett, Thomas. "Army and Society in Eighteenth-century Ireland." In *Kings in Conflict: The Revolutionary War in Ireland and its Aftermath*, edited by W.A. Maguire, 173-82. Belfast: The Blackstaff Press, 1990.

Beaglehole, J.C. "The Royal Instructions to Colonial Governors 1783-1854: A Study in British Colonial Policy." Ph.D. University of London, 1929.

Beckett, Ian F.W. *Riflemen Form: A Study of the Rifle Volunteer Movement 1859-1908*. Aldershot: The Ogilby Trusts, 1982.

Bennett, R.W. "Military Law in 1839." *Journal of the Society for Army Historical Research* 48, no. 196 (1970): 225-41.

Binney, C.R. "An Account of an Extraordinary Instance of Rapid Decay of Girders in the Storehouses at St. John's, Newfoundland." *Professional Papers of the Royal Engineers, New Series* 7 (1858): 135-36.

BIBLIOGRAPHY 213

Bonnycastle, Richard Henry. *Newfoundland in 1842: A Sequel to "The Canadas in 1841."* 2 vols. London: Henry Colburn, 1842.

Bourne, Kenneth. *Britain and the Balance of Power in North America 1815-1908.* London: Longmans, 1967.

Boutilier, Alex. *The Citadel on Stage: British Military Theatre, Sports and Recreation in Colonial Halifax.* Halifax: SVP Productions, 2015.

Brendon, Piers. *The Decline and Fall of the British Empire 1781-1997.* 2007. Reprint, London: Vintage Books, 2008.

Brown, Elizabeth. "Citizen Soldiers: Political Pawns: The Newfoundland Volunteer Companies 1860-1870." B.A., Memorial University of Newfoundland, 1998.

Buckner, Phillip A. "Harvey, Sir John." *Dictionary of Canadian Biography*, vol. 8, University of Toronto/Université Laval, 2003-, accessed March 14, 2017. http://www.biographi.ca/en/bio/harvey_john_8E.html.

———. *The Transition to Responsible Government: British Policy in British North America, 1815-1850.* Westport, CT: Greenwood Press, 1985.

Burroughs, Peter. "Crime and Punishment in the British Army, 1815-1870." *English Historical Review* 100, no. 396 (1985): 545-71.

———. "An Unreformed Army? 1815-1868." In *The Oxford History of the British Army.* 1994. Edited by David G. Chandler and Ian Beckett, 161-86. Reprint, Oxford: Oxford University Press, 2003.

Byrne, Cyril. "Introduction." In *Gentlemen-Bishops and Faction Fighters: The Letters of Bishops O'Donel, Lambert, Scallan and Other Missionaries*, edited by Cyril Byrne, 1-32. St. John's: Jesperson Press, 1981.

Cadigan, Sean T. *Newfoundland and Labrador: A History.* Toronto: University of Toronto Press, 2009.

Candow, James E. "'Beaumont-Hamel and the Trail of the Caribou: Newfoundlanders and Labradorians at War and at Home 1914-1949.' Permanent Exhibition, The Rooms

Provincial Museum, St. John's, NL, 1 July 2016-Ongoing."
Newfoundland and Labrador Studies 31, no. 2 (2016): 367-72.

———. *Cantwells' Way: A Natural History of the Cape Spear Lightstation.* Halifax and Winnipeg: Fernwood Publishing, 2014.

———. *The Lookout: A History of Signal Hill.* St. John's: Creative Publishers, 2011.

Cellem, Robert. *Visit of His Royal Highness the Prince of Wales to the British North American Provinces and the United States in the Year 1860.* Toronto: Henry Rowsell, 1861.

Channing, J.G. *The Effects of Transition to Confederation on Public Administration in Newfoundland.* Toronto: Institute of Public Administration of Canada, 1982.

Chappell, Edward. *Voyage of His Majesty's Ship Rosamond to Newfoundland and the Southern Coast of Labrador.* London: J. Mawman, 1818.

Clode, Charles M. *The Military Forces of the Crown; Their Administration and Government.* London: John Murray, 1869.

Colgan, John. "Leixlip Around 1798." Leixlip History. Accessed Jan. 29, 2018. http://www.kildare.ie/leixliphistory/archives/leixlip-around-1798/.

Colley, Linda. *Britons: Forging the Nation 1707-1837.* 2nd ed. New Haven: Yale University Press, 2005.

Connolly, S.J. *Priests and People in Pre-Famine Ireland 1780-1845.* New York: St. Martin's Press, 1982.

Cowan, Paul. "'Please, write we are starving now'." *Dorchester Review* 6, no. 2 (2016): 65-68.

Creighton, Phyllis. "Troy, Edward." *Dictionary of Canadian Biography,* vol. 10, University of Toronto/Université Laval, 2003-, accessed May 9, 2018. http://www.biographi.ca/en/bio/troy_edward_10E.html.

Cricket Newfoundland and Labrador. "History." Accessed March 4, 2018. http://www.canadacricket.com/nlcricket/?page_id=4.

Crossman, Virginia. "The Army and Law and Order in the Nineteenth Century." In *A Military History of Ireland*, edited by Thomas Bartlett and Keith Jeffery, 358-78. Cambridge: Cambridge University Press, 1996.

Cuff, Robert H., Melvin Baker, and Robert D.W. Pitt., eds. *Dictionary of Newfoundland and Labrador Biography*. St. John's: Harry Cuff, 1990.

Davies, Robertson. *Fifth Business*. 1970. Reprint, Toronto: Penguin Canada, 2005.

————. *For Your Eyes Alone: Letters 1976-1995*. Edited by Judith Skelton Grant. Toronto: McClelland Stewart, 1999.

————. "The Nineteenth-Century Repertoire." In *Early Stages: Theatre in Ontario 1800-1914*, edited by Ann Saddlemyer, 90-122. Toronto: University of Toronto Press, 1990.

Dawe, David. *Riots and Religion in Newfoundland: The Clash between Protestants and Catholics in the Early Settlement of Newfoundland*. St. John's: Flanker Press, 2011.

Day, Fiona. "The Old Garrison Church: St. Thomas', St. John's, Newfoundland." *Journal of the Royal Army Chaplains' Department* 28, no. 8 (1987): 5-7.

Denny, H.L.L. "Lawe of Leixlip." *Journal of the Co. Kildare Archaeological Society and Surrounding Districts* 6 (1909-1911): 230-39.

De Watteville, H. *The British Soldier: His Daily Life from Tudor to Modern Times*. London: J.M. Dent and Sons, 1954.

Donnelly, James S., Jr. "The Whiteboy Movement, 1761-5." *Irish Historical Studies* 21, no. 81 (1978): 20-54.

Dunfield, R.W. *The Atlantic Salmon in the History of North America*. Ottawa: Department of Fisheries and Oceans, 1985.

Durnford, Mary, ed. *Family Recollections of Lieut. General Elias Walker Durnford, a Colonel Commandant of the Corps of Royal Engineers*. Monreal: John Lovell, 1863.

Facey-Crowther, David. "The British Army and Aid to the Civil Power in British North America, 1832-1871." *Journal of the Society for Army Historical Research* 93, no. 376 (2015): 311-31.

216   THE INVISIBLES

Fay, C.R. *Life and Labour in Newfoundland.* Toronto: University of Toronto Press, 1956.

FitzGerald, John. "Conflict and Culture in Irish-Newfoundland Roman Catholicism, 1829-1850." Ph.D., University of Ottawa, 1997.

Fortescue, J.W. *A History of the British Army.* 13 vols. London: Macmillan, 1902-30.

Foster, R.F. *Modern Ireland 1600-1972.* 1988. Reprint, London: Penguin Books, 1989.

Fox, Arthur. *The Newfoundland Constabulary.* St. John's: Robinson Blackmore, 1971.

Fraser, A.M. "The French Shore." In *Newfoundland: Economic, Diplomatic, and Strategic Studies,* edited by R.A. MacKay, 275-332. Toronto: Oxford University Press, 1946.

Gibson, Clare. *Army Childhood: British Army Children's Life and Times.* Oxford: Shire Publications, 2012.

Glascock, William. *Naval Sketch-Book: Or, The Service Afloat and Ashore....* Vol. 1. London: Henry Colburn and Richard Bentley, 1831.

Godfrey, Stuart R. *Human Rights and Social Policy in Newfoundland 1832-1982: Search for a Just Society.* St. John's: Harry Cuff, 1985.

Gosse, Edmund. *The Life of Philip Henry Gosse F.R.S.* London: Kegan Paul, Trench, Trübner, 1890.

Great Britain. Army. *The Queen's Regulations and Orders for the Army.* London: Her Majesty's Stationery Office, 1859.

———. Army Medical Department. *Statistical, Sanitary, and Medical Reports for the Year 1859.* London: Her Majesty's Stationery Office, 1861.

———. House of Commons. "Map of St. John's, Nfld. Showing extent of fire of 1846." London: Standage and Company, 1851.

———. House of Commons. *Sessional Papers.* 1839, Vol. 16.

———. Ministry of Defence. *The Old War Office Building.* London: n.d.

Greenberg, Amy S. *Cause for Alarm: The Volunteer Fire Depart-*

ment in the Nineteenth-Century City. Princeton: Princeton University Press, 1998.

Greene, John P. *Between Damnation and Starvation: Priests and Merchants in Newfoundland Politics, 1745-1855.* Montreal and Kingston: McGill-Queen's University Press, 1999.

———. "The Influence of Religion in the Politics of Newfoundland, 1850-1861." M.A., Memorial University of Newfoundland, 1970.

Gunn, Gertrude E. *The Political History of Newfoundland 1832-1864.* Toronto: University of Toronto Press, 1966.

Guy, Alan J. "The Irish military establishment, 1660-1776." In *A Military History of Ireland,* edited by Thomas Bartlett and Keith Jeffery, 211-30. Cambridge: Cambridge University Press, 1996.

Hall, Henry L. *The Colonial Office: A History.* London: Longmans, Green, 1937.

Hamilton, William B. "Society and Schools in Newfoundland." In *Canadian Education: A History,* edited by J. Donald Wilson et al., 126-42. Scarborough, ON: Prentice-Hall of Canada, 1970.

Harries-Jenkins, Gwyn. *The Army in Victorian Society.* London: Routledge and Kegan Paul, 1977.

Harris, Leslie. "Parsons, Robert John." *Dictionary of Canadian Biography,* vol. 11, University of Toronto/Université Laval, 2003, accessed May 11, 2018, http://www.biographi.ca/en/bio/parsons_robert_john_11E.html.

Hart, H.G. *The New Army List, for 1845.* London: John Murray, 1845.

Herbert, Trevor, and Helen Barlow. *Music and the British Military in the Long Nineteenth Century.* Oxford: Oxford University Press, 2013.

Hewitt, Martin. "Science as Spectacle: Popular Scientific Culture in Saint John, New Brunswick, 1830-1850." *Acadiensis* 18, no. 1 (1988): 91-119.

Hiller, James. "Confederation Defeated: The Newfoundland Election of 1869." In *Newfoundland in the Nineteenth and Twentieth Centuries: Essays in Interpretation*, edited by James Hiller and Peter Neary, 67-94. Toronto: University of Toronto Press, 1981.

———. "James Murray and the 1882 Newfoundland General Election." *Newfoundland and Labrador Studies* 33, no. 1 (2018): 237-58.

Hiller, J.K. "A History of Newfoundland, 1874-1901." Ph.D., Cambridge University, 1971.

———. "Little, Philip Francis. *Dictionary of Canadian Biography*, vol. 12, University of Toronto/Université Laval, 2003, accessed July 6, 2018, http://www.biographi.ca/en/bio/little_philip_francis_12E.html.

———. "Shea, Sir Ambrose." *Dictionary of Canadian Biography*, vol. 13, University of Toronto/Université Laval, 2003, accessed July 26, 2018, http://www.biographi.ca/en/bio/shea_ambrose_13E.html.

Hilton, Phillip J. "'Branded D on the Left Side': A Study of Former Soldiers and Marines Transported to Van Diemen's Land: 1804-1854." Ph.D., University of Tasmania, 2010.

Hollett, Calvin. *Beating against the Wind: Popular Opposition to Bishop Feild and Tractarianism in Newfoundland and Labrador, 1844-1876*. Montreal and Kingston: McGill-Queen's University Press, 2016.

Holman, H.T. "The Belfast Riot." *The Island Magazine* 14 (1983): 3-7.

Holmes, Richard. *Redcoat: The British Soldier in the Age of Horse and Musket*. 2001. Reprint: London: HarperCollins, 2002.

Huffer, Donald Breeze Mendham. "The Infantry Officers of the Line of the British Army 1815-1868." Ph.D. University of Birmingham, 1995.

Hyam, Ronald. *Britain's Imperial Century, 1815-1914*. 3rd ed. Houndsmills, Basingstoke, UK: Palgrave Macmillan, 2002.

Ireland. House of Commons. *Journals 1739-1749*.

Irish University Press. *British Parliamentary Papers*. Vol. 19. Shannon: Irish University Press, 1971.

Janzen, Olaf U. "Newfoundland and British Maritime Strategy during the American Revolution." Ph.D., Queen's University, 1983.

Johnson, J.K. "The Chelsea Pensioners in Upper Canada." *Ontario History* 53, no. 4 (1961): 1-17.

Jones, Frederick. "Bishops in Politics: Roman Catholic v. Protestant in Newfoundland 1860-2." *Canadian Historical Review* 55, no. 4 (1974): 408-21.

———. *Edward Feild: Bishop of Newfoundland, 1844-1876.* St. John's: Newfoundland Historical Society, 1976.

———. "Hoyles, Sir Hugh William." *Dictionary of Canadian Biography*, vol. 11, University of Toronto/Université Laval, 2003, accessed October 4, 2018, http://www.biographi.ca/en/bio/hoyles__hugh_william_11E.html.

Jukes, J.B. *Excursions in and about Newfoundland during the years 1839 and 1840.* Vol. 1. London: James Murray, 1842.

Karsten, Peter. "Irish Soldiers in the British Army, 1792-1922: Suborned or Subordinate?" *Journal of Social History* 17, no. 1 (1983): 31-64.

Laffin, John. *Tommy Atkins: The Story of the English Soldier.* London: Cassell, 1966.

Lahey, Raymond J. "Fleming, Michael Anthony." *Dictionary of Canadian Biography*, vol. 7, University of Toronto/Université Laval, 2003, accessed May 3, 2018, http://www.biographi.ca/en/bio/fleming_michael_anthony_7E.html.

Law, Robert. *Regimental Standing Orders for the Guidance of the Royal Newfoundland Companies.* St. John's: Henry Winton, 1850.

Lindsay, Peter. "The Impact of the Military Garrisons on the Development of Sport in British North America." *Canadian Journal of History of Sport and Physical Education* 1, no. 1 (1970): 33-44.

Lynde, Denyse. "Amateur Theatrical Tradition." Accessed Feb. 25, 2018. http://www.heritage.nf.ca/articles/arts/amateur-theatre.php.

MacKinnon, Robert. "The Agricultural Fringe of St. John's, 1750-1945." In *Four Centuries and the City: Perspectives on the Historical Geography of St. John's*, edited by Alan G. Macpherson, 53-82. St. John's: Memorial University of Newfoundland, 2005.

———. "The Growth of Commercial Agriculture around St. John's, 1800-1935: A Study of Local Trade in Response to Urban Demand." M.A., Memorial University of Newfoundland, 1981.

MacWhirter, W. David. "A Political History of Newfoundland, 1865-1874." M.A., Memorial University of Newfoundland, 1963.

Makepeace-Warne, Anthony, ed. *Brassey's Companion to the British Army*. London: Brassey's, 1995.

Malone, Diane B. "A Survey of Early Military Theatre in America." *Theatre Survey* 16, no. 1 (1975): 56-64.

Mann, Michael. *The Veterans*. Wilby, UK: Michael Russell, 1997.

Mannion, John J. "Introduction." In *The Peopling of Newfoundland: Essays in Historical Geography*, edited by John J. Mannion, 1-13. St. John's: Memorial University of Newfoundland, 1977.

Mason, Philip. *The English Gentleman: The Rise and Fall of an Ideal*. New York: William Morrow and Company, 1982.

Mather, F.C. *Public Order in the Age of the Chartists*. 1959. Reprint, Manchester: Manchester University Press, 1966.

Maunder, John. "The Newfoundland Museum: Origins and Development." Accessed Feb. 15, 2018. http://www.therooms.ca/the-newfoundland-museum-origin-and-development.

McCann, Phillip. "Bishop Fleming and the Politicization of the Irish Roman Catholics in Newfoundland, 1830-1850." In *Religion and Identity: The Experience of Irish and Scottish Catholics in Atlantic Canada*, edited by Terrence Murphy and Cyril J. Byrne, 81-97. St. John's: Jesperson Press, 1987.

———. *Island in an Empire: Education, Religion, and Social Life in Newfoundland, 1800-1855*. St. John's: Boulder Publications, 2016.

McConville, Seán. "The Victorian Prison: England, 1865-1965." In *The Oxford History of the Prison: The Practice of Punishment in Western Society*, edited by Norval Morris and David J. Rothman, 131-67. Oxford: Oxford University Press, 1995.

McCrea, R.B. *Lost Amid the Fogs: Sketches of Life in Newfoundland, England's Ancient Colony*. London: Sampson, Low, Son, and Marston, 1869.

McCullough, A.B. *Money and Exchange in Canada to 1900*. Toronto: Dundurn Press, 1984.

McGowen, Randall. "The Well-Ordered Prison: England, 1780-1865." In *The Oxford History of the Prison: The Practice of Punishment in Western Society*, edited by Norval Morris and David J. Rothman, 79-109. Oxford: Oxford University Press, 1995.

McLintock, A.H. *The Establishment of Constitutional Government in Newfoundland, 1783-1832: A Study in Retarded Colonisation*. London: Longmans, Green, 1941.

Mercer, Keith. "The Murder of Lieutenant Lawry." *Newfoundland and Labrador Studies* 21, no. 2 (2006): 255-89.

———. *Rough Justice: Policing, Crime, and the Origins of the Royal Newfoundland Constabulary, 1729-1871*. St. John's: Flanker Press, forthcoming.

Metcalfe, Alan. *Canada Learns to Play: The Emergence of Organized Sport, 1807-1914*. Toronto: McClelland and Stewart, 1987.

Montague, R.H. "The Royal Veterans in Australia." *Journal of the Royal Australian Historical Society* 68, no. 3 (1982): 238-46.

Morris, E.P., ed. *Decisions of the Supreme Court of Newfoundland 1854-1864*. St. John's: Queen's Printer 1900.

Morton, Desmond. *A Military History of Canada*. 5th ed. Toronto: McClelland and Stewart, 2007.

Moss, Robert. "The Last Duel in Newfoundland." In *The Book of Newfoundland*, edited by Joseph R. Smallwood and James R. Thoms, 4:450-53. St. John's: Newfoundland Book Publishers (1967) Limited, 1967.

Moulton, Edward C. "Constitutional Crisis and Civil Strife in

Newfoundland, February to November 1861." *Canadian Historical Review* 48, no. 3 (1967): 251-72.

Moulton, Edward C., and Ian Ross Robertson. "Bannerman, Sir Alexander." *Dictionary of Canadian Biography*, vol. 9, University of Toronto/Université Laval, 2003, accessed July 26, 2018, http://www.biographi.ca/en/bio/bannerman_alexander_9E.html.

Neary, Peter. "The French and American Shore Questions as Factors in Newfoundland History." In *Newfoundland in the Nineteenth and Twentieth Centuries: Essays in Interpretation*, edited by James Hiller and Peter Neary, 95-123. Toronto: University of Toronto Press, 1981.

Newfoundland. 1833, 1846. *Acts of the General Assembly*.

Newfoundland (House of Assembly). *Journals of the House of Assembly*. 1857, 1862, 1865, 1870.

Newfoundland's Grand Banks website. "Vital Records, Register of deaths, Book 2, 1896, St. John's City District, pp. 437-43." Accessed Oct. 8, 2018. http://www.ngb.chebucto.org/Vstats/death-reg-bk-2-1896-437-443-sjc.shtml-http://www.ngb.chebucto.org.

Noel, S.J.R. *Politics in Newfoundland*. Toronto: University of Toronto Press, 1971.

O'Dea, F.A. "Government House." *Canadian Antiques Collector* 10, no. 2 (1975): 48-51.

O'Dell, Leslie. "Amateurs of the Regiment, 1815-1870." In *Early Stages: Theatre in Ontario 1800-1914*, edited by Ann Saddlemyer, 52-89. Toronto: University of Toronto Press, 1990.

O'Flaherty, Patrick. "Carson, William." *Dictionary of Canadian Biography*, vol. 7, University of Toronto/Université Laval, 2003, accessed May 3, 2018, http://www.biographi.ca/en/bio/carson_william_7E.html.

———. "Kielley, Edward." *Dictionary of Canadian Biography*, vol. 8, University of Toronto/Université Laval, 2003, accessed May 29, 2018, http://www.biographi.ca/en/bio/kielley_edward_8E.html.

———. *Lost Country: The Rise and Fall of Newfoundland, 1843-1933*. St. John's: Long Beach Press, 2005.

———. "Lundrigan, James." *Dictionary of Canadian Biography*, vol. 6, University of Toronto/Université Laval, 2003, accessed May 26, 2018, http://www.biographi.ca/en/bio/lundrigan_james_6E.html.

———. "The Newfoundland Irish." *Newfoundland Quarterly* 86, no. 1 (1990): 20-26.

———. *Old Newfoundland: A History to 1843*. St. John's: Long Beach Press, 1999.

———. *Paddy Boy: Growing up Irish in a Newfoundland Outport*. Lawrencetown, NS: Pottersfield Press, 2015.

———. "Winton, Henry David." *Dictionary of Canadian Biography*, vol. 8, University of Toronto/Université Laval, 2003_, accessed May 9, 2018, http://www.biographi.ca/en/bio/winton_henery_david_8E.html.

O'Mara, M.J. "The Last Duel in Newfoundland." *The Cadet* 6, no. 2 (1919): 9-16, 21-22.

Omond, J.S. *Parliament and the Army 1642-1904*. Cambridge: Cambridge University Press, 1933.

O'Neill, Paul. *A Seaport Legacy: The Story of St. John's, Newfoundland*. Erin, ON: Press Porcepic, 1976.

Parker, Mike. *The Smoke-Eaters: A History of Firefighting in Nova Scotia c. 1750-1950*. Halifax: Nimbus Publishing, 2002.

Philp, John. "The Economic and Social Effects of the British Garrison in the Development of Western Upper Canada." *Ontario History* 41, no. 1 (1949): 37-48.

Plumb, J.H. "The Commercialization of Leisure in Eighteenth-century England." In *The Birth of a Consumer Society: The Commercialization of Eighteenth-Century England*, edited by Neil McKendrick, John Brewer and J.H. Plumb, 265-85. Bloomington: Indiana University Press, 1982.

Poole, Cyril F., and Robert Cuff, eds. *Encyclopedia of Newfoundland and Labrador*. Vol. 5. St. John's: Harry Cuff, 1994.

Preston, Richard A. "The British Influence of RMC." In *To Preserve and Defend: Essays on Kingston in the Nineteenth Century*, edited by Gerald Tulchinsky, 119-37. Montreal and London: McGill-Queen's University Press, 1976.

Proulx, Jean-Pierre. "Placentia: 1713-1811." *History and Archaeology 26*. Ottawa: Parks Canada, 1979.

Prowse, D.W. *A History of Newfoundland from the English, Colonial, and Foreign Records*. London: Macmillan, 1895.

Pulsifer, Cameron. "Beyond the Queen's Shilling: Reflections on the Pay of Other Ranks in the British Army." *Journal of the Society for Army Historical Research* 80, no. 324 (2002): 326-34.

Radzinowicz, Leon. *A History of English Criminal Law and its Administration from 1750*. Vol. 4. London: Stevens and Sons, 1968.

Raugh, Harold E., Jr. *The Victorians at War 1815-1914: An Encyclopedia of British Military History*. Santa Barbara, CA: ABC-CLIO, 2004.

Rewa, Natalie. "Garrison Theatre." In *The Oxford Companion to Canadian Theatre*, edited by Eugene Benson and L.W. Connolly, 222-24. Toronto: Oxford University Press, 1989.

Roberts, Peter J. "The Harbour Grace Elections 1832-1861." M.A., University of New Brunswick, 1969.

Rowe, Frederick W. *A History of Newfoundland and Labrador*. Toronto: McGraw-Hill Ryerson, 1980.

Royster, Charles. *The Destructive War: William Tecumseh Sherman, Stonewall Jackson, and the Americans*. 1991. Reprint, New York: Vintage Books, 1993.

Rudachyk, B.E.S. "The Most Tyrannous of Masters: Fire in Halifax, Nova Scotia, 1830-1850." M.A., Dalhousie University, 1984.

Ryan, Shannon. *The Ice Hunters: A History of Newfoundland Sealing to 1914*. St. John's: Breakwater, 1994.

Senior, Elinor Kyte. *British Regulars in Montreal: An Imperial Garrison, 1832-1854*. Montreal: McGill-Queen's University Press, 1981.

Skelley, Alan Ramsay. *The Victorian Army at Home: The Recruitment and Terms and Conditions of the British Regular, 1859-1899*. London: Croon Helm, 1977.

Smallwood, Joseph R., and Robert D.W. Pitt, eds. *Encyclopedia of Newfoundland and Labrador*. Vol. 1; St. John's: Newfoundland Book Publishers (1967) Ltd., 1981.

Snape, Michael. *The Royal Army Chaplains' Department: Clergy Under Fire*. Woodbridge, UK: Boydell Press, 2008.

Spiers, Edward M. "Army Organisation and Society in the Nineteenth Century." In *A Military History of Ireland*, edited by Thomas Bartlett and Keith Jeffery, 335-57. Cambridge: Cambridge University Press, 1996.

———. *The Army and Society 1815-1914*. London: Longman, 1980.

Stacey, C.P. *Canada and the British Army 1846-1871*. Toronto: University of Toronto Press, 1963.

———. "Halifax as an International Strategic Factor, 1749-1949." *Canadian Historical Association Annual Report* 28, no. 1 (1949): 46-56.

———. "The Withdrawal of the Imperial Garrison from Newfoundland, 1870." *Canadian Historical Review* 17, no. 2 (1936): 147-58.

Stewart, Frances L. "Mess Calls from Signal Hill, Newfoundland." *Northeast Historical Archaeology* 14 (1985): 62-77.

Stocqueler, J.H. *The British Officer: His Positions, Duties, Emoluments, and Privileges*. London: Smith Elder, 1851.

Story, G.M., W.J. Kirwin, and J.D.A. Widdowson, eds. *Dictionary of Newfoundland English*. Toronto: University of Toronto Press, 1982.

Strachan, Hew. *Wellington's Legacy: The Reform of the British Army 1830-54*. Manchester: Manchester University Press, 1984.

Sweetman, John. *War and Administration: The Significance of the Crimean War for the British Army*. Edinburgh: Scottish Academic Press, 1984.

Talbot, Thomas. *Newfoundland; Or, a Letter to a Friend in Ireland in relation to the Conditions and Circumstances of the Island of Newfoundland....* London: Sampson Low, Marston, Searle, and Rivington, 1882.

Taylor, Bayard. *At Home and Abroad: A Sketch-book of Life, Scenery and Men.* New York: G.P. Putnam, 1862.

Tocque, Philip. *Newfoundland: as it was, and as it is in 1877.* Toronto: John B. Magurn, 1878.

Trustram, Myna. *Women of the Regiment: Marriage and the Victorian Army.* Cambridge: Cambridge University Press, 1984.

Tylden, G. "The Royal Canadian Rifle Regiment." *Journal of the Society for Army Historical Research* 34, no. 138 (1956): 59-62.

Vamplew, Wray. *The Turf: A Social and Economic History of Horse Racing.* London: Allen Lane, 1976.

Venning, Annabel. *Following the Drum: The Lives of Army Wives and Daughters, Past and Present.* London: Headline Book Publishing, 2005.

Weaver, John C., and Peter DeLottinville. "The Conflagration and the City: Disaster and Progress in British North America during the Nineteenth Century." *Social History/Histoire sociale* 13, no. 26 (1980): 417-49.

Webb, Jeff A. "William Knox and the 18th-Century Newfoundland Fishery." *Acadiensis* 54, no. 1 (2015): 112-22.

Webber, David A. *Skinner's Fencibles: The Royal Newfoundland Regiment 1795-1802.* St. John's: Newfoundland Naval and Military Museum, 1964.

Wells, Elizabeth A. "Munn, John (1807-79)." *Dictionary of Canadian Biography,* vol. 10, University of Toronto/Université Laval, 2003, accessed July 30, 2018, http://www.biographi.ca/en/bio/munn_john_1807_79_10E.html.

White, A.C.T. *The Story of Army Education 1643-1963.* London: George G. Harrap, 1963.

White, A.S. "Garrison, Reserve and Veteran Battalions and Companies." *Journal of the Society for Army Historical Research* 38, no. 1 (1960): 156-67.

Whiteway, Louise. "The Athenaeum Movement: St. John's Athenaeum (1861-1898)." *Dalhousie Review* 50, no. 4 (1971): 534-49.

Whitfield, Carol M. "Tommy Atkins: The British Soldier in Canada, 1759-1870." *History and Archaeology 56.* Ottawa: Parks Canada, 1981.

————. "Tommy Atkins' Family." *Bulletin of the Association for Preservation of Technology* 5, no. 4 (1973): 65-72.

Whyte, J.H. "The Influence of the Catholic Clergy on Elections in Nineteenth-Century Ireland." *English Historical Review* 75, no. 295 (1960): 239-59.

Williams, N.T. St. John. *Tommy Atkins' Children: The Story of the Education of the Army's Children 1675-1970.* London: Her Majesty's Stationery Office, 1971.

Wolffe, John. "North Atlantic Anti-Catholicism in the Nineteenth Century: A Comparative Overview." In *European Anti-Catholicism in a Comparative and Transnational Perspective*, edited by Yvonne Maria Werner and Jonas Harvard, 25-41. Amsterdam: Rodopi, 2013.

————. *The Protestant Crusade in Great Britain 1829-1860.* Oxford: Clarendon Press, 1991.

Woods, Robert. *The Demography of Victorian England and Wales.* Cambridge: Cambridge University Press, 2000.

NEWSPAPERS

Courier (St. John's). 1853.

Daily News (St. John's). 1906, 1911.

Evening Telegram (St. John's). 1906.

Newfoundland Express (St. John's). 1860, 1861.

Newfoundlander (St. John's). 1827, 1829-31, 1833, 1838-39, 1842-48, 1851-55, 1858-59, 1861-62, 1870.

Patriot and Terra-Nova Herald (St. John's). 1835-36, 1841, 1847.

228   THE INVISIBLES

Public Ledger and Newfoundland General Advertiser (St. John's).
1827-28, 1831, 1833, 1835-36, 1860-62, 1864, 1866.
Royal Gazette and Newfoundland Advertiser (St. John's). 1817,
1834-35, 1843, 1878.
Royal Gazette Extraordinary (St. John's). 1874.
Telegraph (St. John's). 1861
Times and General Commercial Gazette (St. John's). 1845

ARCHIVAL COLLECTIONS

City of St. John's Archives

Maps A 009.2, A 009.5

Library and Archives Canada

R3607-0-6-E. Gustavus Nicolls Papers, F23.
RG8, C Series. British Military and Naval Records. Vols.
369, 1766, 1829.

Memorial University of Newfoundland. Archives and Special Collections

MF-270. D.W. Prowse Scrapbook 1900-1902.
MF-280. "Memoranda on Newfoundland during a residence
from October 25, 1830 to October 12, 1835," by Lieutenant Colonel John Oldfield.

The National Archives of the United Kingdom. Public Record Office

Colonial Office 194. Colonial Office and Predecessors: Newfoundland Original Correspondence. Vols. 74, 82, 83, 87, 88, 109, 111, 112, 116, 125, 147, 156, 160, 161, 165, 166, 168, 180, 186, 207.

War Office 1. In-Letters and Papers. Vols. 549, 551.

War Office 3. Office of the Commander-in-Chief: Out-letters. Vols. 169, 253.

War Office 17. Monthly Returns. Vols. 2252, 2269, 2270, 2284, 2286, 2289.

War Office 25. War Office and Predecessors: Secretary-at-War, Secretary of State for War, and Related Bodies, Registers. Vol. 805, 2242.

War Office 27. Inspection Returns. Vols. 345, 422.

War Office 30. War Office, Predecessors and Associated Departments, Miscellaneous Papers. Vol. 86.

War Office 44. Ordnance Office and War Office: Correspondence. Vol. 163.

War Office 55. Ordnance Office and War Office: Miscellaneous Entry Books and Papers. Vols. 868, 869, 870, 871, 872, 877, 878, 879, 2802, 2988.

War Office 97. Royal Hospital Chelsea: Soldiers' Service Documents. Vols. 1164-70.

Nova Scotia Archives and Records Management

Manuscript Group 12. Great Britain: Army, Headquarters General Orders. Vols. 32, 36, 42, 43, 45, 47, 49, 50, 54, 55.

The Rooms Provincial Archives

GB7.4. British War Office collection. British Army records
(St. John's, NL). 1848, 1852, 1853, 1854, 1855, 1856, 1857,
1858, 1859, 1860, 1862, 1863, 1866, 1867.

GN2.2. Incoming Correspondence, Office of the Colonial
Secretary fonds. 1830, 1831, 1832, 1833, 1834, 1835, 1838,
1839, 1840, 1841, 1842, 1843, 1845, 1847, 1848, 1850,
1851, 1852, 1853, 1854, 1855, 1856, 1859, 1890.

GN2.30. Department of the Colonial Secretary, Blue Books.
1844.

Manuscript Group 543. Phoenix Assurance Company.

INDEX

alcohol. *See also* Royal Newfoundland Companies, crime & punishment. 54-55, 57, 61n, 70
agriculture. *See* St. John's, agriculture
American Civil War, 12, 24
Australia, 13-15, 51, 168

Bannerman, Sir Alexander, Governor, 5, 7, 73, 148, 149, 150-151, 152, 153, 154, 157, 163, 164, 166-167
Bennett, Charles Fox, 83, 94
Bennett, Thomas, Magistrate, 149, 157, 159, 160, 162
Bermuda. *See* West Indies
Blackman, Rev. Charles, 71
Bonnycastle, Sir Richard Henry, 16, 36 72-73, 77
Boulton, Henry John, Chief Justice, 119, 122, 124, 125
Bourne, J.G.H, Chief Justice, 137-138, 149
Brigus, 131
British Empire, xiv, 21, 52, 109, 168, 172, 174

Broomfield, J.J., 88, 96-97
Burke, Johnny, 152n
Burke, Lt. Col. Thomas Kirwan, 7, 83, 182
Byrne, Thomas, 155-156, 165

Campbell, Sir Colin, 120
Canada Commands, 14
Canadas, Upper & Lower, 17, 24, 58, 107, 126
Carbonear, 118, 119, 123, 124-125, 133-134, 136-138, 139, 143, 154-155; – Saddle Hill 118, 132, *132-133*
Carfagnini, Fr. Erico, 162
Carmichael Smyth, Sir James, 16
Carson, William, 84, 112-114, 116, 123, 126, 140
Carter, Frederic, 168
Carter, Peter, Chief Magistrate, 64, 69, 157
Cat's Cove, 155-156
Chambers, Lt. Hugh, 99
charities & fraternal societies, 38, 55, 74-76, 77, 78, 92, 93, 99, 101-102, 104, 141, 151

civil courts of law & magistrates, xv-xvi, 39, 61-62, 84, 94, 104-105, 108-109, 114n, 115-117, 123, 127, 131, 133-134, 136, 137-139, 140, 143, 148-149, 150, 155, 157, 163-164, 165, 174, 143, 144, 149-150, 157, 163-164

civil disorder. *See also* Royal Newfoundland Companies, aid to the civil power. *See also* Riots. 60-62, 107-169

class system. *See* social order. *See* Royal Newfoundland Companies, social profile

Cochrane, Sir Thomas, Governor, 14, 17, 79, 111, 112, 117-118, 122, 131, 137

Coen, Capt. William John, 174

Collington, Lt. John, 84

Colonial Building, *103*

Colonial Office, 2-3, 5, 102, 111, 117-118, 119, 122-123, 125n, 126, 138, 152, 168

Commissariat Dept., 2-3, *6-7*, 6-9, 44, 45, 98

Commissariat House, *6-7*, 44, 173

Conception Bay. *See also* Maps and plans. *See also* individual towns. 39, 107, 119, 124n, 129-141, 142-144, 146, 153-156, 157, 167

courts of law
    civil. *See* Civil courts of law & magistrates
    military. *See* Royal Newfoundland Companies, crime & punishment

Creamer, Pte. James, 59-60

cricket. *See* Sport

crime. *See* Civil disorder. *See* Royal Newfoundland Companies, aid to the civil power. *See* Riots

Crimean War, 3, 22, 79, 174

Crowdy, James, Colonial Secretary, 39, 136

Cupids, 131

Daly, Lt. Edward, 47

D'Alton, Maj. Edward, 74, 78, 79, 153-154

Dalton, Bsp. John, 153-154, 155, 164

Danson, Thomas, Magistrate, 39, 136, 139

Darling, Charles, 7, 37, 105

desertions. *See* Royal Newfoundland Companies, crime & punishment

Dickson, Sir Jeremiah, 58

dogs, 72

Douglas, James, 126-127

Doyle, Maj. Gen. Commanding Charles Hastings, 166

Doyle, Patrick, Magistrate, 140

duel (in 1826), 84

D'Urban, Sir Benjamin, 4

economy. *See also* Fisheries. 75, 76, 83, 92, 101, 130, 143, 150, 171

education, libraries, literary, scientific, agricultural institutes, 55-57, 75-76, 140-141, 169

Edward Albert, Prince of Wales (later King Edward VII), *23*, 145-146

elections. *See* Newfoundland, politics & government, elections

Emerson, H.A., Solicitor General, 136

England, 15, 27, 51, 53, 60, 64, 65, 71, 72, 85, 174

Eyre, Sir William, 5

Fallon, Pte. Luke, 175

Feild, Bsp. Edward, 140-141, 145, 152, 162-163

firearms, 47-48

fires. *See* Royal Newfoundland
Companies, firefighting.
See St. John's, fires
fisheries, xiv, xv, 11, 22, 58, 100,
109, 125, 129, 141, 144-145,
150, 151
sealers' strike (in 1853), 143
Fleming, Bsp. Michael Anthony,
20-21, 102, 109, *110*, 112-114,
117-118, 122-123, 127, 137,
140, 141, 142, 168
food, 40-42, 70, 71, 73, 74
Fort Townshend, 5, 17, 20-21,
31-32, 33, 34, 36, 37, 38, 44,
45, 49-50, 52, 56, 62, 70-71,
82, 99n, 121, 123, 159, 162,
172-174, 184-185
Fort William, 17, 19-20, 31, *32-33*,
33, 34, 36, 37, 38, 44-45, 53, 56,
98, 157, 173-174, 184, 186
France, relations with, 11, 21, 22,
74, 144-145
Fraternal societies. *See* Charities
& fraternal societies
Fredericton, New Brunswick, 4
French in Newfoundland, 11, 22,
74, 144-145
French Revolutionary and Napoleonic Wars, xv, 11, 17, 129
Furey, Charles, 155-157

gambling. *See* Sport
gaols
civilian, 20, 53, 136, 174
military. *See* Royal Newfoundland Companies, crime &
punishment
Garrett, Benjamin G., High Sheriff,
52, 71
George, Prince, Duke of Cambridge, 23
George's Barracks, 36, 37
Gillespie, Lt. John, 47
Glen, Thomas, Receiver General, 152

Glenelg, Charles Grant, 1st Baron
Glenelg, 124-125
Gosse, Philip Henry, 130-131
Goulds, Newfoundland and Labrador, xiii
Government House, 5, *6-7*, 17, 44,
46, 50, 55, 73-74, 173
governors. *See also* Newfoundland,
politics & government. xiv, 2,
4-5, 6-7, 21n, 14, 18, 22, 36, 37,
44, 50, 58, 70-71, 73, 79, 82, 94,
97, 100, 105, 109n, 111, 117,
119, 120, 124-125, 126, 131,
134, 138-139, 147, 148-149,
150, 152, 154, 164, 165, 167,
173, 174
Grant, Lt. John, 121, 122
Grant, Maj. John James, 80-81, 105,
150, 156, 159-164, 182
Great Britain
military history, 1-9, 11-12,
16-17, 23, 27, 167-168
politics & government, 167-168
relations with Newfoundland,
xiv-xv, 2, 3, 4-5, 9, 11, 16,
21-22, 24, 60, 100, 108, 118,
126, 139n, 141, 142, 1443-
144, 146, 148-149, 167, 168
Great Gale (of 1846), 100
Grey, Henry, 3rd Earl Grey, 21, 102

Halifax, N.S. *See also* Nova Scotia
Command. xv, 40, 47, 50, 51, 59,
82, 105, 165
Hanlin, Pte. John, xiii, xvi
Hanrahan, Edmund, 133-135
Hanrahan, Capt. Thomas, 154-155
Harbour Grace, 4, 22, 39, 111, 118,
119, 124, 125, *129*, 130-133,
135-138, 139, 142, 143, 144,
146-150, 153-155, 156-157,
163, 165-167, 169, 174, 175
Court House, *134*
Saddle Hill, 118, 132, *132-133*

Harbour Grace Affray (1883), 169
Harbour Main, 151, 156, 157, 165
Hardinge, Sir Henry, 13
Harvey, Sir John, Governor, 4-5,
    18, 22-23, 36, 58, 70-71, 82, 97,
    98-99, 100, 139, 140, 141
Hayward, John, 154
Hendrik Willem Frederik, Prince
    of the Netherlands, 70-71
Higgins, Thomas, 150-151
Hill, Sir Stephen, Governor, 167
Hobhouse, Sir John, 13
Hogsett, George James, Attorney
    General, 149, 155, 156, 157, 164
Hogan, Timothy, 112-114
Horse Guards, 1, 15-16, 55
horse-racing. See Sport
horses, 71, 72, 73, 81, 89
hospitals. See St. John's, hospitals
Hoyles, Hugh, 140-141, 146, 152,
    163, 168, 176

India, 168
infantry regiments
    40th Regiment of Foot, 189n.4
    62nd Regiment of Foot, 59, 163,
        165
    71st (Highland Light Infantry)
        Regiment of Foot, 65, 66
    81st Regiment of Foot, 14
Ireland, 112-113, 115-116
Irish in Newfoundland, 7, 27-30,
    51, 65, 74, 81, 108-109, 112,
    113-114, 118, 122-123, 131, 175

Jacob, John, 139
Jamaica. See West Indies
jealousy between towns, 131,
    137-138
Jones, Jenkin, 87-88, 92
Jukes, J.B., 90-91, 130, 131
justice. See Courts of law & magis-
    trates. See also Royal Newfound-
    land Companies, crime
    & punishment

Kent, John, Colonial Secretary, 104,
    112, 123, 125, 148, 149, 150,
    151-152, 162, 168
Keough, Patrick. See Kough, Patrick
Kielley, Edward, 125
Kirkland, Sir John, 9
Kitchin, William, 157-158
Kough, Patrick, 124

Labouchere, Henry, Colonial Sec-
    retary, 22
Law, Lt. Col. Robert, 7, 37, 38, 39,
    42, 47, 57-60, 61, 64, 65-68, 66,
    69, 72, 83, 85, 98, 99, 100-102,
    104-105, 119, 121-122, 124,
    125, 136, 144
Le Marchant, Sir John Gaspard,
    Governor, 4, 5, 100, 141
libraries. See Education, libraries,
    literary, scientific, agricultural
    institutes
Little, John, 168
Little, Philip Francis, Prime Minister
    (later Supreme Court Judge),
    104-105, 142, 148, 151, 162
loyalty, patriotism, nationalism, 23-
    24, 28, 80, 82, 140, 144-146, 172

Mackesey, Henry, 83
"Mad Dogs." See Religion
magistrates. See Civil courts of law
    & magistrates
maps & plans
    Conception Bay, 128
    St. John's, 95, 158, 184-188
marriage, See Royal Newfoundland
    Companies, marriage
Mason, Lieut. William, 139
McCoubrey, John Williams, 164
McCrea, Lt. Col. Robert Barlow,
    73, 85
merchants & mercantile interests,
    92-93, 115-116, 124, 125,
    126-127, 130, 131, 139, 144,
    147-148, 149-150

INDEX   235

Mexican-American War, 21
militias, 5, 22-24, 117, 137
Mitchell, Ensign Arthur Bambrick, 69-70
Molloy, Edward, 118
Monroe, James, President of the United States, 16
Montreal, Quebec, 88, 168
Moore, Henry, 154
Morris, Patrick, 113, 123, 126
Mount Pearl, 83
Mullock, Bsp. John Thomas, 74, 145, 151, 153, 162, 163, 164, 166, 168
mummering, 76
Munn, John, Magistrate, 130, 146-147, 149, 150, 165
music, 79-81
mutiny. *See* Royal Newfoundland Companies, crime & punishment
Myrick, Patrick, 175-176

nationalism. *See* Loyalty, patriotism, nationalism
Neaven, Sgt. John, 120-122
New Brunswick, 16-17
New Zealand, 168
Newcastle, Henry Pelham, Duke of, 145-146, 148-149, 164-165, 166
Newfoundland
    politics & government, xv-xvi, 4-7, 21, 92, 99-100, 104-105, 107-109, 111-112, 116-118, 119, 125, 130, 138-139, 141-142, 144, 146, 147n, 148, 149, 151-152, 156-157, 164-166, 167, 169, 176
    elections, 119-127, 129-135, 139, 141-143, 146-151, 152-159, 165-166
    military history (overview), xiii-xvii
    union with Canada, 167, 168-169

Newfoundland and Labrador, name of Canadian province, xi
Nicol, Pte. John, 175
Nicolls, Lieut. Gen. Gustavus, 17
Noad, Joseph, Surveyor General, 99
Nova Scotia Command, xv, 4-5, 8, 14, 15-17, 22, 24, 28, 43, 44, 53, 54, 58, 60, 76, 91, 120, 125, 163, 166, 167, 174
Nowlan, Patrick, 151, 155-156, 157, 165
Nugent, John Valentine, 126-127, 140

O'Brien, Laurence, 74, 127, 168
O'Donnell, Fr. Jeremiah, 56, 159-160, 175
O'Flaherty, Patrick, 6n
Oldfield, Lt. Col. John, 19-20, 31, 55, 111
Ordnance, Board of. *See also* Royal Artillery. See also Royal Engineers. 1-2, 3, 8, 17, 19, 32-33, 36, 40-41, 53, 75, 94, 98, 99, 103, 104, 123, 173-174, 184-188, *188*
Ormsby Family, 76-77

Parsons, Robert John, 119-120, 123, 124, 127, 141, 146
patriotism. *See* Loyalty, patriotism, nationalism
penitentiary. *See* Gaols
Peters, Joseph, Magistrate, 165
Petrie, Lt. Martin, 76
Philpott, Ensign John, 84
Pinsent, Robert John, Magistrate, 134-135, 147, 150, 154, 155
Pippy, Virtue, 39-40
Placentia, xiv, 51
police & policing. *See also* Royal Newfoundland Companies, aid to the civil power. xvi, 91, 98-99, 115, 116, 117, 136-137

poor relief. *See* Charities & fraternal societies

Port de Grave, 139

Portugal Cove, 130

poverty & the poor. *See also* Charities & fraternal societies. 28, 38, 72n, 99n, 104, 141

Power, James, Magistrate, 39

Prendergast, James Luke "Mad Luke," 133-135, 150-151, 153

Prescott, Capt. Henry, Governor, 94, 118, 122, 124-125, 126, 133, 136-137, 143

Prime, Pte. Joseph, 59, 174

Prince Edward Island, 168

Prince of Wales' visit. *See* Edward Albert, Prince of Wales (later King Edward VII)

prisons
civilian. *See* Gaols, civil
military. *See* Royal Newfoundland Companies, crime & punishment

Prowse, D.W., Judge, 17

Prowse, Robert, 74, 119

Quebec City, Quebec, 88

Queen's Letter Fund. *See* Charities & fraternal societies

Quill, Lt. Arthur Saunders, 47, 74, 159-161

recruitment. *See* Royal Newfoundland Companies, recruitment & statistics

regimental bands. *See* Music

religion, 29, 49, 56, 102, 108-109, 111-118, 119, 123, 126-127, 133, 137-138, 139-141, 145-146, 148-149, 151, 152-154, 162, 166, 168-169, 176

Rice, Lt. Stephen, 83, 84, 114-115

Ridley, Thomas, Magistrate, 119, 130, 135, 146-147, 149-150, 165

riots. *See also* Civil disorder. 115-116, 119, 121, 123, 127, 135-136, 147-148, 150, 151n, 153-166, *158*, 168-169

Robe, Maj. Alexander Watt, 36, 53, 98, 99

Robinson, Brian, Judge, 163

Rowan, Sir William, 4

Royal Artillery, 1, 3, 6n, 8, 14, 22, 24, 31-32, 33, 34, 36, 44, 47-48, 51, 55, 61, 73, 75, 90, 91, 93-94, 97, 98, 99, 105-106, 144, 167, 182

Royal Canadian Rifle Regiment, 15, 24-25, 31, 70, 79, 167

Royal Engineers, 1, 3, 6n, 35, 46, 55, 90

Royal Navy & naval matters, xiv-xv, 2, 54, 70n, 74, 76, 77, 81, 82, 111, 125, 169

Royal Newfoundland Companies
accommodations. *See* Royal Newfoundland Companies, living conditions
aid to the civil power, xvi, 52, 107-169
composition, 181-183
crime & punishment, 50-60, 69-70, 120
diet, 40-43
duties, 43-49, 68
early years, 14-16
firefighting, xvi, 49, 53, 87-106
formation, 11-14
health, 14, 16, 27, 30, 36, 40, 42, 44
legacy, 85, 171-176
living conditions, xiii, xvi, 29-40, 42, 44, 70
marriage, xvi, 57, 62
officer corps, 67-69
rank & file, 31, 34, 36-38, 60
military experience, 63-65
overview, xiii-xvii, 4-9

parades & ceremonies, 49-50
pay, 13-14, 16, 30-31, 64
recruitment & statistics, xvii,
13-16, 24, 28-29, 31, 37, 42,
53-54, 57-58, 64, 181-183
reduction and disbandment,
21-25
relations with townspeople,
60-62, 74
social profile
officer corps, 63-70, 70-85
rank & file, 27-29
surgeons, 3, 8, 54, 69, 76, 83,
163
Russell, John, Lord (later 1st Earl
Russell), 136-137, 139
Royal Newfoundland Regiment of
Fencible Infantry, 51
Royal Newfoundland Veteran
Companies. *See* Royal Newfoundland Companies
Rudkin, Capt. Mark, 84
Ryan, Joseph, Magistrate, 155

Saint John, New Brunswick, 88
St. John's
agriculture, 20-21, 40-41, 75
churches, 20-21, 98, 102, 162,
173
Court House, *161*
description, 171-174
fires. *See also* Royal Newfoundland Companies, fire-
fighting. 77, 87-89, 90-91,
94-105, 141, 143, 162-163
Harbour, xiv-xv, *19-20*, *48*, *158*,
hospitals, 5, 32, 33, 36, 45, 120,
121n, 143, 173, 184, *187*
neighbourhoods & streets,
5-6, 19-20, 32-33, 38, 62,
72, 83, 84, 88, 94, *96*, *97*,
98-99, 104, 106, 157n, *161*,
172-174

maps & plans. *See* Maps &
plans, St. John's
military sites. *See* Maps & plans,
St. John's
Regattas, 80, 81
Signal Hill. *See* Signal Hill
society, 65-66, 70-74, 108-109
town planning, 99-100, 101,
102-104
water supply, 89, 103-104
St. John's Garrison. *See* Royal New-
foundland Companies
St. Pierre & Miquelon, 11, 22
Sall, Lt. Col. William, 15, 30n, 83,
120, 124, 182
Salmon Cove, 155, 156
Scottish in Newfoundland, 27, 65,
67, 76, 112-113, 126-127, 175
Shea, Ambrose, 152, 168
Shea, Edward, 78, 104, 116-117,
142, 168
ships
HMS *Electra*, 75, 82
HMS *Eurydice*, 68
HMS *Hydra*, 165
HMS *Niobe*, 167
HMS *Spiteful*, 165
HMS *Tamar*, 167
HMS *Tyne*, 74
Signal Hill, 16-18, 20, 32-37, 41,
45, 46, 52, 53, 55, 57, 70n, 93-
94, 103-104, 111, 120, 173
signalling service, 8, 48-49, 91
Simms, Charles, 149, 156
Simms, James, Attorney General,
124
social order, xvii 23, 70, 72, 73, 75,
77, 81, 82-83, 85, 90, 100, 104,
108-109, 113, 125, 131, 139-
140, 142, 145, 151, 167, 169, 171
Spaniard's Bay, 139
Spence, Gilbert William, Assistant
Surgeon, 76

sport, 81-85
Stanley, Edward, 14th Earl of
    Derby, 138
Stark, John, Magistrate, 136, 139,
    147
Stephen, James, Colonial Under
    Secretary, 138
Stevens, William, Deputy Assistant
    Commissary General, 77
Stewart, Sgt. Alexander, 47
Strapp, Patrick, 156

Tarahan's Town. *See* St. Johns,
    neighbourhoods & streets
Taylor, William, 155
Telegraphy, 144, 154
theatre & theatricals, 76-81
Thomas, William, 71
Trollope, Col. Charles, 5
Troy, Fr. Edward, 114-115, 118, 123
Tucker, Richard Alexander, Chief
    Justice, 111
Tulloch, Lt. Col. Alexander, 42

ultramontanism, 109, 113
uniforms, 9, *15*
United States, relations with, 11, 16

veterans' regiments, 12-15, 16, 28,
    31, 33, 38, 52, 54, 55, 111, 114-
    115, 119
Vigoureux, Lt. Col. Henry, 83, 84
volunteers. *See* Militias. 5, 12, 15-16,
    23-24, 47, 58-59, 60, 153

Walsh, Fr. Kyran, 155, 156
Ward, Fr. Patrick, 123
Weir, T.C., Assistant Commissary
    General, 99
Wellington, Arthur Wellesley, Duke
    of, 3, 15-16, 17, 27, 56
West Indies, xv, 17, 51, 168
Western Bay, 133-134

Whiteway, Sir William Valance,
    176
William Henry, Prince (later King
    William IV), 70n
Winter, George, Deputy Ordnance
    Storekeeper, 99
Winton, Henry, 93-94, 112, 116-
    117, 118, 122, 125, 132
women, 31, 34, 36-40, 104
Wright, Maj. H.R., 99